Remembering Jefferson

Remembering Jefferson

Who He Was, Who We Are

Mary E. Stuckey

UNIVERSITY PRESS OF KANSAS

Published by the University Press of Kansas (Lawrence, Kansas 66045), which was
organized by the Kansas Board of Regents and is operated and funded by Emporia State
University, Fort Hays State University, Kansas State University, Pittsburg State University,
the University of Kansas, and Wichita State University.

Library of Congress Cataloging-in-Publication Data is available.
LCCN: 2025025190
ISBN (cloth): 9780700639991
ISBN (epub): 9780700640003
British Library Cataloguing-in-Publication Data is available.
EU Authorised Representative Details: Easy Access System Europe
Mustamäe tee 50, 10621 Tallinn, Estonia | gpsr.requests@easproject.com

Jacket design and illustration by Karl Janssen, adapted from the official presidential
portrait of Thomas Jefferson by Rembrandt Peale, 1800.

Contents

Acknowledgments vii

Introduction 1

1. The Presidential Jefferson 21

2. The Monumental Jefferson 49

3. The Collective Jefferson 80

4. The Popular Jefferson 107

5. The Children's Jefferson 134

Conclusion 161

Notes 175

Selected Bibliography 213

Index 227

Acknowledgments

Working with the University Press of Kansas is always a joy. David Congdon is a terrific and caring editor, and the production staff are equally superb. So thanks to Andrea Laws, Erica Nicholson, Michelle S. Asakawa, and all the others who helped with the production of the book. I'm grateful to the reviewers as well, whose input improved the project.

Deepest thanks to the College of Liberal Arts and the Department of Communication Arts & Sciences at Penn State University. I am privileged to be a Sparks Professor, and to receive extremely generous research support, which enabled travel to various Jefferson sites and relevant archives. A sabbatical leave meant that the research and writing went much faster than would otherwise be the case. And the support the college and department offer for subventions is unmatched and very much appreciated. It's an honor to be part of such a vibrant intellectual community, and I'm more grateful than I can say that I am at PSU.

I have the best colleagues on the planet. They are super smart, even more generous, and always helpful. They are people to whom I can show a bad draft, knowing that they will treat it with generosity, even while acknowledging that it is, in fact, bad. Both Lisa Flores and Steve Browne are consistently and graciously those colleagues for me. Thank you.

The work I do would be impossible without the support and assistance of archives, archivists, and those who work at presidential libraries. I'm grateful to Kirsten Strigel Carter, Patrick F. Fahy, Matthew

C. Hanson, and Sarah Navins for their archival help, and to Cliff Laube, who always makes my visits to the FDR Library special. Bob Clark's knowledge and generosity are always appreciated. Thanks also to Audrey Tepper, the historical architect at the National Park Service (NPS), who taught me a great deal about monuments and their preservation. Librarians are, of course, closely allied to archivists, and I'm equally grateful for the help Jeffrey Knapp and Ellysa Cahoy of the PSU Library provided. I'm grateful beyond measure to all of the rangers, especially interpretive rangers, who work at NPS sites across the country. Research for this trip ranged from coast to coast, and I'm grateful to all the NPS employees and volunteers who took the time to talk with me and answer my questions about interpreting Jefferson.

Various people endured conversations about how we remember Jefferson, and many people traveled with me as I visited places where he is remembered. Steve and Carolee Stuckey spent considerable time traveling with Jefferson in mind, and Carolee developed a somewhat disturbing knack for finding bonus Jefferson artifacts, sometimes in the unlikeliest of places. Their perspectives taught me a lot about how Jefferson is interpreted and viewed. Maren Richter's curiosity and willingness to experience places from a variety of viewpoints proved invaluable. My niece Amanda deserves special recognition as well—her insights on childhood education were immensely valuable. And, as always, my work was improved by conversations with Nancy Kassop, Jim and Laura Parsons, Christa Olson, Allison Prasch, and Sam Martin.

I'm always grateful for those who find time for me, and the work for this project was lightened by the time I got to spend with family and friends. Linda McCarty, Jennifer Beese, and Beth Gylys have once again made everything better. And so have the trainers and clients at One on One, my local gym, where I am always welcomed, encouraged, and well taken care of. Stephen Heidt and Rob Mills are the best interlocutors one could hope for; thank you for your wisdom and humor.

This year especially, I have been reminded of how very much I love, admire, and appreciate the women in my family. So Mom, Carolee, Amanda, Aryn, and Paisley, this one is dedicated to you, and to the memory of my sister Pamela.

Introduction

Remembering Jefferson

This is not actually a book about Thomas Jefferson. It is a book about how contemporary US Americans remember him and what that says about how they understand themselves. This means it is a book about how we define "us," who gets to be included in "our" community, and who is either left out or made unwelcome in it. So it is also a book about how we remember the past, because that influences who we are in the present, and those memories change over time and across circumstances. US Americans have not always remembered Jefferson in the same ways, and not all US Americans remember him the same way now. For some, he is primarily a model to be emulated, a Renaissance man ahead of his time and a symbol of American ingenuity and enterprise. For others, he is primarily an enslaver, a man who owned more than six hundred men, women, and children over his lifetime, who fathered children with one of the women he enslaved, and who owned some of his own children. Still others primarily find him an example of the complexities inherent in claiming any substantive national identity—like US Americans, they argue, Jefferson encompasses multitudes. I am interested here in what it means that so many interpretations of one person collide at this particular moment.

I treat Jefferson as a rhetorical artifact rather than as an orator or politician in his own right.[1] That is, I am less interested in Jefferson himself than in how he is used as a justification for political action and as a marker of national identity. I focus on how presidents used him to advance their agendas, how various actors created monuments and memorials to him and to the other members of the founding generation, how he appears in popular culture, and what we teach our children about him. All of these sites reveal, in their own ways, how various US Americans understand Thomas Jefferson and how they use him to understand themselves and each other.

Rhetoric Is Everywhere

Too often, rhetoric is equated with empty talk, with the absence of meaningful action. But rhetoric is better understood as "the fine and useful art of making things matter."[2] How we define something helps us understand it, and rhetoric can be understood as the choices we make when we offer definitions. To see politics as a "race," for example, is to accept winners and losers as inevitable, but to see politics as a "neighborhood," is to encourage mutuality and community rather than competition. In another example, the line and the practice of lining up are manifestly democratic; they enact the principle of "first come, first served," and reject social hierarchies and political privilege. They are democracy in action. The democracy of lines matters little to us when lines work smoothly—grocery stores and banks come to mind. But consider, too, all of the ways that the democracy of lines can be subverted and how those of us from democratic cultures react to those subversions: when someone jumps a line, or the ways that they are circumvented at places like Disney World through things like Fast Passes and other mechanisms, or how hierarchy is made obvious as we queue up at airport boarding gates. These things grate because lines are supposed to be democratic, and in these cases, they are not. We probably think about these more in terms of "fairness" than as "democracy," and this is itself revealing, because it indicates how closely we connect democracy and some idea of what fairness looks like. It also serves as a reminder than even in a democratic nation, some places are more democratic than others, and we react to each of those places differently even though their rhetoricity is largely invisible to us, and we do not consciously think, "I am unhappy with airport lines because they violate democratic norms."

Places more generally can also be considered through this lens. The nation's capital is also rhetorical. It was designed to highlight the importance of Congress, for example, and the city's layout was intentional and political, as were the choices of certain kinds of architecture, which were meant to underline republican values and traditions. Various monuments and memorials were placed with both aesthetics and politics in mind, and were designed to evoke specific feelings of awe and reverence. That is rhetoric in action.

Rhetoric operates most obviously in speech, and so in this book, I first rely on presidential discourse to get at historical uses of Thomas Jefferson. The presidency is a conservative institution. While there have been exceptions, historically and in general, presidents do not advocate radical changes, but tend to move slowly and cautiously, arguing that their preferred policies are consistent with previous practices. Because he was an early president, because he is revered as a member of the founding generation, because he left behind a large corpus of often eloquent language, and because he had and expressed opinions on a wide range of topics, Jefferson is consistently useful to presidents arguing that their preferred policies are aligned with national history. And because he was useful to presidents, Jefferson is also useful to us, as we seek to understand how he is used historically and at our present moment to define national identity.[3]

Rhetoric, however, isn't confined to the spoken word. Commemorations, whether presented as monuments and memorials or as rituals (such as reading the Declaration of Independence on the Fourth of July) are rhetorical; they make some people and some events matter.[4] By doing so, they tell us who and what serve as models for us as citizens, and in their absences, who and what don't. Again, Jefferson, who has been consistently memorialized since the founding, is useful to us. By noting when and where he appears, and by recognizing the contexts of those appearances, we are reminded that choices were made to celebrate his achievements and accomplishments; those celebrations took specific forms; they occurred in political, social, and material contexts; and considering all of these things tells us something about those times and also about our own. Think, for example, about the difference in presenting Jefferson as the author of the Declaration of Independence in the Jefferson Memorial and in the Museum of African American History and Culture (MAAHC), just a short distance away.[5] In his memorial, the Declaration is not nearly as complicated a document as it is in the MAAHC. Looking at monuments and memorials individually, then, can provide us with one kind of understanding about what matters. Looking at various commemorations of the same individual provides us with different kinds of grounds for judgment, because not all spaces are created equal, and how things are placed in relation to other things affects their meaning.[6] So we might ask why Jefferson is so often commemorated and other founders have fewer memorials. We might look at how other members of the founding generation, or other presidents, or other figures with complicated histories have been remembered. We might consider what it means when they are treated as members of groups (and which groups) and when they stand alone as individuals. And we might ask why and how some memorials remain important, others adapt and change their meaning, and others become irrelevant.

Making things matter, then, is also a matter of individual and collective judgment, because in the act of making something matter we are delineating reasons for that significance. Making meaning out the past is a social practice; it is done collectively, by members of a given community.[7] We might go alone to visit a monument or memorial, but once we are there we are enmeshed in a web of social meaning even as we help create and modify those meanings by our participation. It is significant that Monticello hosts a naturalization ceremony every year; and it matters that so many presidents, for example, participate in those ceremonies. We might ask why those in charge at Monticello decided to do this, and why so many presidents take part in the annual ceremony. But the very fact that this place is the site of such ceremonies, and the fact that they are endorsed and celebrated by so many presidents, makes claims upon a shared sense of national identity. At those moments, Monticello becomes quite explicitly a site of national citizenship.

Monticello points us to another important element of this

Presidents often speak at and participate in naturalization ceremonies at Monticello, as President Bush is doing here on July 4, 2008. Courtesy of the George W. Bush Presidential Library.

discussion: that negotiations over national identity also occur in popular culture, where artifacts are created from the ground up rather than from the top down. Vernacular rhetoric intersects and interacts with official rhetoric, and does so in complicated ways. While the presidential Jefferson might, for example, still be an object of reverence, the popular Jefferson is more subject to criticism, more able to be parodied and challenged. Jefferson is interesting not least because he is so frequently fictionalized, and, increasingly since the revelations about his treatment of Sally Hemings, not always in flattering ways. Some of these fictional Jeffersons are offered to children, as they are taught the national political culture, its implicit hierarchies, and their place within them.

Rhetoric is everywhere, and there are multiple ways of approaching it. In this book, I focus on specific sites, and do so a little differently in each chapter. When I concentrate on presidential rhetoric, for example, I also concentrate on how that creates community; when I turn my attention to children's literature, I focus on the educational capacities of rhetoric. In every chapter, then, I illuminate something about Jefferson, something about how we create communities and citizens through rhetoric, and something about how those things can be discovered in certain places. I do so with regard to Jefferson because more than perhaps any public figure (except Abraham Lincoln), he has a prominent place in the nation's self-understanding. And that, too, is a product of the rhetoric concerning him.

The Manifold Jefferson

There are many reasons to examine US national identity by focusing on remembering Thomas Jefferson. First, from the founding forward, Jefferson has been ubiquitous. There are buildings, streets, cities, counties, schools, universities, and mountains named for him. As early as the eighteenth century and as recently as 2014 there have been proposals to create new states using his name. Close to half a million people visit his home at Monticello every year. The National Park Service lists eleven separate sites with connections to him.[8] He has his own memorial in Washington, DC, and his name was only recently removed from the Jefferson National Expansion Memorial (now Gateway Arch National Park) in St. Louis, where exhibits dedicated to him remain. His face is on the nickel. He has a namesake fort in Florida. He is among those collectively memorialized as national "founders" and among those remembered as "great" presidents. A recent survey listed him as the nation's fifth most popular president (behind Lincoln, Kennedy, Washington, and Theodore Roosevelt).[9] He is one of the presidents on Mount Rushmore, he is prominent among those remembered for signing the Declaration of Independence, and he is, with other founding-era presidents, revered for his work fomenting the US American Revolution and the creation of the US nation.[10] The interest in him is international; there is, for example, a statue of him in Paris. This level of commemoration is not a relic of history. He continues to be one of the nation's most studied presidents.[11] His complexities and controversies have figured large in popular culture, from Broadway musicals such as *Hamilton* (2015), to

movies like *Jefferson in Paris* (1995) and *Sally Hemings* (2000), and documentaries like Ken Burns's *Thomas Jefferson* (1997). His presidency,
his politics, and his private life continue to absorb US Americans,
much as they always have.[12]

Second, this vast amount of commemoration has often been connected to arguments about US national identity.[13] Scholars have long
recognized Jefferson as instrumental both in nation building and in
influencing the national character.[14] This influence is especially interesting because Jefferson can be and is used to justify such a wide
variety of political positions and very different senses of what it means
to be a good citizen of the United States.[15] He has even been used to
blur distinctions among and between those positions.[16] He is useful to
those who occupy nearly every place along the political spectrum. No
matter what policies are preferred, no matter how one understands
national identity, Jefferson can be wielded in support of those arguments.[17] He seems to be almost infinitely flexible.[18]

Third, and relatedly, there is really no consensus about who
Thomas Jefferson was.[19] Everyone, of course, agrees that he was the
slave-owning primary author of the Declaration of Independence, the
nation's third president, and an important figure in the US founding. The basic facts of his life are largely undisputed. There is accord
among historians and probably among the US public that he was a
multitalented and complicated man, who in at least some ways represents important national paradoxes. There is also agreement around
the belief that there is something elusive about Jefferson, that his essence is never fully captured, nor is it fully capturable.[20] It is a curious
fact about the scholarship on Jefferson that it tends to define him
through lists. Dumas Malone, for example, one of Jefferson's most renowned biographers, wrote, "Thomas Jefferson appears to have been
half a dozen men rolled into one. He was dedicated to public affairs,
and he held public offices ranging from county magistrate in Virginia
to President of the United States. But—besides being a legislator, a
diplomat, an executive—he was a father, a scientist, an architect, an
inventor, a patron of education and the arts. He was no soldier, like
George Washington, but he fought for what he believed in. He was

no orator, like Patrick Henry or Daniel Webster, but he was a remarkably good writer. His words have become famous and are quoted around the world."[21] Walter Groom, a more recent biographer, argues, "Thomas Jefferson was a true Renaissance man. He was a student of philosophy and law, a scientist, inventor, architect, musician, and lover of fine things—a man of vision. He was a planter, a Virginia gentleman, expert horseman, and owner of slaves. He was a brilliant writer and, as the new nation formed, he became an important politician."[22] It is as if Jefferson was so many things that he cannot be understood without reference to all of them, as if he is somehow more than the sum of his multitudinous parts.

The many things that Jefferson was, however, were not always consistent, and a number of scholars focus on one or another of the many contradictions and paradoxes Jefferson presents.[23] He was a professional politician who consistently argued that he preferred a quiet life at Monticello. He argued for limited government and as president did not hesitate to wield federal power. He was an advocate of individual liberty who did not extend those views to women and an eloquent proponent of human rights who enslaved some people and advocated for the removal of others from their homelands. Because of his contradictions, inconsistencies, and paradoxes, Jefferson is often considered to be a perfect representation of the United States as a nation.[24] This observation brings us to the question of what national identity is and how we might know it when we see it.

What We Remember Is Who We Are: National Identity and Public Memory

It is common for people to refer to national identity without realizing they are doing so. We make observations about what Brazilians "are like," or how something is "typically Italian," or believe that the Congolese are different from Sri Lankans. In the US context, politicians and especially presidents are fond of referring to "the national character," often when they are advocating for a specific policy that they perceive as being in line with their understanding of that character.

Which is to say that all presidents define what it means to be a member of the nation and make arguments about what kinds of things "good citizens" believe, think, and do. These arguments can be as simple as "voting is a privilege; do your civic duty and get to the polls," or as complicated as "we must fight to defend our nation" from foreign or domestic threats—claims that define the nation by announcing what threatens it. These are examples of "constitutive rhetoric," language that creates community.[25] When presidents speak, they generally have short-term policy or political goals in mind. They want support for their presidencies and for the specific programs they espouse. But they offer arguments in ways that are inevitably, if often implicitly, tied to a specific version of national identity. They argue that "we should enact this policy" because of "who we are as a people."

Because they are presidents, the one elected office in the United States that speaks for and to the entire nation, their visions of what it means to be a citizen has a kind of authority that visions possessed by most other citizens lack. And because presidents all govern at different historical moments and have different needs and preferences, their visions vary across time.[26] But they all offer specific visions of the nation and what it means to be a good member of it. These visions are both inclusive and exclusionary—all visions of any community draw lines between who is inside and who remains outside of it.[27] These are the terms of national identity at any given moment. Because presidents speak for the nation, their views tend to dominate their historical moment, but they are never fully definitive.

Presidents are the most obvious source of arguments about national identity, but nations are actually awash in such arguments—they appear all over, in places like advertising, the ways we organize space, and in monuments, memorials, and movies.[28] All of these are forms of collective action, and they are also forms of collective memory.[29] Collective memory, how groups of people remember the past, is distinct from individual memory in that it is the larger structure within which our individual memories reside. Individual memories of childhood, for example, may be associated with "the 1990s"; in that case, the larger general sense of what "the 1990s" were helps structure those individual memories. Collective memories are cultural refer-ents as well as anchors for individual attitudes and beliefs. But these referents are inventions; they do not arise naturally or inevitably.[30] In much the same way that an individual's view of their childhood may vary across time as they age, a community's view of the past changes to suit present needs.[31]

Because collective memory represents shared consensus about the meaning of the past, creating, changing, and maintaining it is some-thing that communities do together, most often as various kinds of commemoration—celebrating the Fourth of July, for example, or ded-icating a monument to a fallen hero.[32] These aren't always obviously "political," in the way most citizens think about politics—the side-walk stars along Hollywood Boulevard, for instance, are examples of collective memory, and reveal something about what those in charge of authorizing them think is important at any given moment. When sportscasters compare contemporary athletes to past ones, they are engaging in acts of collective memory. Collective memory is rooted in these kinds of commemorative practices, and because it reflects the shared values of a community, collective memory is closely tied to collective identity.[33] Our collective memories are coexistent with our conceptions of the community or nation, who serve as our models of excellence, how to be a member or citizen of it, and what kinds of things look to us like fairness and equity.[34]

Being engaged in the processes of collective memory marks one as a member of the community—people whose voices are not heard in these processes are also those who are being excluded from the com-munity, and those whose values are reflected in public commemora-tion are marked as included in the community. Think, for example, of the increasingly widespread practice of celebrating Juneteenth, now a federal holiday commemorating the end of slavery. Once largely confined to Black communities, celebrating this day at the federal level is a marker of the lessened exclusion of those communities.[35] The need for months dedicated to Black, women's, and Indigenous history also underlines the limits of such inclusion as those histories remain siloed from, and often ancillary to, "national" history, which is still often understood in terms of white history. Choices are always made concerning what to celebrate, and those choices reveal the nature and locus of power within the community.[36] Understanding community depends on understanding the relationships between and among memories in a given polity, to see memory practices in light of what they can tell us about relationships and hierarchies within a community.[37]

For example, the strength with which some community members may hold on to their version of events and how those events are celebrated is an indicator of their commitment to retaining control over present forms of social organization. Collective memory is not about accuracy—it is about how a community needs to understand itself.[38] There are bad versions of history, of course. Claiming that the Boston Tea Party took place in 1775 instead of 1773 is empirically wrong. Claiming that it was about rejecting a strong federal government is also wrong, but more interestingly so, because it reveals something about the commitments of those making the claim.[39] As Gail Bederman puts it, "Every society is known by the fiction that it keeps.... The issue is not whether a society tells fictions to itself and others, but which fictions it calls true, which false, which art, which entertainment."[40] Public memory is always managed—and it is generally managed in ways that accrue benefits to those with the power to offer a given construction.[41] And because power can shift over time, commemorations also shift.[42] Collective memory is best understood as a process, not a product.[43]

Because collective memory is a process, repetition is important.[44] The more often a person or event is commemorated, the more interpretive weight it bears. This is one of the reasons why the sheer number and scale of monuments to the Confederacy and the absence of significant competing commemorations matters so much; the disparity in numbers literally enshrines one interpretation and erases others.[45] Monuments and memorials represent at least some degree of public consensus about the past.[46] But no community is ever monolithic; even families have different perceptions of shared history and shared identity. Communities are no different, and memory sites are always multivocal, often inconsistent, and protean.[47] Despite frequent presidential claims to the contrary, there is no singular definition of what it means to be a US American citizen, no complete agreement on who ought to be included—and who ought to be excluded—from the polity.[48]

Memory sites have dominant meanings, and this matters because they are pedagogical. They teach not only about history but also about the community and what it means to be a "good" member of it.[49] Author Washington Irving, for example, is commemorated in his hometown Sleepy Hollow, New York—visitors are taught to admire both the individual and his writing.[50] Near the site of the famous "Headless Horseman Bridge" is another kind of commemoration—this one marks the spot where Major John André, Benedict Arnold's infamous coconspirator, was caught by three local patriots.[51] Both kinds of commemoration—one to the person often credited with inventing the American short story, and the other marking the capture of a Revolutionary-era British spy—offer information about the area's past and the character of its residents. The act of marking contributions to the fine arts and to the nation's founding is also an act of projecting those contributions and the implied character of the locals into the future. They are things to be proud of and to emulate.

But they are not entirely representative. In our eagerness to present the best face of our communities, we elide or ignore its less savory tendencies, and it is difficult to find ways to offer such commemorations even when a community chooses to do so.[52] In noting the patriotism of those who captured André, for example, we are not told that at the time, slavery was legal in the state of New York. This is not unreasonable; slavery had nothing to do with André's capture. But it is also true that there are infinitely more memorials to Revolutionary patriots than to those they enslaved. This tilts our understanding of history. Collective memory is, as in the case of Sleepy Hollow, constructed both out of what we collectively choose to remember and out of what we choose to forget or ignore.[53]

It is therefore especially interesting to note who, what, why, and how some people are remembered and others are not, for those choices tell us much about the community. The founding era, for example, is one of the more managed aspects of the national history. Its monuments are among the oldest in the nation (the memorial dedicated to General Richard Montgomery in New York was established by the Continental Congress in 1776) and among the newest (the memorial to George Mason on the National Mall dates back only to 2002). In between, there have been hundreds of monuments, many of them placed as the nation was descending into civil war.[54] The reason isn't hard to find: fear that the nation was falling apart led its citizens to seek unity in the memory of the Revolution.

This connection between what is commemorated and when also underlines the importance of the selectiveness of memory. As in the case of relying on the founding in a moment of national division, national unity has often depended on focusing on the salutary aspects of the fight for independence: the heroes, their ideals, their bravery, and not their inconsistencies, hypocrisies, and commitment to white supremacy.[55] As Nikole Hannah-Jones notes in this regard, "the United States is founded on both an ideal and a lie."[56] If the nation is invested in preserving the ideal and the only way it can do so is by perpetuating the lie, then the exclusion of some people is always going to be the result, because their history must be erased to preserve that lie.

Even within the context of an idealized past, different people within the same era are remembered differently. Most obviously, Benedict Arnold is one of the Revolution's villains, and George Washington is one of its heroes. But not all heroes are the same.[57] Jefferson is remembered because he is both accessible and flexible and has been so from his day to ours.[58] Because public memory is malleable, although not infinitely so, Jefferson has been, variously, "freedom's philosopher, racist-in-chief, the champion of liberal government, and the champion of small government. . . . His is the first name Americans associate with representative democracy. He is the 'founding father' whose political sentiments reverberate loudest. Here and around the world, he is democracy's muse."[59] However one views Jefferson, other aspects of him linger, casting shadows on any singular interpretation of him.[60]

Jefferson made extensive efforts to control (or at least influence) the public memory of his presidency and his role in the larger history of his time.[61] He wrote his own epitaph; he left letters and documents defending and explaining his role in various events; he famously asked James Madison to take care of how he was to be remembered. But he could never completely control the public perception of him, and US Americans have had distinct views of Jefferson over time—views that correspond to how those in power viewed the nation at the time.[62]

Because the legacies of slavery and the complexities of race more broadly are so deeply embedded in US national identity, and because those things are so much a part of contemporary conversations about that identity, and are so controversial and so contested, discussions of slavery and race are integral to how Jefferson is now remembered. Some ignore issues of Jefferson and race, which reflects a preference that current racial hierarchies go uncontested, and that current national identity remain unaltered. Others finesse these issues, reflecting a greater sense of ambivalence about how to deal with matters of race and national identity. Recognizing the importance of race, they are uncomfortable with the implications of dealing with it openly. Still others center questions of race in conversations about national identity, seeking to highlight and upset current racially based hierarchies. These choices are central to how Jefferson is remembered, and are therefore prominent throughout this book.

Similarly, Jefferson in his own time was lauded as a president who, by completing the Louisiana Purchase, "doubled the size of the nation" and opened the West to settlement. But what the United States bought from France was not actual land but only the right to negotiate with Indigenous peoples for it; and the West was, in fact, already occupied by those peoples.[63] Choices were made to dispossess those peoples, and while the nation has long resisted any accounting for this history, it continues to shadow national history and national identity. So this is also a prominent theme in the book.

I am interested here in how we remember Jefferson on the 250th anniversary of the founding. I consider Jefferson's actual biography, of course, but also how this biography has been and is understood. Because memory is associated with national identity, and because our collective memory of Jefferson is so fluid, how he is remembered and by whom is a good indicator of the varied valences of contemporary national identity, in all of its complexities. I take seriously the idea that the different ways we remember (through presidential speeches, monuments and memorials, popular culture, and children's literature) all speak to different audiences and do so in different ways, creating different kinds of memory communities, which overlap, parallel, combine, and collide to produce the rich, contradictory, and elusive sense of what it currently means to be a US American.[64] These forms of memory do not create Jefferson out of whole cloth, but are grounded in the facts of his life.

Considering Jefferson

I am, as I have noted, relatively uninterested in litigating the facts of Jefferson's life. There are many excellent biographies of him already.[65] That said, in order to understand how he is remembered, and what that might tell us about current national identity, we need at least some understanding of those facts. In what follows, then, I offer a very brief account of his life and career.

Thomas Jefferson was born on April 13, 1743, on the family plantation in Shadwell Virginia. He grew up as the privileged son of a slave-owning family. His first memory, cited over and over in biographies of him, is of being placed by one of his family's enslaved workers on a pillow, and being conducted via horseback to a nearby plantation where he was to live for several years. That his first memory is of slavery is not remarkable; slavery infused his whole life. After a childhood of private education typical for one of his status and wealth, he attended William and Mary before becoming a lawyer in 1767 and member of the House of Burgesses in 1769. In that capacity, he persuaded his cousin to advocate for some mild reforms to the institution of slavery, such as providing owners rather than the governor the right to emancipate enslaved persons. The measure faced strong opposition and failed. As a lawyer, he took the cases of some enslaved people seeking their freedom; in at least one case, he grounded his case in natural law. These elements of his career are often stressed by those seeking evidence that despite his ownership of enslaved persons, he was a life-long opponent of slavery.

In 1772 he married Martha Wayles Skelton and moved to Monticello, a home Jefferson constructed (and continuously reconstructed) near Charlottesville. When Martha's father died, she and Jefferson inherited eleven thousand acres of land, considerable debt, and 135 enslaved people, including Martha's half-sister, a child named Sally Hemings. Martha bore six children (only two of whom, Polly and Martha, survived into adulthood) and suffered from poor health for much of their marriage, dying in 1782.

In 1775 Jefferson became one of the youngest members of the Second Continental Congress. As a member of that Congress, he quickly developed a reputation for rhetorical skill, and was one of the Committee of Five charged with drafting a declaration declaring colonial independence from Great Britain. After resigning from Congress, he returned to Virginia and was elected to the House of Delegates, where he sponsored legislation intended to improve the judicial system, protect religious freedom, create a system of public education, and eliminate primogeniture.[66] Elected governor in 1779 and again in 1780, he moved the state capital from Williamsburg to Richmond and continued to work for religious and educational reforms. Not a particularly good wartime governor, at one point Jefferson was forced to flee troops under the leadership of the traitorous Benedict Arnold, an event that created considerable controversy.[67]

In 1780, at least partly in response to claims by a French naturalist that the flora and fauna of the Americas were inferior to those of Europe, Jefferson began work on *Notes on the State of Virginia*, a compendium of observations about Virginia's geography, wildlife, laws, and customs, published in 1785. It was also a collection of racist opinions presented as empirically grounded observations concerning African Americans and Indigenous peoples. Appointed to the Congress of the Confederation following the British surrender, Jefferson crafted the Land Ordinance of 1784, which served as a model for the Northwest Ordinance (1787), which provided a process by which territories become states, and the (often forcible) reappropriation of land from Indigenous people to the US government.

In 1784 he was sent to France to join the ministerial delegation there. He took his daughter Martha with him and was later joined by his younger daughter Polly, who was accompanied by a young enslaved woman, Sally Hemings, with whom Jefferson began a sexual relationship.[68] He spent several years in France, and was there during the debates over reforming the Articles of Confederation and the new US Constitution.[69] He returned to the United States in 1789, already confirmed as the new nation's first secretary of state.

As a member of George Washington's cabinet, he developed both political and personal animosity to Secretary of the Treasury Alexander Hamilton, whom he considered a monarchist, and thus a threat to democracy in the United States.[70] The disputes between the two continued to escalate until Jefferson resigned from the cabinet in 1794; those disputes contributed to, among other things, the creation of the US party system and the partisan press.[71] Jefferson consistently supported state and local control above that of the central government. Elected John Adams's vice president in 1796, he and James Madison secretly authored the Virginia and Kentucky Resolutions in response to Adams's Alien and Sedition Acts. These resolutions made the case that the Constitution was a compact among sovereign states that gave limited power to federal government and claimed, contrary to the Constitution, that states had the power to overrule actions of the federal government.[72]

Following the bitterly contested 1800 presidential election, Jefferson took office claiming unprecedented national unity and the victory of "true" republicanism.[73] As president, Jefferson proved to be more of a pragmatist than an ideologue, however, keeping, for instance, the US National Bank that he considered a symbol of Federalist power. Committed to national expansion, Jefferson's administration is probably best known for the Louisiana Purchase. Jefferson considered the deal itself to be of dubious constitutionality, but this defender of small government nevertheless exercised one of the most sweeping acts of presidential power in history.[74] Understanding that the United States did not have title to western lands, he sent Meriweather Lewis and William Clark, captains of the Corps of Discovery, on an expedition designed to establish that title.[75]

Other matters of foreign policy were also important to Jefferson's administration.[76] He managed armed skirmishes between the United States and Tripoli,[77] he ended US support from the Haitian revolutionaries led by Toussaint Louverture,[78] and he authorized an extremely unpopular embargo in 1807, aimed at both France and Great Britain.[79] Domestically, he had to contend with the controversy caused by his former vice president Aaron Burr's trial for treason.[80] He advocated Indigenous assimilation and removal.[81] Despite any ambivalence he may (or may not) have cherished on the subject of slavery, he remained a consistent defender of the institution, even though he signed legislation outlawing the domestic slave trade.

Following his presidency, he retired to Monticello, his Virginia plantation and the home of both his acknowledged white daughter's family and his unacknowledged enslaved one. There he died, on the fiftieth anniversary of the signing of his famous declaration, just before fellow patriot, friend, and antagonist John Adams.

Jefferson's Legacies

On April 13, 1943, President Franklin Roosevelt dedicated the Thomas Jefferson National Memorial in Washington, DC. Later that day, Archibald MacLeish, the Librarian of Congress, convened an impressive panel of Jefferson scholars in a symposium in his honor. Celebrations were also held at Jefferson's home at Monticello, outside of Charlottesville, Virginia; in Philadelphia, where he had drafted the Declaration of Independence; and in St. Louis, Missouri, the embarkation point of the Corps of Discovery, popularly known as the Lewis and Clark Expedition. It was quite the birthday party for someone who had been dead for more than a hundred years.

Few presidents have been remembered as lavishly or as often as Jefferson. In the chapters that follow, I look at the different ways he is remembered now and the different meanings contemporary US Americans attach to his memory. The first chapter, "The Presidential

Jefferson," offers a brief history of how US presidents have used Jefferson to serve different political agendas over time, noting how presidents of different parties have and continue to use Jefferson to authorize their various definitions of national identity. Institutionally, the presidency often relies on precedent, and we can learn a great deal about both the presidency and the evolution of national identity by looking closely at who and what serves as presidential precedent, and why.[82] Here, I contribute to our understanding of how presidents rely on their interpretations of national identity to craft both a version of who Jefferson was and a vision of what the nation has become.

Chapter 2, "The Monumental Jefferson" focuses on how Jefferson is remembered in monuments and memorials. Monuments can be understood as attempts to render one understanding of politics lasting if not timeless, but as controversies since the 2020 police murder of George Floyd have indicated, they do so with varying degrees of success. The Revolutionary moment tends to get re-memorialized in times of national stress and threatened disunity, which points to both the continuing need to reassert that unity and the fragility of those assertions. Here, I think through how and why some versions of history remain central to national self-understanding, why others might need to be rethought, and how still others become irrelevant.

Chapter 3 continues that discussion, this time examining how Jefferson is remembered as part of a group—most often, the members of the founding generation, but also as the progenitor of the Lewis and Clark Expedition. These collective memorializations render their subjects (sometimes literally) larger than life, and make criticism of them or their policies difficult.[83] In this, I add to our understanding of how both the monuments themselves and the contexts in which they find themselves affects how they might be received, and why depictions of a group (like "the founders") or a moment (like "the Revolution") condenses complicated histories into simple moral tales, glossing national history and impeding a nuanced sense of national identity.

In chapter 4 I take up the question of how Jefferson is remembered in popular culture, with particular attention to him as the subject of collective moral judgments, and what that tells us about how we understand the dilemmas of US American citizenship.[84] Because it is vernacular and often local rather than official and national, depictions of time-honored characters like the founders are moved off of the more sacred ground of many official memory sites, and become more humanized, more complicated, and more readily open to criticism. These bottom-up versions of national identity are more flexible than many official versions, more easily able to adapt to changing views and new information. They can be more immediately revealing of changes to conceptions of national identity within the broader culture.

In chapter 5 I focus on the lenses through which children are taught about Jefferson, and the consequences of each for conceptions of citizenship and belonging. Despite the commonplace that "children are the future," literature and other media specifically aimed at children are not often the subjects of rhetorical analysis, although they are potentially interesting sites for understanding the kinds of contestations that occur over what children are taught.[85] In focusing on this important slice of popular culture, I hope to add to our understanding of how rhetoric operates in explicitly educational and didactic forums. In these forums, lessons of citizenship and belonging are offered not as the obvious subjects of the stories, but as entailments and consequences of stories presented as factually based histories. These consequences and entailments thus appear as both natural and inevitable, beyond questioning. But they are also always contingent, always invented.

These chapters all focus both on different sites of public memory and on different aspects of national identity. Through these lenses, we have access to the history of how presidents have wielded Jefferson in the service of their agendas and what agendas he may be serving now; to contemporary understandings of the ideals Jefferson stood for and what the nation ought to value; how we ought to understand the founding generation, and to what extent we should be guided by them; how he should be understood as an individual, and what that tells us about the national character and national moral struggles; and how we want children to understand their place in the nation, and how its ideals might be enacted in the future. I conclude with a discussion of what this tells us about national identity.

1

The Presidential Jefferson

Thomas Jefferson and John Adams, close associates, political enemies, and (sporadically) personal friends, died within hours of one another on the fiftieth anniversary of the date usually associated with the signing of the Declaration of Independence, July 4, 1826. Given the nation's ongoing tumultuous relationships with slavery and with itself (the Missouri Compromise was a mere six years in the past and the Civil War only thirty four years ahead), these two deaths, occurring in tandem and on that date, were widely understood as ominous portents for the future. In his famous eulogy, Massachusetts senator Daniel Webster called upon his audience to treat this occasion as a call to much-needed national unity. Webster considered the tears shed by the nation at the loss of these two political giants a sign "that the nation itself might be immortal." He continued, "Their work doth not perish with them. The tree, which they assisted to plant, will flourish, although they water and protect it no longer; for it has struck its roots deep; it has sent them to the very centre; no storm, not of force to burst the orb, can overturn it; its branches spread wide; they stretch their protecting arms broader and broader, and its top is destined to reach the heavens."[1] Webster used the deaths of these two Revolutionary patriots to argue that sentiment for national union ran deep and reached broadly. His metaphor made the implicit argument that the nation could survive its present tensions because all of its citizens, northern and southern, in slave states and in free states, were equally dedicated to the legacy left by Adams and Jefferson, equally loyal to the union the US Revolution had created.

Webster was not making a statement about the stability of the federal union, but a plea for it. We do not need to speak to certainties. Rhetoric concerns the contingent, that which must be argued for, not that which is taken for granted. This is one of the reasons "rhetoric" is so often associated with politics, for in politics, many things are contingent. Politics is the realm in which communal choices are made, and rhetoric is the mechanism for deciding among those choices. In US national politics, few people make more arguments, or make them to larger audiences, than presidents. As they make their arguments, presidents reach for past precedents as well as for future possibilities. In doing so, they speak very clearly to questions of national identity. They often find, as Webster did, that Thomas Jefferson is signally useful to them. Jefferson's words, his life, and his symbolic stature have been wielded by a surprising number of presidents for a surprising number of often disparate—and sometimes even directly opposed—purposes.

Presidents use Jefferson to help them authorize their understanding of national ideals, and thus they use him as they endeavor to create national community. They also create national community by collecting "the people" around specific kinds of policy choices, both internationally and domestically. That is what this chapter is about. I first discuss the connections between rhetoric, community, and presidential speech. Next, I offer a brief history in broad strokes of how presidents have generally used Jefferson, paying particular attention to Franklin Roosevelt, who reshaped Jefferson into his own image, and Ronald Reagan, who reshaped Roosevelt's Jefferson into his own. I then turn to some specific examples that flow across presidencies so we can see how more recent presidents remember Jefferson, what they do with those memories, and what those uses tell us about national identity.

Creating Community

Communities are not created by geography, ethnicity, race, or common interests, but through rhetoric.[2] We give meaning to geography, ethnicity, race, and common interests through language. That is, geography, ethnicity, race, and common interests only become meaningful as categories in the context of arguments that tell us both that they are meaningful and how they matter. Race, for example, only matters in a context in which it is created, defined, and given purpose. Such creations, definitions, and applications always both divide and unite people. Whenever people create communities, they do so by drawing lines between who is included and who is excluded from those communities—creating an "us" also creates a "them."[3] In the US American example, for instance, the claim that "Americans" have a unique and definable identity goes back at least as far as the Declaration's claim that the "political bonds" holding them to the British were both dissolvable and dissolved, that "one people" were separate enough from another that independence was both warranted and necessary. J. Hector St. John de Crevecoeur elaborated on this argument in his 1782 publication, *Letters from an American Farmer*, in which he argued that the former colonists were unique because of their access to land, which gave them the ability to avoid poverty and live independent, self-sufficient lives.[4] Both the signatories to the Declaration and Crevecoeur claimed that something about the geography and the lived experiences of those in the North American British colonies made them distinctly different from their European cousins. Creating a community out of these new people meant finding ways that they were like one another, despite religious, regional, and cultural differences, and unlike the British, despite their many obvious similarities.

But not all those who lived in the places comprising the former British colonies were therefore automatically included in the newly created community. Indigenous and enslaved people, those who did not trace their ancestry to Europe, and all women were excluded as equal members of this new community, and even among those who were included, some (wealthy landowners, for example) were preferred to others (indentured servants, say). Creating community necessarily means creating inclusions, exclusions, and hierarchies.[5] Sometimes constitutive rhetoric, the language of community creation, might be quite explicit; someone might declare, "People of this community believe this, prefer these people to those, and do these kinds of things as a result." But generally speaking, the language of community is more subtle than that. A community leader, retelling a well-known story of the community's origins, will call upon certain values that their audience probably takes for granted—as they take for granted the origin story in general. So a speaker on the eastern seaboard might recall the Pilgrims; in the Midwest, the pioneer heritage might be foregrounded; in the West, it might be the missions established by the Spanish, the Bear Flag Rebellion, or the gold rush—communities often have a large repertoire of stories to choose from. None of these examples, or the many others like them, are just origin stories. They are also claims to belonging that bring with them different hierarchies. Audience members can see themselves as the actual or the ideological descendants of the Pilgrims, the pioneers, or those who settled the West. Those who are not among those descendants, or who do not in some way represent the values and heritages associated with them, are usually placed at the bottom of the resulting hierarchies.

Note also that because these consequences are inherent in the stories of communities, they seem both natural and inevitable. The values and beliefs, for example, that are claimed in these stories as foundational to a community—the devotion to God of the Pilgrims, the hardworking resilience of the pioneers—are treated as universals. Not all members of the "Greatest Generation" shared the ideals and beliefs commonly associated with that phrase any more than all members of "Generation Z" share the attributes often ascribed to them. But at the level of the nation, these generalizations are so vaguely defined and so often repeated that they are also never quite heard. Any individual member of "Gen Z" might quibble with a description of their era, but when presidents laud "American values" on ceremonial occasions, those values are so much a part of the fabric of national conversations, and presidential treatments of them are generally so bland, that they are likely to be widely accepted—at least by the audience that is most obviously addressed at such moments.[6]

Presidents are expected to speak to the positives in national history, to base community on national successes. A president speaking on the Fourth of July who attempted to modify their claims about US American freedom and commitment to democracy by mentioning slavery or its legacies of continuing inequities would be considered by their probable audience to be failing at their ceremonial celebratory task.[7] Consequently, while those whose experiences run counter to these presidential narratives are also those who are usually at the bottom of the national hierarchies, or are those who are excluded from the nation altogether, these erasures and exclusions are generally accomplished almost invisibly, at least to those who are included in the community. Claims to belonging, especially at the national level, are not made as if that belonging is contingent. They are enunciated as *statements* that do not need to be proven and should not be contested, not as *arguments* whose merits are up for debate. And the implied exclusions and limitations are almost always ignored by those who are not directly affected by them.

But those exclusions and limitations are still there, and they still matter. Any definition of community will be both inclusive and exclusionary. Any one claim to belonging necessarily limits the claims of others, either by erasing them (as in the Pilgrim replacement of Indigenous people), by making them villains (as in the "savage Indians" of many a white western tale), or by limiting the roles they are allowed to play (the treatment of women in almost all origin stories).[8] These stories do not offer these exclusions arbitrarily. There is always a reason—now usually rooted in behavior or ideology, but sometimes also located in race, or gender, or class—for why a group of people must be excluded to protect the community (think about many a contemporary rhetorical treatment of immigrants seeking to enter the United States via its southern border, and how that is different from the treatment of those coming in from its northern border).[9] Not all of these exclusions are the same. There is obviously a difference between claiming that violent white supremacists are acting in "un-American ways" and claiming that women, or Chinese, or Muslims, are by definition unable to act as US American citizens, although different presidents have made, at different times, both kinds of claims. And that difference is tricky; once it is agreed that people can be excluded for being "un-American," that category can expand and contract in a variety of ways, some more dangerous to democratic values than others. Those who might be liable to exclusion at any given moment depends on the stories the community is willing to accept about itself.

I label these as "stories" rather than as "histories" for a reason. Although many of them are historical, or at least reference history, they are also all constructions—they are simplified versions of complicated pasts that tell one version of events and neglect or ignore others. As with all public memory, the past serves the present; we tell stories of the past that help us navigate our own moment. These stories have varying degrees of accuracy, but accuracy is never the point. They serve to define "us," to draw communities together. On the national level, presidents strive to create an "Unum" out of "E Pluribus." This is almost never easily accomplished.

Presidents are the only political actors authorized to speak for the entire nation, and they draw much of their authority and power from this ability.[10] In making their claims about the contours of the nation and the nature of its good (and bad) citizens, presidents have considerable, but not complete, power. Sometimes, presidents offer visions that the nation rejects, and even successful visions are also always contested—in the current moment, for example, Democrats and Republicans have starkly different views of what the nation stands for, who ought to be included in it, and on what kinds of terms.[11] That said, visions of national identity are less likely to find controversy when they are grounded in "what everybody knows," which is also to understand that the "everybody" in question is already considered a member of the community. When former enslaved person and orator Frederick Douglass asked in 1852, "What to a Slave Is the Fourth of July," he was disrupting the commonplaces of Independence Day celebrations in a caustic demand for recognition of the gap between national ideals and national practices.[12] Such disruption is almost always made by those who are marginalized or excluded from the community, and are almost never welcomed by those who are already included in it.

Much more common—especially among presidents—are claims that place ideals and practices together and beyond such demands.

Constitutive rhetoric succeeds when enough of the people being addressed see themselves as willing members of the community being described, and see the values being associated with that community as reflecting their aspirations. So presidents laud the patriotism of volunteers, of military personnel, of teachers, of whatever individual or group they are using as a model of citizenship. The argument on such occasions is something like, "We all agree that patriotism is good; these people show patriotism by doing/being/believing these specific things, and so we admire and want to be like them." This kind of identification between values and nation has consequences. Audience members see themselves as part of the community and also as willing to act as such.[13] As members of the US American community, for example, people might see themselves as both dedicated to "freedom" and willing to act in its defense. Depending on how those actions are defined, those people might be willing to engage in volunteerism, to vote, to join the military, or to storm the national Capitol.

This list indicates how flexible different presidential visions of national identity might be. But whatever the variation, when presidents offer their visions to the public, they do so as if there is only one option; as if that one option is widely, if not universally, agreed upon; and that they are clearly speaking as heirs to a long line of similar understandings of "American" values and actions. The most obvious way to do this is to rely on the words and examples of previous presidents. When it comes to useful words and examples, no one comes in more handy to more presidents than Thomas Jefferson.

Jefferson over Time

As both Merrill Peterson and Joseph Coglinano have documented, Jefferson's popularity has ebbed, flowed, and changed in content over time.[14] So too has his usefulness as a warrant for political action. Revered in the immediate aftermath of his death in 1826, as the nation stumbled closer to Civil War he was more likely to be wielded as a justification for states' rights and secession than as a philosopher of national union. Southerners seeking justifications for secession found those justifications in a variety of places; important among them were both the Declaration of Independence and the Virginia and Kentucky Resolutions, secretly authored by Jefferson and James Madison.[15]

While abolitionists relied on the claims to human equality embedded within the Declaration, the document also provided secessionists with a clear justification for political division based on the maintenance of structural inequality—the system of chattel slavery. Secessionists are not alone in this, of course; the argument that any "one people," however understood, has the right to their "separate and equal station" has been used to authorize various kinds of political disunion throughout US history, ranging from the peaceful to the violent.[16] Michael J. Lee and R. Jarrod Atchison argue that the Declaration is a useful warrant for secession for at least three reasons: it sets up a rationale, arguing that denial of human rights is sufficient cause for separation; it claims the right of a people to "alter or abolish" a government; and it argues that separation can be justified based on racial or cultural difference.[17] Antebellum Southerners tended either to ignore the claims to human equality or to contextualize them as intended only to apply to white men, but they latched onto the argument that cultural differences justified separation with both tenacity and ferocity.[18] Jefferson's Declaration provided them with what they considered to be an irrefutable argument for secession. Partnered with the Virginia and Kentucky Resolutions, which made (poorly reasoned) arguments about the states' ability to nullify actions of the federal government, secessionists claimed that their actions—up to and including human enslavement—were consistent with the ideals of the founding.

Following the war, Jefferson's association with the Confederacy greatly diminished his authority as a spokesperson for the nation, and presidents in the postbellum era, concerned as they were with crafting union in the aftermath of civil war, relied on other sources for those arguments. By the early twentieth century, even though the federal union itself seemed stable, the nation still contended with internal divisions, and presidents like the first Roosevelt worried about

Jefferson's legacy as one that potentially inspired insurrectionists and anarchists.[19] Thus, from the antebellum era through the 1930s, Jefferson was considered more as a source of authority for those people presidents tended to consider dangerous to the federal union than for those interested in maintaining it. But there is a distinction between using Jefferson to secede from the Union, as the Confederates did, and to demand fairer treatment or inclusion within it, as many of those whom Theodore Roosevelt considered dangerous did. This shift is important, because once the Civil War seemed to solve the question of union, the Declaration—and Jefferson with it—were then available as sources of authority for those arguing that the nation was founded on the ideals of equality and human rights. Advocates for labor, for women's rights, for Black civil rights, for Indigenous rights, and so on used the Declaration to ground their arguments in the US political tradition, and to therefore argue that they were not radicals asking for a different kind of nation, but solidly within the nation, asking only to be recognized as such.[20]

By the 1930s, when ardent Jefferson admirer Franklin D. Roosevelt assumed the presidency, the nation's survival again seemed threatened, but this time the crisis was one that Roosevelt hoped could be used to unite the country, and Jefferson became one of his strongest allies in the effort.[21] For Roosevelt, the nation could only be saved through the efforts of a strong national government, so his reliance on Jefferson, philosophically an advocate of state and local governments over that of central federal power, was decidedly incongruous.[22] But Roosevelt did what many other presidents do as well—he remade Jefferson, Jefferson's memory, and Jefferson's legacy into shapes that suited his needs. In this case, Roosevelt first relied on Jefferson's optimism and his faith in democracy to buttress his own actions in response to the unprecedented crisis posed by the Great Depression. He then depended on Jefferson's frequently avowed if unevenly practiced dedication to human freedom to make arguments regarding US intervention in the war in Europe. As his attention shifted from the Depression to the war, FDR's faith in the nation—and in Jefferson as a powerful advocate for a symbol of it—remained steadfast. In memorializing Jefferson, FDR also memorialized his own view of the United States.

Like many other Democrats in the 1920s and 1930s, Franklin Roosevelt saw in Jefferson a way to legitimate the New Deal and its underlying philosophy by drawing a line from the Roosevelt administration back to Jefferson. Because his dedication to what he called "Jeffersonian principles" was long-standing, FDR could use Jefferson as a warrant for his own actions without seeming to be stretching the Virginian's legacy beyond which it could not plausibly go.[23] For Roosevelt, those principles, like his own, centered on the idea that governments should be inclusive of the entire nation, not merely responsive to elites. Roosevelt tended to rely on Jefferson as a hero of the "common man" and to ignore Jefferson's disapproval of strong federal power. In 1925, for example, in a message to the Thomas Jefferson Memorial Foundation, FDR wrote, "The world may view American [*sic*] as a young country, yet it recognizes that we were the first among all nations to establish a government representative of the whole people. In the conception and in the application of this great advance, Thomas Jefferson was the steadfast, clear-thinking leader."[24] Roosevelt consistently argued that Alexander Hamilton, Jefferson's nemesis, was the same as his own political enemies, striving to restrict governmental access to the wealthy, and that he, like Jefferson, was engaged in fighting for the rights of the common people.[25]

Roosevelt was not alone in his understanding of Jefferson, nor was he alone in hoping that Jefferson's legacy could be wielded to contemporaneous political purposes. Josephus Daniels, the former secretary of the navy, FDR's former boss and frequent correspondent, wrote to the president calling Jefferson "the greatest American liberal." Daniels claimed, "He breathed the breath of life into the new republic in his Declaration and saved freedom by writing the guarantees of freedom of religion, freedom of the press, and the Bill of Rights into the Constitution after the Convention had omitted those basic guarantees essential for a free government."[26] This is, of course, a minor misreading of history (Jefferson was not especially active in either writing or passing the Bill of Rights; that credit more appropriately goes to his friend Madison). But Daniels was less interested in historical accuracy than in connecting Jefferson to Roosevelt and the ideological battles Jefferson fought to the ones Roosevelt and members of his coalition were engaged in.

In 1933 FDR was elected one of the honorary presidents of the "Jeffersonians of America," a group "dedicated to educational work for preservation of fundamental American ideals [of] civil liberty[,] religious freedom[,] and universal education we all inherit from Thomas Jefferson." Writing to inform FDR of this honor, the organization's president told him, "you are fighting the same battle that Thomas Jefferson, James Monroe, Andrew Jackson, Abraham Lincoln and TR [Theodore Roosevelt] fought against the power of the privileged few for the salvation of the masses of American people and in your heroic effort please be assured that you have the best wishes and whole-hearted loyal support of the Jeffersonians of America."[27] This list is instructive, including as it does a collection of US presidents who span a fairly wide ideological spectrum. The list, and others like it, indicate both Jefferson's utility across party lines, and the ways that the New Deal was seeking to reshape those lines. FDR himself insisted that his administration's goals encompassed not party, but nation.[28] Laying the cornerstone for the Jefferson Memorial in 1939, Roosevelt said, "He lived, as we live, in the midst of a struggle between rule by the self-chosen individual or the self-appointed few and rule by the franchise and the approval of the many. He believed, as we do, that the average opinion of mankind is in the long run superior to the dictates of the self-chosen."[29] Note here not only that FDR equated his own struggle with Jefferson's, but also his use of constitutive rhetoric: he is speaking to what "we" believe, and thus also to who "we" are.[30] And he pitted not Democrats against Republicans, but "the few" against "the many."

This use of Jefferson stood FDR in good stead as the Second World War loomed, and he increasingly made arguments detailing threats to global democracy and encouraging action in its defense. He did not hesitate to use Jefferson as he made these arguments. Despite his claims to the contrary, FDR was both deeply interested and deeply involved with design decisions for the Jefferson Memorial; he offered opinions on the statue, the memorial's design, and its inscriptions.[31] In doing so, he was consciously calling upon Jefferson's connection to democratic republicanism and consciously avoiding the less savory aspects of his legacy.[32] Speaking at the dedication of the memorial in 1945, for example, Roosevelt called Jefferson the "Apostle of Freedom" and said, "He lived in a world in which freedom of conscience and freedom of mind were battles still to be fought through—not principles already accepted by all men. We, too, have lived in such a world. He loved peace, and loved liberty—yet on more than one occasion he was forced to choose between them. We, too, have been compelled to make that choice."[33] For Roosevelt, Jefferson was a model of both correct thinking about government and the necessary sacrifices that had to be made to deliver and protect human freedom. Speaking about the quotations selected for engraving on the memorial, Roosevelt said, "The words which we have chosen for this Memorial speak to Jefferson's noblest and most urgent meaning; and we are proud indeed to understand it and share it: 'I have sworn upon the altar of God, eternal hostility against every form of tyranny over the mind of man.'"[34] Roosevelt here used Jefferson to liken the world war to the founding; they were the same struggle, fought across centuries. Yet the quotations on the memorial, as we will see in the next chapter, are intentionally misleading. They had to be because Roosevelt's Jefferson was primarily an advocate for the common person, a spokesperson for human freedom, and a dedicated adherent to human liberty. Because he was all of these things, he was also an appropriate model for US Americans engaged in a world war that Roosevelt understood as pitting the traditions of western democracy against the forces of tyranny.[35] Jefferson's views on race and his support of slavery were inconveniences, to say the least.

After Roosevelt's death and the end of the war, presidents of both parties largely relied on this view of Jefferson, generally depicting him, especially in the context of the Cold War, as a global citizen, a defender of democracy, and a "believer in progress."[36] In the hands of these presidents, Jefferson came to symbolize US American ingenuity, its vast potential, and its capaciousness. Dwight Eisenhower, for instance, marking the 150th anniversary of the Louisiana Purchase, called it "typically American."[37] Democrats shared this view. Probably the most famous presidential invocation of Jefferson, of course, is when John F. Kennedy, hosting a dinner for Nobel laureates, welcomed them to the White House saying, "I think this is the most extraordinary collection of talent, of human knowledge, that has ever been gathered together at the White House, with the possible exception of when Thomas Jefferson dined alone."[38] It is worth noting that this dinner honored not all Nobelists, but those of the Western Hemisphere. Jefferson was invoked as a US American, and as superior to the hemispheric best, in the context of the Cold War.

Unsurprisingly, the national bicentennial in 1976 brought with it even more praise for Jefferson.[39] That March, the Library of Congress building was renamed for Jefferson. April 13, Jefferson's birthday, was named "Thomas Jefferson Day" by President Gerald Ford, who called Jefferson "the greatest of this inspired group of patriots" and the nation's "most articulate champion of individual freedom."[40] Note here that Ford used the adjective "individual" to modify "freedom." Roosevelt had used Jefferson as an "apostle of freedom," by which he meant both individual and collective freedom, both of which he opposed to totalitarian regimes. As a conservative, Ford was shaping Jefferson to fit his own politics. In doing so, he was also arguing for Jefferson's continued relevance. Not only was Jefferson's name now on the Library of Congress, not only did he get his own day, but his was the face on the new $2 bill; Jefferson continued to circulate as a symbol of the nation. Ford argued, "We are all his successors, and it is up to us, not history, to see that Jefferson's faith survives. . . . In every generation, Americans have turned to Jefferson for comfort and inspiration. They have found new meanings, often conflicting meanings, in his words. In their search for Jefferson's spirit, Americans have sought themselves," specifically linking Jefferson to the national search for identity.[41] For Ford, Jefferson's legacy was one that encompassed both substantive policies and an orientation toward politics: "We find he believed that not every difference of opinion is a difference of principle, and that he tolerated error in confidence that truth would triumph."[42] It is not at all clear that this is a particularly good analysis of Jefferson's approach to politics. It is very clear that Ford, governing in the wake of Watergate and the Vietnam War, badly needed a unifying figure, and Jefferson was useful in that endeavor. But he was also limited—acceptable to Ford's political coalition, in the context of the 1970s, Jefferson was much less appealing as a national symbol to others. Black US Americans, for example, found little to admire in Jefferson's legacy as an enslaver, and probably had difficulty seeing themselves as welcome in a nation that relied on him as its symbol.[43]

Perhaps for this reason, Southerner Jimmy Carter found other sources to justify his commitment to human rights, and relied relatively little on Jefferson.[44] His successor, Ronald Reagan, however, followed Ford in appropriating Jefferson from the Democratic purposes to which he had long been put, and used Jeffersonian references quite frequently.[45] In Reagan's hands, Jefferson was useful primarily as an advocate for individual freedom and small government. Roosevelt's Jefferson might be seen as the Jefferson of the Louisiana Purchase, wielding executive power even he was not sure he actually possessed. His Jefferson was a man who used government power to protect the people from a selfish elite. Reagan's Jefferson was a strong advocate of states' rights and a critic of strong federal power. His Jefferson defended the people from their government. Speaking at a conference of state legislators shortly after his election, for example, Reagan said, "It was Jefferson who reminded us that against the invasion of the people's liberty, the only 'true barriers . . . are the state governments.' So today, fresh from our victories together, I ask you to join me in another great cause, another great revolution, and a great experiment."[46] What Reagan had in mind was nothing less than dismantling the New Deal—the creation of which FDR had justified with reference to Jefferson. It is not a coincidence that he placed himself alongside Jefferson as a revolutionary and experimenter, bolstering both his policies and his own stature.

Reagan argued, for example,

Thomas Jefferson said, "I know no safe depository of the ultimate powers of the society but the people themselves". . . . And that conviction is embodied in our 10th amendment—the Federal Government will do only those things called for in the Constitution, and all others shall remain with the States or the people. Would you not agree that we have strayed much too far from that noble beginning, and that the whole idea of our Revolution—personal freedom, equality of opportunity, and keeping government close to the people—is threatened by a Federal spending machine that takes too much money from the people, too much authority from the States, and yes, too much liberty with our Constitution?[47]

This is not necessarily a good reading of Jefferson's philosophy, but it doesn't stretch him more than Roosevelt did—it merely stretches him in the opposite direction.

Reagan, like Roosevelt, used his version of Jefferson to good political effect. But Republicans were not going to keep Jefferson without a fight. Coming into office in 1992, Bill Clinton was quick to adopt aspects of Jefferson, especially those that favored an experimental, forward looking, progressive politics.[48] He said, for example, "Thomas Jefferson believed that to preserve the very foundations of our Nation, we would need dramatic change from time to time. Well, my fellow Americans, this is our time. Let us embrace it."[49] Much as Reagan had adopted specific pieces of a Jefferson already present in the public mind (defender of individual liberty), Clinton took pieces of Reagan's Jefferson (his forward-looking experimentalism) and focused on those pieces that fit his own approach to politics.[50] But as Democrats were less certain that Jefferson was useful in uniting their coalition, Jefferson was increasingly used by those advocating against the federal government, against taxes, and against the Democratic agenda.[51]

A couple of things are worth noting here. First, Clinton notwithstanding, from the 1960s on, Democrats have generally become increasingly leery of Jefferson. His history as an enslaver became more relevant to more national politicians in the wake of the civil rights movement, especially once the revelations about Sally Hemings (detailed in chapter 4) exploded into public consciousness. In addition, Jefferson's views on US American Exceptionalism, the belief that there was something not only unique but also morally superior about the United States, was a difficult assumption for Democrats to make in the aftermath of the Vietnam War, and absent a Cold War context. Republicans, more willing to accept the premises of US American Exceptionalism and less willing to advocate for civil rights, were more comfortable with the Jefferson they had crafted—one dedicated to small, local government, who abhorred federal power and federal taxation, and who could be used to defend their vision of US American global hegemony. The next section delves into some of these differences with specific attention to how presidents have used Jefferson to make claims about national identity.

The Useful Jefferson

Presidents have long relied on Jefferson as the archetype of US democracy, as the defender of "the people." Since we've already heard from some of these early presidents, I pick up this story in the middle of the twentieth century, after World War II. As the United States sought to globalize its version of democracy following the Second World War, presidents found Jefferson and the universals he had articulated in the Declaration particularly useful. Speaking after the Soviets crushed the Hungarian Revolution in 1956, Eisenhower said, "But the human spirit knows, as Thomas Jefferson says, that the God who gave us life, gave us liberty at the same time. The courage and sacrifices of the brave Hungarian people have consecrated that spirit anew."[52] For Eisenhower, the Hungarians were representing the ideals of the US founding, which were global in scope. His Democratic successor agreed with this interpretation of Jefferson, greeting Ghana's president in 1961 by saying, "Thomas Jefferson also once said, 'the disease of liberty is catching.' It has been the object of our guest's life to make sure that the disease of liberty spreads around the globe. He fought for it in his own country. He fights for it in Africa—he fights for it around the globe."[53] In JFK's hands, as in Eisenhower's, Jefferson had become an international symbol of human rights and democratic freedom. This was possible because both presidents shared the same broad goal: Jefferson was useful to them both as they sought to defend a specific view of the United States in the context of the Cold War. Jefferson's stress on liberty allowed them to argue that the United States had always stood for freedom against the kind of tyranny they associated with the USSR.

So it is not surprising that Lyndon Johnson used Jefferson to explain his policies in Southeast Asia in 1966, which he understood as one of the Cold War's proxy wars, saying, "No better words could describe our present course than those once spoken by the great Thomas Jefferson: 'it is the melancholy law of human societies to be compelled sometimes to choose a great evil to ward off a greater,'" acknowledging that in his view, he had no good choices when it came to the war in Vietnam.[54] But he made choices nonetheless, and used Jefferson to justify continuing the war, telling US troops, "At this moment in Vietnam, thousands of young Americans march with Jefferson."[55] Nixon too found Jefferson useful in justifying the war, quoting him in 1971 on the point that the United States acted "not for ourselves alone, but for the whole human race."[56] This idea, that the United States had a moral responsibility to defend global freedom, was of course a hallmark of Cold War discourse.[57] The more unsavory those actions were, the more likely presidents were to justify them by grounding them in national ideals, and the more important Jefferson became.

Richard Nixon, for example, used the same quotation as Johnson, and to the same end. In his 1970 State of the Union Address, he said,

Two hundred years ago this was a new nation of two million people, weak militarily, poor economically. But America meant something to the world then which could not be measured in dollars, something far more important that military might. Listen to President Thomas Jefferson in 1802: We act not "for ourselves alone, but for the whole human race." We had a spiritual quality then which caught the imagination of millions of people in the world. Today, when we are the richest and strongest nation in the world, let it not be recorded that we lack the moral and spiritual idealism which made us the hope of the world at the time of our birth.[58]

For Nixon, Jefferson's vision was one that called upon the nation to preserve its heritage, to retain its idealism, and to continue to inspire the world. That inspiration required continuing the war.

Once the Cold War ended and the United States was no longer pitted against one clear ideological foe, it was more difficult for presidents to easily apply foundational US values to global conflicts. In defining the War on Terror, however, George W. Bush also defined a clear ideological enemy. As his project of democracy promotion in the Middle East seemed frustratingly slow, he called upon Jefferson to ask the nation for patience. In a 2003 press conference he said, "I remind some of my friends that it took us a while to go from the Articles of Confederation to the United States Constitution. Even our own experiment with democracy didn't happen overnight. I never have expected Thomas Jefferson to emerge in Iraq in a 90-day period."[59] Years later he was still asking for patience, and still using Jefferson to do so. Speaking to the American Legion in 2006, he said, "In the early years of our Republic, Thomas Jefferson said that we cannot expect to move 'from despotism to liberty in a feather bed.' That's been true in every time and place."[60] Bush here made the implicit argument that all democratic revolutions are the same, that they all adhere to the same principles and follow the same path. And that the United States was the model for those principles and that path.

For these presidents, the United States not only believed in certain things but had a moral obligation to both model those principles and to support them around the world. Its role as a superpower legitimated the claim that US Americans inherently had both the responsibility and the right to act internationally. As George W. Bush put it, "Thomas Jefferson understood that these rights do not belong to Americans alone; they belong to mankind. . . . We honor his legacy by aiding the rise of liberty in lands that do not know the blessings of freedom."[61] For Bush, US values were world values, and his actions in the Middle East were not only justified, but were required, by the legacy left by Jefferson.

In his first term, Donald Trump justified not war but trade by relying on Jefferson and the founders. Tracing the historical centrality of Pacific trade to the United States on a visit to Vietnam, he said, in part, "In 1804, Thomas Jefferson sent the explorers Lewis and Clark on an expedition to our Pacific Coast. They were the first of the millions of Americans who ventured west to live out America's manifest destiny."[62] Trump here not only claimed the Pacific coast as part of the United States long before it actually was, but in doing so attached that claim to "manifest destiny" not as an ideological relic of the past, but very much as part of the present. For Trump, US American global rights were things to be asserted, not negotiated.

As useful as Jefferson was in explaining the US international mission as integral to its national character, Jefferson is also useful as a way of connecting domestic policy to national character. It is not easy to determine which policies are or are not "Jeffersonian," as his name has been invoked in the service of a wide variety of objectives. Dwight Eisenhower, for example, approved of Jefferson as a model of "the simple, old-fashioned virtue of not spending more than you make," as part of Virginia's "great heritage for efficiency in government, elimination of extravagance, strong local government—these concepts were as clear to Thomas Jefferson as they are to your leaders today."[63] That Eisenhower would attribute "lack of extravagance" to Jefferson, who lived out his retirement adding to his already crushing debt, seems absurd. But such was Jefferson's symbolic power that he could be mobilized in many, usually more plausible, ways.

Jefferson is, for example, quite reasonably every president's favorite source on religious freedom.[64] As Herbert Hoover noted in 1930, Jefferson's well-known efforts on behalf of freedom of conscience "decisively helped to fix it in the national policy, with results beneficent beyond calculation."[65] Bill Clinton called him "the father of religious freedom in America."[66] Barack Obama relied on Jefferson when hosting one of his Iftar dinners, noting that the diversity of religion is "an affirmation of who we are as Americans."[67] Donald Trump quoted him on the central importance of religious freedom.[68] US Americans, according to almost every president who spoke on religion, owe their tradition of religious tolerance to Jefferson, and this tradition is deeply and uncontroversially embedded in the national character.

Education is similarly tied to Jefferson, and is similarly tied by presidents to national identity, although they have had, of course, very different views on the specific policies and particular identities that these connections imply.[69] But presidents also tie Jefferson to a startling array of political positions. Lyndon Johnson used him to argue for an increase in military pay.[70] Richard Nixon found that Jefferson agreed with him on revenue sharing and campaign financing.[71] Gerald Ford quoted him on health policy.[72] Ronald Reagan cited him again and again on tax and economic policy and as a source of inspiration for policies allowing prayer in schools.[73] George H. W. Bush argued that Jefferson would agree with him on the question of union dues, and Bill Clinton implied they saw eye to eye on his National Service Initiative.[74] George W. Bush argued that Jefferson's faith in democracy would prove itself in Iraq.[75] Barack Obama saw Jefferson as an environmentalist.[76] Donald Trump used him to argue that "fake news" is as old as the republic.[77]

Lyndon Johnson stretched him even so far as to serve as a warrant for civil rights. Speaking at Swarthmore's commencement in 1964, Johnson said,

> The truth is—far from crushing the individual, government at its best liberates him from the enslaving forces of his environment. For as Thomas Jefferson said, the care of human life and happiness is the first and only legitimate object of good government. Upon the rock of that conviction, this Government is fighting—fighting to free 20 million Americans whose rights have been denied and whose hopes have been damned because they were born with dark skin.[78]

It is somewhat startling that Johnson would quote a man who owned more than six hundred humans over his lifetime on civil rights, but this reveals how presidents use Jefferson's values as transcendent and timeless to argue that the United States is on an arc of always coming closer to enacting its ideals. This idea, that the United States is an imperfect democracy, always striving to better enact its own foundational principles, is basic to how presidents use Jefferson. For much of US history it was possible for presidents to uncritically offer the United States as the best, most enduring example of democracy the world had ever seen. At least since the 1960s, that has proven much more difficult. Presidents are more likely to argue that the nation has acted undemocratically in the past, but is always involved in an ongoing process of correcting those mistakes. And they use Jefferson to do so.

Gerald Ford, for instance, argued that Jefferson shows us that "the American adventure is a continuing process," and Reagan relied on Jefferson's example when he said, "We in America have been blessed with a sacred opportunity and a sacred quest," to enact freedom.[79] Bill Clinton claimed that Jefferson helped create "a system that would always be in the act of becoming, that his unshakeable belief that the future could be better than the present extended even to himself and his contemporaries, to their failures and their successes. And that is what we must always believe."[80] Presidents could—indeed had to—avoid Jefferson the enslaver in favor of him as the country's "most articulate champion of individual freedom" because they increasingly tend to recognize the gap between national ideals and national actions without making that gap too large, or challenging belief in the national commitment to those ideals.[81] Celebrating the Bicentennial at the National Archives, Ford said, "We are all born free in the eyes of God. That eternal truth is the great promise of the Declaration, but it certainly was not self-evident to most of mankind in 1776. I regret to say it is not universally accepted in 1976. Yet the American adventure not only proclaimed it; for 200 years we have consistently sought to prove it true."[82] Here, Ford elides the fact that if God-given equality was self-evident to Jefferson, he managed to avoid acting on it. Ford did so not because he somehow failed to realize that Jefferson owned enslaved persons, but because Jefferson's example was useful to him as a way to argue that the nation has made progress in achieving the goals Jefferson left it.

Ford is not alone. In order to make unequivocal arguments about the laudatory nature of US American national identity, presidents of both parties tend to defend Jefferson and preserve his iconic status even while admitting to his flaws. Bill Clinton said, "Remember, it was Thomas Jefferson, not Abraham Lincoln—Thomas Jefferson the slave owner—who said, '"I tremble when I think of slavery to consider that God is just.' There were people who knew in their hearts the truth but denied it a long time."[83] Jefferson here is treated as worth emulating because he understood and articulated an important principle, not because he acted on that principle. By forming the argument this way, both Jefferson and his principles remain useable as the basis for a positive interpretation of national identity. As Ford said, "To be American is to subscribe to those principles which the Declaration of Independence proclaims and the Constitution protects—the political values of self-government, liberty and justice, equal rights, and equal opportunity. These beliefs are the secret of American unity from diversity—in my judgment the most magnificent achievement of our 200 years as a nation."[84] Jefferson in this sense serves presidents as a touchstone, allowing them to tie their visions of democracy to him. Ronald Reagan said, "Much has changed in the last two centuries, but the principles Thomas Jefferson espoused still lie at the heart of our democratic society."[85] George H. W. Bush echoed this claim, saying, ""For Jefferson understood that the essence of America lies not in shared real estate but in shared values, not in common ancestry but in a common vision."[86] That vision, the national goals of "freedom" and "equality," are never quite spelled out by these presidents when they make these largely ceremonial speeches, because to specify is to create disagreement. US Americans can agree on the centrality of "equality" and "liberty" to their sense of what it means to be "American." But they do not share the same definitions of those terms when it comes to political action, and translating those values into policy is another matter altogether.

Increasingly, as claims to national unity become harder for presidents to plausibly make, and as more has become known about Jefferson's own private life, presidents have taken his personal deficiencies into account and used them as a metaphor for the nation's imperfections. Celebrating Jefferson's birthday in 1995, Bill Clinton said, "Despite his flaws, Jefferson imbued us with his powerful faith that justice would ultimately transcend our seeming inability to do what we know is right. And I believe he would rejoice to know how far we Americans have come toward winning equal justice under all."[87] Like Jefferson, the nation sometimes failed to act on what it knew was right; but the nation had nonetheless come a long way in its moral development, and had done so because of his inspiration. As George W. Bush put it,

Our world echoes with Jefferson's ideals, even though Jefferson did not always act as if they were true. The same Thomas Jefferson who wrote the original ordinance banning slavery in the Northwest Territory lived on the labor of slaves. The same Jefferson who denied racial equality spoke ringing words of equal rights. He doubted the existence of the Christian God, but he trembled for his country when he remembered that the God he doubted was just. No wonder America sees itself in Thomas Jefferson. He was what we are: marked with faults, inspired by strong ideals.[88]

This vision of national identity—a nation united by its commitment to foundational principles, always striving to enact those principles, always getting closer to doing so, is bipartisan and powerful.[89] Speaking on the anniversary of the dedication of the monument to Martin Luther King Jr., Joe Biden said, "Across the Tidal Basin stands another giant of our history: Thomas Jefferson, whose words declared the very idea of America that we are all 'created equal . . . endowed by our Creator with certain unalienable rights,' and we all deserve to be treated equally throughout our lives. To state the obvious—no audience knows it better than this one—we've never fully lived up to that idea. But we've never walked away from it fully."[90] For these

The Jefferson Memorial is one of the nation's pilgrimage sites, where parents, like the Obamas, take their children to learn about what it means to be a US citizen. Courtesy of Barack Obama Presidential Library.

presidents, US Americans are defined by their commitment to the task of enacting national values, not by their failure to do so. This allows them to always celebrate that identity, even while acknowledging a history of inequities and injustices. This acknowledgment is an effort at inclusion, but it is also true that ignoring past injustices and their continuing consequences silences and excludes those who experienced them. The flawed Jefferson, representing a flawed nation, is an attempt to find a more inclusive Jefferson.

Of course, not all US Americans are comfortable with this vision of the nation; some cannot see in him a model worth emulating, and some presidents, like Jimmy Carter, do not rely on him. However, not all members of the national community see Jefferson or the nation as flawed. Speaking on Independence Day amid the controversies over statues and other memorials that erupted after the police murder of George Floyd in 2020, Donald Trump said. "Two hundred and forty-four years ago in Philadelphia, the 56 signers of our Declaration of Independence pledged their lives, their fortunes, and their sacred honor to boldly proclaim this eternal truth: that we are all made equal by God. Thanks to the courage of those patriots of July 4, 1776, the American Republic stands today as the greatest, most exceptional, and most virtuous nation in the history of the world." He continued, "All Americans today are the heirs of this magnificent legacy. We are the descendants of the most daring and courageous people ever to walk on the face of the Earth. We inherit their towering confidence, unwavering enthusiasm, their unbridled ambition, and their unrelenting optimism. This is the untamed spirit that built this glorious nation, and this is the spirit that burns brightly within the soul of every American patriot."[91] Trump's vision of the nation was unapologetic in both his first and second terms. Jefferson represented—in this example, at least—a return to a former, uncritical celebration of a nation united by its values, and inclusive because of those values. It is a different view of the nation than one shared by most recent presidents, and it is one that reveals one of the gulfs in national identity at this particular moment. It also reveals gulfs between opposing sides on national policy preferences.

Jefferson had no opinions on most of these policies, and he would have objected strenuously to others, but because over his lifetime he offered enough general philosophical observations about how government ought to conduct itself, presidents have been able to find a quotation to suit nearly every argument on nearly every policy domain. This tells us little about Jefferson. It tells us a great deal about how presidents ground their own policy preferences in the precedent of the founders. When they use Jefferson (and others) this way, it brings the founding moment into the present, and dates the present back to the founding. But it does so in ways that are not especially useful in understanding either our moment or theirs, because the connections being crafted between them are not really connections at all. The argument is, "Jefferson thought the people should rule; this policy is consistent with that argument; therefore, we should enact this policy." But Jefferson's thoughts on popular sovereignty (for example) were inconsistently applied in his own administration, were never intended to refer to policies like, say, campaign finance, and thus form a poor logical ground for justifying such policies.

Logic is not the point. The point is to associate presidents and their policy preferences, with a source that they hope will put the matter beyond debate. This practice shows us what a fluid thing national identity is. US Americans follow in "the tradition" of the founders, but that tradition is almost infinitely malleable and is used to support a wide variety of actions and beliefs, and so claims about national identity that stem from them, on the one hand, are very tenuously rooted indeed, and, on the other, have an ideological heft and staying power that is hard to overcome.

Conclusion

Governing during the Civil War, Abraham Lincoln made extensive use of the founding and the founding documents. He reflected on the deaths of Jefferson and Adams as he celebrated Union victories at Gettysburg and Vicksburg. He said, "Precisely fifty years after they put their hands to the paper it pleased the Almighty God to take them both from the stage of action. This was indeed an extraordinary and remarkable event in our history." That event, he continued, was made all the more remarkable when James Monroe also died on July 4, a mere five years later. Then he continued, "On this last Fourth of July just passed, when we have a gigantic Rebellion at the bottom of which is an effort to overthrow the principle that all men were created equal, we have the surrender of a most powerful position and army on that very day."[92] Lincoln could not help but see the hand of Providence in this auspicious fact. Jefferson was deeply embedded not only in the Fourth of July but also in Lincoln's understanding of the cardinal principle undergirding the union.

Lincoln was not the last president to see God, Jefferson, and national purpose intertwined. A hundred and twenty some odd years after Lincoln spoke, Ronald Reagan recalled that Fourth of July, and told the nation that "it falls to us to keep faith with them and the great Americans of our past."[93] A year later, he argued, "We're still Jefferson's children, still believers that freedom is in the unalienable right of all God's children."[94] Laying aside the paternalism of this claim, it is worth noting that while Lincoln had constituted a nation grounded in human equality, Reagan located the same nation in its commitment to freedom. His successor, George H. W. Bush, blurred this very important distinction when he evoked that same moment, arguing on the fiftieth anniversary of Mount Rushmore National Monument that the nation should "express our undiminished devotion to the ideals of Washington, Jefferson, Lincoln, and [Theodore] Roosevelt, ideals as towering and solid as the monument that honors them."[95]

Unlike Bush, I argue that neither the ideals nor presidential applications of them are, in fact, solid. We can see their fluidity when we look at presidential uses of Jefferson across time, across party lines, and across policy domains.[96] These traditions and ideals do not exist independently of their rhetorical lineages, and those lineages may have only the most tenuous of connections to the figures we associate with them. In many ways, this doesn't matter very much. If a policy is passed with specious justification, it will still do much of what it was intended to do. In other ways, it matters a great deal, because members of any community hold tightly to their origin stories and grasp firmly the identities that those stories provide. If those stories tell us who we are, we ought to be careful about which stories we tell, and to what ends.

Presidents are intentional about the stories they tell—the aspects of the founders and of Jefferson that they evoke. Presidents with politics as different as FDR and Reagan found Jefferson equally useful. Presidents relied on him to make arguments about the US American role in the world and the role of government at home. In all of these areas and in all of these ways, different versions of the US American community—who is included in it, the hierarchies that are implied, and the purposes to which government ought to be put—are deeply embedded. We are the stories our leaders tell. And as we will see in the next chapter, we are also who and what we choose to remember as we tell those communal stories.

2

The Monumental Jefferson

Many people probably wish they could write their own epitaphs. Thomas Jefferson actually did. The obelisk marking his grave is inscribed, "Here was buried / Thomas Jefferson / Author of the Declaration of American Independence / of the Statute of Virginia for religious freedom / & Father of the University of Virginia." These, he wrote, were the accomplishments through which he wished "most to be remembered."[1] But the headstone on his grave at his home Monticello is not the original; in the years following Jefferson's death, so many people chipped off pieces of the obelisk as souvenirs that it had to be first moved indoors and then replaced entirely. In 1878 Congress authorized funds for a new marker on the condition that the grave be deeded to the US government. The family would not agree, and the project stalled until 1882, when Congress again authorized a replacement, this time with no conditions.

The replacement created the minor problem of what to do with the original; there are not a lot of precedents for determining the appropriate disposition of a decommissioned grave marker. The president of the University of Missouri was among those requesting receipt of the stone, making the argument that the university's status as the first land grant institution west of the Mississippi gave it a claim to the obelisk, citing Jefferson's dedication to education, his contribution to the Northwest Ordinance, and his role in the Louisiana Purchase in his request. Jefferson's heirs found this argument persuasive, and the grave marker was installed on the university's campus in 1885.[2] Along with a statue of Jefferson, donated by the university's Jefferson Club in 2001, the obelisk and plaque were located on the main quad in the Jefferson Memorial Garden.

While students occasionally pressured the university asking for the removal of the statue, marker, and plaque, following the murder of George Floyd on May 25, 2020, that pressure intensified.[3] That June, Roman Leapheart, a student, started a petition for removal, arguing that "'Mizzou has no room for a racist slaveowner on our campus, in the Quad, where thousands of black students pass by every day, forced to deal with imagery of the past in the future where we should be promoting equality, diversity, and inclusion."[4] The university's chancellor refused to remove the artifacts, and replied in a statement that said in part, "We learn from history, we contextualize historical figures with complex legacies. We don't remove history."[5] In September 2020 the Jefferson statue was splashed "with a liquid" that "appeared to be chocolate milk" during a protest for stronger COVID-19 safety measures on campus. The grave marker was also splashed. When the administration again refused to remove the statue, it was defaced with graffiti. Two people were cited for property damage, and the grave marker is now encased in acrylic.[6] The university agreed to consider the matter of the statue and headstone, and the chancellor appointed a Task Force on Recontextualization, which subsequently recommended adding signage including text about both Jefferson's strengths and his "shortcomings." In June 2021 the University of Missouri System Curators voted against adding this signage by a margin of 7–1. And there the matter, along with the statue, plaque, and obelisk, rests.[7]

This case is interesting for many reasons: it's illustrative of the history of statues and commemoration; it's one example among many of the kinds of controversies that now envelope statues and commemorative sites; it reveals the power that officials have over commemorative sites; and it displays all the elements of how we remember Jefferson in the context of commemorative practices in the current United States and what that might tell us about national identity.[8] In this chapter I argue that there are three lenses through which we might understand public monuments in general, and those related to

Jefferson's original headstone, now encased in plexiglass at the University of Missouri. Photo by the author.

Thomas Jefferson in particular. First, most monuments, most of the time, show a great deal of what I call *monumental stability*. Statues, plaques, and other kinds of commemorative architecture are erected at specific moments in time, for specific kinds of reasons, and they remain, relatively uncontroversially, doing the political work they were intended to do. Think, for example, of the Jefferson Memorial in Washington, DC, under this heading. These monuments display consistent attributes of a shared national identity.

Second, there is also some *monumental adaptation*. That is, the memorial may remain, but its location might shift, and/or its meaning might accrue additional layers, lose some of its significance, or adapt to changing circumstances. Here, the best example is the interpretive history of the Jefferson National Expansion Memorial, now Gateway Arch National Park. These sites illustrate the more fluid and changeable aspects of national identity. As aspects of the national character evolve, change, and adapt, those changes are revealed in memory places.

Finally, there is a small category of commemorations that I call *monumental detritus*, relicts of previous moments in which some form of commemoration was thought to be important but whose meaning is often lost, and whose presence is all but invisible. My examples here include the Jefferson stone at the base of the Washington Memorial in Washington, DC, and various busts and statues of him that have essentially become statutory wallpaper, occupying physical space but lacking ideological presence. In these places, we see aspects of national identity that were once presumed to be important enough to warrant commemoration but whose staying power has lapsed, and they are no longer collectively useful or relevant to how the nation defines itself.

In making this argument, I begin with a brief discussion of statues, monuments, and commemoration, and their relationship to national identity. Then I treat each kind of monumental character in turn, concluding with some observations on what monumental commemoration contributes to our understanding of what it means to be a citizen in this particular moment.

Commemoration, Public Memory, and National Identity

Thomas Jefferson is one of the nation's most widely commemorated presidents. Some twenty-two counties and one parish are named in his honor; at least fourteen cities, towns, and villages bear his name, including one state capital (Missouri); roughly 350 elementary, secondary, and high schools are named for him (in this he is second only to Abraham Lincoln, whose total is a staggering 650); and one university (in Philadelphia) honors him.[9] There are Jefferson hotels in Philadelphia, Pennsylvania, Richmond, Virginia, and in Washington, DC; one of the buildings of the Library of Congress is named in his honor, as is the library at the University of Missouri and one of the wings associated with the History Museum in St. Louis. At least one mountain (in Oregon), several state parks, a fort (in Florida), a national highway, a research lab and national accelerator, and a "minor planet" are all named Jefferson. Add to this the number of statues and monuments dedicated to him: there are at least three such statues, for instance, on the campus of the University of Virginia, and several can be found on the grounds of the state capitol in Richmond. He has his own national memorial in Washington, DC, and used to have one in St. Louis, where a statue of him remains. There are statues in every region and possibly in every state honoring him. Jefferson is everywhere. So much so, in fact, that the smartphone app Roadside Presidents lists eighty-one Jefferson sites, including an "Appeal to Divine Providence" dating to the 1990s, which depicts John Adams, Benjamin Franklin, and Thomas Jefferson kneeling in prayer after writing the Declaration. There are several versions of this statue, the largest of which weighs nearly two tons. There are markers to Jefferson outside of a saloon (St. Bernard, Ohio); banks (Birmingham Alabama; Monticello, Indiana), and in a rest area (Alexandria, Virginia). There is a marker at the Los Angeles Forest Lawn Cemetery and at the grave of the person who designed the Jefferson nickel (Owosso, Ohio). He appears in a hotel lobby in Richmond, Virginia, and in re-creations of Mount Rushmore (Santa Clara, California; Lehi, Utah), one of which is constructed out of Legos (Winter Haven, Florida). He appears with other chief executives as an animatron in Disneyland and in Sparks, Nevada.[10]

He is ubiquitous for a reason. One of the presidents most strongly connected to the ideals associated with the nation's founding, he has been, as we saw in the previous chapter, useful to a wide variety of political ideologies, policies, and programs. By commemorating Jefferson, advocates also commemorated their political preferences. By setting him in stone (or bronze, or a variety of other materials), they also sought to set their version of him—and their vision of the nation—in stone as well. Public monuments are designed to be both permanent and timeless.[11] As Pierre Nora argues, memory places are efforts "to stop time, to block the work of forgetting, to establish a state of things, to immortalize death, to materialize the immaterial."[12] They are intended to render politics above the fraught nature of a particular moment.[13]

Monuments are designed to be visited. They exist in partnership with their viewers. Monuments and statues are thus a part of civic tourism, the travel that teaches citizens (and others) which parts of history are worth remembering and worth honoring. Historical tourism, and the monuments and commemorative sites associated with it, performs national history and helps create and reinforce specific views of the nation and national identity.[14] What we choose to remember about the past and how we choose to remember it helps create how we understand the present. Tourists, as they participate in these sites, are also participating in acts of public memory and the creation of civic identity.[15] Tourists thus participate in the creation and maintenance of specific versions of history. Those versions always serve contemporaneous needs. Sites that are designed with one version of the past in mind thus privilege certain tourists above others in a self-perpetuating commemorative cycle. One version of history and the national past becomes sacralized, inviolable.[16] And out of that version of the past arises a specific definition of national identity.[17]

Historical tourism in particular is designed to make better citizens. Visiting such sites is a pilgrimage of sorts.[18] Tourists intentionally select sites that will educate them about historical events and model for them the correct way to engage the nation.[19] They view sites, purchase related material at them, and participate in civic discourse through tours and conversations about them.[20] These sites thus help create a common sense of the past, and a common sense of who the nation is in the present—at least among those who access them, and among those whose versions of events are included at them.[21] It is notable that when the sites include the perspectives of those previously ignored at these sites, there is considerable pushback, as when discussions of slavery as one of the primary causes of the Civil War was included at Gettysburg.[22]

This impulse to favor the history that fits with ideological preferences marks the distinction between heritage and history. History presents facts; heritage makes use of those facts for present purposes.[23] Monuments and statues are efforts to freeze one vision of heritage into a widely received history. Several things are worth noting about this. First, this process has generally favored the perspective of the white majority, as national monuments and national histories tell a version of the past that makes white citizens feel at home in the nation and comfortable with the progress it has made. It does so by neglecting the perspectives of those who might challenge this view. This kind of "management of memory" allows and even encourages people to remain ignorant of other perspectives on events that shaped and continue to shape the nation.[24]

Second, this process is always incomplete. No one version of history is ever entirely uncontested or unchallenged. Sites are leaky—they seep out into their surrounding environment, and the environment flows into them.[25] The fact that Jefferson's statue in the Capitol in Washington, DC, is surrounded by paintings depicting colonization and conquest of the land that is now the United States inflects the interpretability of the statue itself. And Jefferson's presence, amid paintings of continental conquest, inflects the interpretability of those paintings as well.[26]

Third, monuments convey the impression that they are somehow above politics, that they commemorate a history that is not contingent or incomplete in either the past or the present, when this is patently not the case.[27] This pretense can create a kind of empty patriotism, in which allegiance is offered to vague conceptions of the nation and its ideals without consideration of what those ideals may have meant, or how they might have enacted (or enacted differently) in either the past or the present.[28] This is especially important given the fact that monuments respond not only to past events but also to contemporaneous political needs. That is, commemorations of the US Revolution, for instance, might have different valences depending on when the commemoration was created. This fact is most marked in the ways that Confederate monuments proliferate during moments of civil rights gains.[29] What gets commemorated at any given moment is always a reflection of political and social power and is always an effort to maintain that hierarchy.[30] Such efforts are always incomplete and are always contested. We saw this in the first months of the second Trump administration, for example, as he signed an executive order mandating a specific view of US history at sites funded by the federal government.[31]

Monuments, then, as important sites of collective memory are also important sites of collective identity.[32] They offer what purports to be (but never quite is) a stable and permanent rendering of the past. They also offer, without seeming to do so, a singular version of the national past. But that past is always contestable, and is always contested, so monuments and statues have differing degrees of permanence. Some monuments are, of course, more stable than others. It is worth considering why that might be, and what kind of consensus those monuments create.

Monumental Stability

All statues, like all monuments, are efforts at projecting a current political hierarchy into the future. Some of these efforts are more successful than others, at least insofar as they seem to draw little public criticism—and often seem to earn even little public comment. They are, in short, accepted as part of the public landscape. Once erected, monuments tend to remain in place unless those with the power to make choices about them have pressing reasons for their removal. It is particularly interesting to think about the question of monumental stability at this historical moment, when statues are being torn down, removed, or contextualized.[33]

Jefferson has not been immune from this process. A statue of him at Hofstra University was moved from its place in front of the student center into an academic building, where presumably the sight of it would cause less controversy.[34] Another, incongruously placed on the Square in Decatur, Georgia, in honor of a deceased state senator, was removed at the donor's request to protect it from damage.[35] His removal from the New York City Council Chambers was more controversial, as that took over two decades of efforts on the part of Black and Latino council members and created considerable discussion over the question of removal versus contextualization.[36] Some considered Jefferson's "history as a slaveholder" ample grounds for removing the statue. Others, such as renowned Jefferson historian Annette Gordon-Reed, objected to removal, arguing, "This represents a lumping together of the Confederates and a member of the founding generation in a way which I think minimizes the crimes and the problems with the Confederacy."[37]

Equally controversially, another statue, located in front of Thomas Jefferson High School in Portland, Oregon, was toppled, and its remains were placed in storage.[38] That event caused then president Donald Trump to declare, "The left-wing anarchists tore down a statue of Thomas Jefferson. . . . Two days ago, leftist radicals in Portland, Oregon, ripped down a statue of George Washington and wrapped it in an American flag and set the American flag on fire. Democrat, all Democrat. Everything I tell you is Democrat."[39] Trump clearly understood the removal of statues to be both political and partisan in a way that leaving them in place was not.

Whether leaving them in place is partisan doesn't concern me here, but I do want to emphasize that both leaving them in place and removing them are indeed political choices, and monumental stability tells us a great deal about what a community sees as worth preserving, reflecting of how they understand themselves and one another. Here, then, I look at a couple of examples of Jefferson, as he continues to be revered, both locally and nationally.

Local Jeffersons, Local Meaning

Richmond, Virginia, is deeply invested in its own history, both as a site of important events related to the US Revolution and, especially, as the capital of the Confederacy. It is littered with museums, place names, monuments, and statues commemorating the Civil War and those people Southerners saw as its heroes. Its famous Monument Avenue is a roughly fourteen-block stretch of some of the most expensive real estate in Richmond. Up until 2022, there were statues and monuments commemorating Confederates and the Confederacy—including statues of A. P. Hill (who was actually buried under his statue), J. E. B. Stuart, Stonewall Jackson, and Jefferson Davis. An enormous statue of Robert E. Lee anchored one end of the avenue, and tennis great and hometown hero Arthur Ashe was placed at the other end, a placement that caused no small amount of controversy.[40] Between 2020, when the recent statue controversies first arose, and 2021, when Lee was taken down, all of the Confederate statues on Monument Avenue were removed (A. P. Hill was reburied elsewhere).[41] The only statue that remains on display is Jefferson Davis, whose graffiti-covered image lies on its side at the Valentine Museum in downtown Richmond.[42]

There was considerable Confederate commemoration on the state capitol grounds as well. That site, designed by Thomas Jefferson (in 1785, with help from Charles-Louis Clérisseau), is the first state capitol constructed after the Revolutionary War, and the first public building in the "New World" in the form of a classical Greek temple. It's a National Historic Landmark, has been nominated for inclusion as a World Heritage Site, and is on the National Register of Historic Places.

Jefferson appears all over the capitol grounds. He is part of a huge statue honoring George Washington at the entrance to the grounds; a large statue of him holding the plans for the building is inside the capitol; and a bust of him is ensconced, along with those of all other presidents from Virginia (and the Marquis de Lafayette), in niches surrounding a statue of George Washington. These remain, even when other statues and busts were removed from the House chamber—including busts of noted Confederate general Joseph E. Johnston, Alexander Stephens, Matthew Fontaine Maury, Jefferson Davis, J. E. B. Stuart, and Stonewall Jackson. A statue of Robert E. Lee was also removed from the chamber, and a statue of former Virginia governor and US senator Harry Byrd (d. 1966) was removed from the grounds.[43]

Jefferson, it appears, remains present because in Richmond, he is associated with the state of Virginia, which has its own complicated history with slavery; with the Revolution; and with the founding of both Virginia as a state and the nation as a whole. None of these are enough to create sufficient impetus to remove him. Local commemorations are subject to local judgments and local power. Those may or may not parallel more national concerns. In Richmond, at least, a distinction was made between (some) statues of Confederates (in most cases) and an avowed twentieth-century segregationist (in the case of Byrd) and founders who were also enslavers. It is worth noting that the (Democratic) Speaker of the House had the power to order the removal of statues and busts from the House chamber. She had no such unilateral power over the statues on the grounds. In general, no matter how widespread the controversy, judgments about monuments are made locally. In Washington, DC, those judgments are inevitably national.

National Jeffersons, National Meaning

Jefferson is ubiquitous throughout Virginia and in its capital. He is also ubiquitous in the nation's capital, where there are a large number of statues, busts, and sites associated with him. There is no place in the nation where monumental real estate is more precious than on the National Mall. The Mall in Washington is strongly associated with expression of foundational national values; the Mall is thought to "belong to the nation."[44] It is considered to be "where American society expresses its national ideals of democracy, liberty, and freedom,"[45] a "sacred space,"[46] and a symbol of "the nation and its democratic values, which serve to inspire the world . . . a testament to America's past and present where the values of the nation are presented in a masterful blending of formal history and tradition with contemporary life."[47] It is the site of numerous public events, especially "First Amendment activities."[48] The Mall is a "designed historic landscape," often referred to as a "America's front yard" and thus "representative of our national character."[49] Over two million people visit the Mall every year, from every state in the nation and nearly every country in the world. So many people traverse the grass there that the National Park Service (NPS) lays down ten tons of grass and nearly three thousand yards of turf annually.[50]

The Mall is a more complicated site than these descriptions indicate.[51] It is important to note, for example, that the city of Washington was long associated with the slave trade, and racial inequities have always underlain the construction of the city's public spaces, including the Mall itself.[52] It is therefore perhaps unsurprising that the majority of US American visitors to the Mall are white.[53] And while "US American values" are thought to be represented on the Mall, since September 11, 2001, security was heightened throughout the Mall, and it was increased again after 2020. Though the Mall is a place where the exercise of foundational rights is celebrated, protests near the Washington, Lincoln, and Jefferson memorials are limited by law. In short, the Mall represents many of the contradictions of national history, even if it is not obviously doing so.[54]

As Jefferson is well represented on the Mall, I briefly discuss his commemoration at the Library of Congress (LOC) and the National Museum of African American History and Culture (NMAAHC) and then spend considerably more time on the best example of monumental stability, the Jefferson Memorial.

The LOC is but one of the many places in the capital city that bears Jefferson's name. In Richmond, he is honored as author of the Declaration of Independence (as part of the Washington statue), as architect of the building, and as a Virginian who was also president.

At the LOC, Jefferson's personal library is showcased, as is his role in promoting the library during his presidency. Here, his famous quote "I cannot live without books" gets special prominence. But the history is a little obscured. The LOC brochure, for example, notes that Jefferson sold his personal library to the LOC. Congress did indeed appropriate $23,950 for more than six thousand of Jefferson's books in 1815. But Jefferson's contribution to the LOC was not the magnanimous act of charity that it is sometimes portrayed as being.[55] Jefferson was deeply in debt; he needed the money even more than Congress needed the books. Jefferson was an important benefactor of the Library of Congress. He was also a beneficiary of congressional largesse. But one side of this coin is much more stressed than the other, and interpretation depends heavily on Jefferson's generosity rather than his debt.

In 1942, for instance, the then Librarian of Congress, Archibald MacLeish, wrote to President Franklin Roosevelt, asking that the LOC be considered as part of the events commemorating the bicentennial of Jefferson's birth, as MacLeish argued that the LOC was "Jefferson's foster child, if he ever had one."[56] MacLeish held a symposium at the Library associated with the bicentennial (when Jefferson's national monument was also dedicated), on "the application of the Jefferson experience to our experience."[57] This is an important aspect of monumental stability, although it is rarely expressed so clearly. For monuments and commemorations to be stable, they need to be understood as continuing to have some relevance not only in their own time, but in the contemporaneous moment as well. In the LOC, Jefferson continues to have this relevance. One of the Library's buildings was named in his honor in 1980, and in 1991 the LOC started looking for duplicate copies of Jefferson's books that had been subsequently lost to a fire. And now, visitors to the LOC are told and told again of Jefferson's role in the creation and support of the Library, and of his continuing legacy as the Library itself. His presence there is a friendly one; the staff have been known to adorn his bust with hats and T-shirts. The more controversial aspects of Jefferson's legacy, such as his relationship to slavery and to continental conquest, remain undiscussed at the LOC, as they do not pertain directly to his relationship to the Library.

Jefferson's relationship to slavery, however, is central to his depiction in the NMAAHC, which contains a statue of Jefferson that is likely to prove quite stable.[58] Docents there say that prior to the second Trump administration, their statue had not proven controversial, a fact that they attribute to how he is presented. The statue of Jefferson is in a corner of the lowest floor. Visitors encounter it only after passing detailed information on the transatlantic slave trade and slavery in North America. His statue is surrounded by statues of those he disparaged and/or who challenged his views (scientist and physician Benjamin Banneker, poet Phillis Wheatley, Elizabeth Freeman (who successfully sued for her freedom), and Haitian revolutionary Toussaint Louverture). Behind him is a wall of 609 bricks, each one representing a person he enslaved. The exhibit includes a quotation from the Declaration of Independence along with the words of Black US Americans like Absalom Jones, Harriet Tubman, and Frederick Douglass. The exhibit underlines the presence and contributions of Jefferson's contemporaneous African Americans.[59] It also marks Jefferson as a symbol of the manifold contradictions and tensions between the language used to legitimate the Revolution and the material practices of most of the white members of the founding generation.[60]

Other stable sites around Washington tread more carefully around Jefferson's complicated legacy, but are largely untroubled by it. While the curators of the National Museum of the American Indian have chosen to omit him from their exhibition space and gift shop, the famous desk upon which he wrote the Declaration of Independence resides in the National Museum of American History, where he is well represented in the gift shop. He is among those celebrated in the National Archives, where the Declaration of Independence and Constitution are on view. There is a statue of him in the Capitol rotunda, and his memorial on the Tidal Basin is one of the "big three" memorials in the capital's monumental core.[61]

The Jefferson Memorial comprises 19.2 acres just south of the Tidal Basin. It sits on land reclaimed from the Potomac River, a fact that means that the memorial is constantly imperiled by water and drainage issues. It is a large structure, in the style of a Greek temple, containing an enormous statue of Jefferson (it is nineteen feet tall and weighs ten thousand pounds). The interior walls of the memorial, surrounding the statue, are inscribed with quotations from Jefferson's public and private writings. It is a pastoral site, famous for its cherry trees, located just off a major thoroughfare, which gives it both a romantic and an urban feel.[62] The NPS considers it significant "as America's foremost memorial to its third president, as an original adaptation of Neoclassical architecture, and as a key landmark in the monumental core of Washington, DC."[63]

Plans for the memorial date to the early years of Franklin D. Roosevelt's administration.[64] Long a fan of Jefferson, FDR found him both personally inspiring and politically useful—as was made clear in the previous chapter—considering Jefferson to represent the most important national values. He was not alone. Advocating for a national memorial to Jefferson on the House floor, for instance, Thomas Ludlow (D-IN) said, "As one who has profound faith in the philosophy of Thomas Jefferson and who prides himself on being called a 'Jeffersonian Democrat,' I am glad that, at last, a memorial to the great statesman is to be erected in the capital of the country which, thanks largely to his wisdom and vision, is, and for all ages to come will be, the common man's greatest land of opportunity."[65] Like Roosevelt, Ludlow connected Jefferson's historical moment to his own. He said,

> At a time when tyrannical dictatorships are rising to the zenith all over the world and popular government is sinking to the nadir everywhere, it is particularly appropriate that we should erect in the city of Washington, the political center of the Western Hemisphere, this memorial to Jefferson so that the whole world may know that in America, at least, the ideals of humanity are still our ideals, and we have not lost, nor in any degree surrendered, our appreciation of the value of the franchise of freedom.[66]

This is the key element of monumental stability: the values that are understood as being represented in a given act of commemoration are understood as continuing from that moment into the present, and to be important in determining the future. At the time of the monument's construction, Jefferson's battles and Jefferson's values were understood—at least by Democrats—to speak to the battles in which they engaged and the values that they revered. The monument remains stable because those values continue to be considered integral to national identity. It is this Jefferson that President Trump seeks to preserve.

FDR himself often disavowed his interest in or influence over the memorial. This was disingenuous, to say the least, as correspondence indicates that the commission consulted with him frequently.[67] And he had very specific opinions about the statue and the inscriptions accompanying it.[68] But he absolutely didn't want his influence becoming known, writing to Stuart Gibboney, the president of the Thomas Jefferson Memorial Foundation and a member of the Memorial Commission, "I have no objection to your showing my memorandum to the members of the Jefferson Memorial Commission, but, under no circumstances, should it leak out that I have had anything to do with the choice or nonchoice of a statue. That is not my function!"[69] Whether it was his function or not, Roosevelt had considerable influence over the location, design, and content of the memorial.[70]

At the time, both the location and the design caused considerable controversy.[71] First, there was an uproar concerning the Tidal Basin's iconic cherry trees, which were threatened with removal to make way for the memorial.[72] The issue received extensive media coverage when local women attached themselves to the trees to prevent removal.[73] Roosevelt, as was typical for him, disavowed any role in decision making, and recommended that people contact their members of Congress.[74] So great was the controversy that the NPS was asked to provide information to the White House about the average lifespan of the trees, how many were being removed, how many were being replanted, and so on.[75] It turned out that there was less damage to the beloved trees than was feared, and the furor died down.

The second matter was more closely related to issues that concern us here, because it went to what kinds of commemoration were best

suited to a democracy in the 1930s and 1940s. Roosevelt himself preferred neoclassical designs, and most of the public buildings designed
and constructed in Washington during his time in office reflected this
preference.[76] Others, members of the Fine Arts Commission and the
Planning Commission among them, argued that the approved design
was ponderous and dated; an unsuitable style for either its subject or
its time.[77] Frank Lloyd Wright was so offended by the design that
he offered his opinions in print.[78] Roosevelt, of course, had more influence than Wright, however loudly he denied it, and the memorial
remained neoclassical in style.

Of more import now, although noncontroversial when the memorial was constructed, are the edits done to the quotations inscribed on
the memorial's walls. Saul Padover, FDR's secretary of interior, and
author of a hagiographic biography of Jefferson, chose the quotations
with considerable help from his boss in the White House. James W.
Loewen has carefully documented the misleading result.[79] "The first
panel misquotes the preamble and conclusion of the Declaration of
Independence. . . . The second panel, on religious freedom, takes three
quotations from Jefferson's Act for Religious Freedom, passed by the
Virginia Assembly in 1779, and adds a sentence from a letter he wrote
to James Madison a decade later. That sentence is ripped out of context." The third panel is accurate, but the fourth is "a hodge podge of
quotations from diverse writings by Jefferson from widely different
periods in his life. The effect of this medley is to create the impression
that Thomas Jefferson was very nearly an abolitionist. In their original
contexts, the same quotations reveal quite a different Jefferson conflicted about slavery—at times its harshest critic, often its apologist."[80]

At the time, these quotations served Roosevelt's interest in honoring a Democratic president while minimizing Jefferson's commitment
to maintaining racial hierarchies.[81] Engaged in a war he considered
essential to the survival of democracy, Roosevelt wielded Jefferson
and his legacy as a powerful symbol of the stakes at play in that conflict, and offered a very specific interpretation of Jefferson in doing so.
That interpretation sits uneasily alongside developing understandings
of Jefferson and his commitments, but the memorial remains stable,

despite a few calls for its removal, one of which has come from a descendant.[82] As of this writing, the memorial is being renovated. The interpretation offered in the museum portion of the memorial will change, and of this writing there were plans to offer discussion of the quotations as well as of Jefferson's relationship to slavery. It remains to be seen what effect, if any, Trump's executive order will have on these plans, but the memorial itself will in any case will not be altered.

Consequently, neither will its connection to a specific conception of national identity. The NPS makes this connection clear, stating,

> Thomas Jefferson—political philosopher, architect, musician, book collector, scientist, horticulturalist, diplomat, inventor, and third President of the United States—looms large in any discussion of who Americans are as a people. . . . With his strong beliefs in rights of man and a government derived from the people, in freedom of religion and the separation between church and state, and in education available to all, Thomas Jefferson struck a chord for human liberty more than 200 years ago that resounds through the centuries.[83]

Similarly, the current web page for the memorial has links that delve more deeply into Jefferson as a "Founding Father," to the design of the memorial, its status as a "Shrine to Freedom," his role as a "Spokesman for Democracy," and to the memorial as a "Pantheon Among Cherry Blossoms." The "Founding Father" tab has links to "History and Culture" that include discussion of the memorial's architecture and structure and to "the Man," which is a biography—but one that contains no mention of Sally Hemings, very little on his private life, and nothing on slavery.[84] This text grounds both Jefferson and the nation in an unwavering and unnuanced commitment to human rights and personal political freedom.

The context of memorials matters a great deal to both their meaning and to their stability. Like local monuments that remain stable when their meaning reflects the shared concerns among those who exercise power in the locality, national monuments experience stability when they are perceived by those with national power as continuing to represent matters that concern the nation. The Jefferson of the Library of Congress represents the nation's commitment to knowledge. The Jefferson of the National Museum of African American History and Culture is an enslaver who advocated ideals he did not enact, emblematic of the nation's struggle between its values and its practices.[85] Both of these are national, but are also representations that occur in more narrow spaces than the statue of him at the Jefferson Memorial. That Jefferson is dedicated to democracy and individual freedom. If the planned changes to interpretation at the Jefferson Memorial are enacted, they are likely to offer nuance on the inscriptions and the meaning attached to them, complicating the figure of Jefferson without affecting its stability. There are other monumental sites where the alterations have been so extensive that the meaning of the site itself has changed, and it is to those that we now turn.

Monumental Adaptation

Monuments and other commemorations are intended to endure, and they most frequently do. Sometimes, however, the meanings attached to commemorative sites never quite grab hold, or become outdated as the community moves on, rejects, or substantially reinterprets those meanings. When this happens, it is because either the values that were originally associated with a memorial never really resonated with the community or that they no longer do so, signaling either misinterpretations or changes in community identity. Think, for example, of local reinterpretations of some of the religious iconography at the University of Notre Dame: the enormous depiction of Jesus with outstretched arms on the library ("Touchdown Jesus"); the large statue of Moses with a raised hand and an extended index finger, leading his people to the Promised Land ("Number One Moses"); and the statue of a Notre Dame alumnus who served as chaplain to the Civil War's Irish Brigade, Father William Corby, one arm raised in benediction ("Fair Catch Father Corby"). These icons haven't entirely lost their intended religious meanings, but they are substantially revised to suit the local obsession with football. Or consider what happens when a protestor defaces a statue, an act that can be understood as reappropriating the monument itself, marking it in ways that inevitably and permanently alter its meaning.[86] The statue of Jefferson Davis, for example, covered in graffiti and lying on its side inside of a museum, is a very different statue than it was when it was located on Monument Avenue. Its previous meaning has gone beyond recovery.

There are two examples of this process located in St. Louis, Missouri, the first of which I will discuss only briefly before moving to the more extended example. The first is the Jefferson Memorial/Missouri History Museum. The memorial was built with proceeds from the 1904 World's Fair, whose theme was "The Louisiana Purchase," and the building is located at what was the entryway to that event. Dedicated in 1913, it is the first national monument to Jefferson. Neoclassical in design, the building contains a large statue of a seated Jefferson, looking sternly into the West. The unsmiling visage is unusual, as Jefferson is typically depicted with a slight smile on his face. The building is a city landmark (#107), and that protected status means that it is practically guaranteed at least some level of stability.

But it is not entirely stable. The memorial is attached to the Missouri History Museum, but on tourist maps of the city, the site itself is referred to not as the memorial but as the museum; its identity has been submerged into that of the museum. More importantly for my argument here, in 2022 the museum added contextualizing panels to the base of the statue.[87] Those panels detail the history of the statue and include material on "freedom and enslavement" and "expansion and removal." The museum consulted with relevant groups on the content of these panels, including members of the Osage nation. The exhibit now asks visitors questions like, "Should the Louisiana Purchase be celebrated?" rather than offering authoritative interpretations. There are still elements that will cause some consternation among some visitors: the panels refer to Hemings and Jefferson as having a "relationship," for instance. And the history is misleading: while the exhibit acknowledges the one-sided nature of treaties, one panel offers the common inaccuracy that the Louisiana Purchase "doubled the size of the United States" rather than informing visitors that the United States actually bought from the French the exclusive right to negotiate with Indigenous peoples, not the land itself.[88]

In general, the new panels complicate the portrayal of Jefferson as worthy of a memorial because of his role in westward expansion, and asks visitors to contemplate national history in a way that the original designers of the memorial would not have anticipated and probably would not have approved. This kind of contextualization is a middle ground between leaving monuments and statues in place, relocating, and removing them, and provides one example of monumental adaptation, indicating some of the ways that outdated commemorative forms might be repurposed for contemporary sensibilities, reflecting changes in shared communal identity.[89] Contextualization, however, can be problematic, especially if it happens in piecemeal fashion or leaves other problematic elements of a museum unaddressed.[90] Contextualization is not necessarily the solution to political controversy some might hope it is.

The Jefferson National Expansion Memorial (JNEM), now Gateway Arch National Park, is a more complicated version of adaptation. Once dedicated to commemorating the Louisiana Purchase and the pioneers, and then offering a more layered but unnuanced version of a "clash of cultures," the monument's museum is now a more complicated set of exhibits, and the park itself, while bearing remnants of its prior incarnations, is really all about its signature arch.[91] The name, the exhibits, and the purpose of the site have all adapted over time to meet contemporary needs.

The original motivations for the site included a desire to garner federal funds to ameliorate unemployment problems caused by the Great Depression, to reinvigorate the St. Louis riverfront, and to lessen the "cultural gloom of the 1930s" by focusing on a period of optimistic expansion.[92] The actual construction of the memorial was lengthy and troubled.[93] But one thing remained constant across the decades that construction took: the point of the memorial was to valorize the US American westward expansion and Thomas Jefferson's role in promoting it, and to revitalize St. Louis through the vehicle of a national foundational myth extolling the virtues of the frontier experience.[94] Bernard Dickmann, the mayor of St. Louis, wrote to FDR asking for his support of the planned memorial. He argued, in part, "The far-seeing and unconquerable spirit of the explorers and frontiersmen, the "unknown Pioneers" of earlier days, and the vision and genius of Thomas Jefferson,—from whom we inherit our abiding trust in the plain people, which is the foundation stone of democracy—should be thus adequately and inspiringly memorialized."[95] Dickmann was not alone in his understanding of the memorial. The American Historical Association, for example, offered the following reasons for its endorsement of the proposed memorial:

> Jefferson, as President of the United States, ensured through the Louisiana Purchase and the Lewis and Clark Expedition the expansion of our national domain to the Pacific. . . . The great westward movement [that] . . . followed closely upon the Louisiana Purchase and the Lewis and Clark Expedition . . . the national expansion of our country from its original confines along the eastern seaboard to a continental empire stretching from the Atlantic to the Pacific, is to a most important degree the result of the vision and genius of Thomas Jefferson . . . and the American people feel a deep debt of gratitude to Thomas Jefferson for his great achievements in behalf of national expansion, and particularly for the Louisiana Purchase and the Lewis and Clark Expedition.[96]

Note here that westward expansion is treated both as the unique product of Jefferson's actions and as natural and inevitable, and the frontier as integral to the entire national experience. St. Louis assumes pivotal status in national history. This is not a local memorial but one that promised to explain the nation to itself. The NPS "Foundation Document" overview states, "The American West is both a symbol and a physical reality that attracts people from all over the world and continues to shape national identity."[97]

But as important as the frontier myth is to the US American psyche, and as important as St. Louis was to westward expansion, the attraction of JNEM was never primarily about the opportunity to learn more about the pioneers. While the site consists of a small museum, the Old Courthouse, an explorer's garden, five miles of paved trails, a museum, and a visitors' center, visitors come to the park to experience its iconic arch, not to educate themselves about westward expansion. According to the NPS, "The park was orginally [*sic*] named after President Thomas Jefferson. Jefferson's acquision [*sic*] in 1803 of the Louisiana Territory from France known as the of the Louisiana Purchase doubled the size of the United States. This new land was to be explored and encouraged westward expansion. The previous name has simply never been adopted by the millions of people that visit Gateway Arch National Park. The bill to rename the park was signed into law in February 2018."[98] The park's name now reflects the purposes and meaning the public has always assigned to the site.

The Gateway Arch was designed by Eero Saarinen, and from the beginning, interpreters worked hard to connect the structure to the ostensible point of the site. Saarinen's biographer writes of the original plan for the arch: "The clearing from which the arch would rise, in single magnificence, was the image of the primitive clearings, in which they had camped while the great Virginian—our only architect President—wished them westward, ever westward, carrying forward the destiny of the nation and the world, and this selfless spirit of discovery, by men for other men, is what the monument should commemorate forever."[99] But the arch itself is determinedly modernist and doesn't hail back to the frontier experience in any easily discernible way.[100] The interpretive focus is on the construction of the arch, not its symbolic meaning.[101]

There is a small museum that, along with some of the remaining signage dating from its earlier incarnation as JNEM, remains on the site. That museum is very different from its predecessor, having been redesigned in 2018 with the collaboration of local Indigenous peoples and other stakeholders with the specific intent of increased inclusivity.[102] Visitors must pass through the museum's central hallway in order to access the arch, and at least some spend time there as they await their timed entrances to the arch and/or the movie about its construction.

As visitors pass through security and enter the visitors' center, they are met with six screens that portray scenes settlers would have seen, and are thus immediately positioned as settlers, a position that is quickly destabilized if they choose to enter any of the six galleries leading off of the central corridor (Jefferson's Vision, Colonial St. Louis, Riverfront Era, Manifest Destiny, Building the Arch, and New Frontiers). In each of these galleries, common assumptions about US American history are presented and also challenged; in the colonial gallery, for example, displays note that there were people in St. Louis long before Europeans arrived, and signage informs visitors that "you could have been born a slave." The Manifest Destiny gallery greets visitors with a large panel titled, variously, "The West Was Won" (with a picture of President James Polk), "El Norte Fue Robado" (with a picture of Margarita "Chata" Bandini, and "The West Was Stolen" (with a picture of an unnamed Indigenous person). The curators clearly made efforts to complicate standard narratives of westward expansion.

The gallery dedicated to Jefferson's Vision is of primary interest to us here. It begins with Sacagawea, and visitors are given the opportunity to "Join an Expedition," which pluralizes both the roles available to visitors—visitors can be a cook, or a hunter, or a scientist, for example—and also the number of journeys west—Lewis and Clark are not the only explorers included. Visitors can examine western flora via microscopes, participating in discovery as well as learning about it. There are exhibits dedicated to the Indigenous peoples Lewis and Clark encountered, to the fur trade and fur traders, and examples of Jefferson's rhetoric on and about the West and Indian peoples. There is a small plaque on York, the enslaved Black American who accompanied the Corps of Discovery.

A statue of Jefferson—notably without his usual copy of the Declaration or quill pen—stands in the center of the gallery. It is surrounded by screens, maps, books, and artifacts. The screens display quotations from Jefferson that both praise Indigenous peoples and disparage them. One quotation, for example, concerns his plan to drive them into debt so they would be forced to cede land. As

While the national park in St. Louis, Missouri, is no longer named after Jefferson, exhibits continue to include him and the history of US western expansion, often doing so in ways that allow visitors to interpret that history in a number of different ways. Photo by the author.

elsewhere in the museum, the displays offer information and pose questions for visitors to consider, such as "Whose land?"

When I visited, it was evident from visitor comments that many of them didn't know that this site had anything to do with the commemoration of westward expansion or that it had material on US history at all. Many visitors made comments like, "Oh, that's interesting," and "I didn't know that" when encountering displays on treaties and the treaty-making process, or exhibits on Indigenous peoples. This material was treated by many of the visitors I shared my visit with as bonus material, and was obviously not the primary reason they were visiting the park. There is no better evidence of monumental adaptation. The NPS had taken the site's history into account and has renovated the museum space to reflect that history. Interpretive rangers were available, and happy to provide information about the history, while also recognizing that it is ancillary to the purposes of most visitors.[103] The park has accommodated itself to those purposes—it is now named for the arch, not for Jefferson or expansion. It has adapted its meaning, and so it survives as a site that over a million and half people visit every year. Its ideological purpose has changed as well: it now strives to educate visitors about the complexities of westward expansion rather than valorizing it. The monument and its interpretation have changed to reflect more contemporary understandings of national identity and the place of the frontier in it. Other monuments have not proven adaptable, and have become detritus.

Monumental Detritus

Monumental detritus is a category of objects that take up physical rather than ideological space. Some monuments and statues have been around for so long that they have become part of the landscape, perhaps barely noticed by those who pass by them regularly. These statues and monuments may still carry ideological meaning—failing to register, for example, the ideological heft of a Confederate statue does not remove the heft from that statue. Such a statue is not monumental detritus, because it retains meaning; detritus has lost ideological and perhaps even historical meaning.

The entire University of Virginia, for example, is something of a monument to Thomas Jefferson, who designed its rotunda, lawn, and pavilion. The statue of him on the rotunda is apparently so true to life that upon seeing it, his niece famously fainted. Visitors are also directed to a statue of him located in a niche off of the lawn facing the rotunda, and campus ambassadors were able to identify one other statue of him on the campus. All of these are, of course, noncontroversial and not especially interesting—they are examples of monumental stability. But there are also bonus busts of Jefferson located in other buildings. In one such example, visitors come to view other exhibits related to the founding, such as a copy of the Declaration of Independence, provenanced to George Washington. The document's primary author lurks in a pair of niches off to the side, dirty, chipped, unnoticed, and possibly unrecognized. There are no labels and no effort at interpretation.

Similarly, there is a bust of Jefferson on the second floor of the Daughters of the American Revolution (DAR) Library in Washington, DC. There is no accompanying labeling and no interpretive material. No one on duty the day I visited was able to tell me anything about the bust or its provenance. It was simply there, in a niche, opposite Benjamin Franklin. One could, of course, argue that the very presence of these busts has ideological meaning, especially as they are placed within the DAR building, a site and an organization that have specific ideological associations.[104] But I argue that because they reference the founding without attaching any meaning to it, and because they are essentially wallpaper even in (perhaps especially in) the context of this particular site, they accrue no actual meaning.

The Jefferson Pier Stone is another example of monumental detritus. Located on the grounds of the Washington Monument, the stone marks the intersection of the east-west line of the Capitol and the north-south line from the White House. Jefferson urged that the north-south line, connecting to the White House, be the "Washington Meridien," which he hoped to use as a navigational aid for sailors. As a piece of historical trivia, the stone is perhaps interesting. But it attracts no attention at all. During my visit several National Park Service rangers, on the National Mall to help manage an unrelated event, were all unaware of the stone. Visitors walked past it without noticing or regarding it. As an act of physical commemoration, it is less than meaningless. No one currently considers it important to declare that this spot in Washington, DC, is an important navigational reference point. Such a claim is irrelevant to contemporary national identity, which now centers the United States in the global arena in a different way.

This example is especially interesting because it is located between monuments to Washington and Lincoln. A tourist's gaze is directed from one monument to the other; the stone fails to even register as an obstacle between them. Detritus is useful because it marks what we are being directed to see, and what was once an object of focus but is now all but invisible. We are directed to see some things—the tower of the Washington Monument, the temple to the Great Emancipator—and we are directed away from others—the legacy of slavery, for example, left by Washington and his contemporaries. Most of the things we are directed away from obviously go unmarked. But monumental detritus reminds us that there is much that escapes our attention. Even monumental absences might have more ideological weight than these examples. There is no mention of Jefferson, for example, at the National Museum of the American Indian. There are not even any books concerning him in the bookstore's library. Given his stance on Indian Removal, it is hard to believe that this absence is unintentional.

Washington, DC, is littered with monuments, so it is perhaps unsurprising that it would also be home to a good amount of monumental detritus. But such detritus is everywhere. Of the counties, schools, and streets named after Jefferson, many of them have undoubtedly lost any connection to the person of the nation's third president. These sites lack controversy because they lack enough ideological heft to render them controversial. But that residual meaning remains, perhaps waiting for a moment when it might matter for some interpretative purpose.[105]

Such detritus is not limited to the nation's capital. In East Liverpool, Ohio, for example, there is a memorial to the beginning spot for surveying for westward expansion under the Northwest Ordinance. "Though it doesn't exactly say so," Simon Winchester has written, "it truly is a memorial to the two most Jeffersonian ideas, private land ownership and public westward expansion."[106] It's not that the monument "doesn't exactly say" this about Jefferson. It doesn't say anything about Jefferson at all. His name is not on the monument. So even if his ideas continue to be commemorated here, however vaguely, Jefferson himself has been erased and is not connected to those ideas. Nothing about this monument centers Jefferson's ideas to national identity.

It is always possible that some of these sites will get reenergized, will develop new or renewed ideological meaning. Someone, for example, might care enough about the nomenclature to advocate changing the name of one of the schools currently dedicated to Jefferson, or some event might trigger a resurgence in admiration for him. Such things happen.[107] But we tell stories that hold meaning for us, that contribute in some way to our collective understanding of ourselves and our communities. Once monumental stability becomes calcified in ways that fail to contribute that kind of meaning, the monument itself become detritus.

Conclusion

One way to understand public monuments is to see them as intending to set politics in stone, to preserve the ideologies that buttress given political arrangements, and to render them uncontestable. They do this by claiming, however implicitly, to represent a consensus among a given community. But because they can never actually represent a consensus, they can also never really be uncontested. All public arguments, whether made in speeches, as in the previous chapters, or in material form, as in this one, are always partial. Some members of the community are not asked their opinions. Their consensus is neither valued nor sought.

But they have opinions, nonetheless. No interpretation of any given monument is ever definitive. These works have dominant meanings, and those meanings are produced and maintained by those with the power to make decisions. The Jeffersonian Memorial is protected space. The statue inside of it is not going to come down in the foreseeable future, and while there are plans to modify the interpretive exhibit, even if that happens, its overall meaning will remain largely unchanged. Other memorials, located in places more open to change than the National Mall, can be subject to alteration, as decision makers either decide to absorb them into other kinds of commemoration, as at the Missouri History Museum, or to adapt the interpretation of them to how they perceive the public interpretation has moved, and to bring them in line with evolving understandings of national identity. Monuments and commemorations that fail to resonate in the present risk becoming detritus. They lack any ideological weight, and remain as lingering relics of the past, no longer relevant to how the nation understands itself.

The idea of monumental stability allows us to see what versions of national (or regional or local) identity have staying power. In much the same way as presidential uses of Jefferson provide insight into how one figure can be adapted over time and across circumstance to authorize very different views of national politics, monuments offer a longitudinal perspective on events and values. When a monument is constructed, it is an effort to make a specific value material. We revere certain people or events in certain contexts, for certain reasons. Sometimes, those people or events continue to represent those values in ways that speak to their audiences. Sometimes a gap may open between the person or event and the value in question, forcing adaptation. And sometimes that gap may become so large that the monument or memorial becomes detritus. This is not just true for monuments and memorials of Jefferson, but for all efforts at memorialization.

Looking at Jefferson through the lens of monumental commemoration, then, allows us to understand some things about national identity. First, it is always a product of political power. Like monuments, the contours of national identity are inflected by the preferences of those empowered to make decisions. Second, that power is

not definitive. As in the changes of monumental adaptation, definitions of national identity are only as powerful as the consensus they
can command. Monuments and memorials, like the definitions of national identity they enshrine, must resonate with their intended audiences if they are to continue being meaningful. As we will see in the
next chapter, the vaguer the terms, the more likely consensus becomes.

3

The Collective Jefferson

We do not normally think of statues as being especially mobile. They are, as we saw in the previous chapter, intended to be stable reflections of the past and usually are meant to be permanently placed in specific locations. But at least one statue of Thomas Jefferson has moved around the nation's capital quite bit.[1] Commissioned by Uriah Levy (a Jefferson admirer who also bought Monticello and saved it from ruin), this statue was finished in 1834. It was intended as a gift to Congress, but its members were unsure of the propriety of such a gift, and the statue, not officially accepted by Congress, wandered around the Capitol until 1847, when it was placed on the north lawn of the White House—the only presidential statue ever to be located on the executive mansion's grounds. Neglected and subject to the elements, it began showing its age. In 1874 Uriah Levy's brother Jonas wrote to Congress, reminding them that the statue was donated to be displayed in the Capitol, and if they refused to accept it, the family wanted it back. Congress officially accepted the statue, authorized its restoration, and put it in the Capitol's Statuary Hall. In 1900 the Jefferson statue moved again, this time to the rotunda, the symbolic heart of the national government, where it remains.[2]

This statue's adventures are interesting because they point to a couple of additional things about monuments and memorials and their relationship to national identity that weren't as clear in the previous chapter. First, while this is a statue of Thomas Jefferson, it is also a statue of a member of the founding generation. Jefferson stands (literally, in this case) for himself; he also stands for the ideals of the founding. Second, this statue occupied specific places: first in the Capitol, then on the White House grounds, then back at the Capitol. Those charged with the statue's disposition were conscious of its meaning, and were equally conscious that this meaning was impacted by its immediate context. They understood that memorial sites affect and are affected by the places where they are found.[3] Context helps to define in particular ways things that are contingent.[4] On the White House grounds, for instance, Jefferson's statue risked becoming detritus; neglected and largely unseen, it lacked the kind of ideological heft it has when displayed in the rotunda.

So we now focus on the question of context. Like statues, national identity comes with a context; similar claims resonate differently in different historical and geographical contexts. For example, because of the multiple layers and many possibilities of defining the nation, a bust of Jefferson placed near one of Robert E. Lee calls up different aspects of his legacy than one placed near a bust of John Adams (who never owned any enslaved persons) might. Place matters in other ways as well. A statue of Jefferson as one of forty-six chief executives lining the streets of Rapid City, South Dakota, carries different associations than the giant carving of his head and those of three of other presidents on Mount Rushmore, roughly twenty-five miles away. In this chapter I focus on these kinds of contexts, first offering a quick discussion of space and place and why they matter to national identity, and then briefly describing the treatment of Jefferson in the Capitol rotunda, at Independence National Historic Park in Philadelphia, Pennsylvania, and on Mount Rushmore. In all of these contexts, Jefferson is an individual, of course, but he is also a member of a group, the "founding generation," and as a member of this collectivity he represents, variously, the colonial era and its transition to independence, the revolutionary era and its transition to a new government, and westward expansion. The Jefferson of the early republic is remembered as an advocate of national independence and individual freedom. But that Jefferson is also an imperial Jefferson, and how he is remembered in that context helps put the question of US American territory and how it was obtained beyond the realm of political debate, which in turn privileges one specific view of what it means to be a US American while making other possibilities more difficult to imagine.

Focusing on groups of people, and periodizing the eras in which they lived and acted, works in three ways. First, it allows us to conceive of collective choices as the product of individual action—larger political trends become reduced to the acts of one person, usually a president, or are reduced to one event. So when we think of "the Age of Jackson," we also collapse Andrew Jackson and numerous other political actors into the same category, which suppresses the overlaps and continuities with other moments and elides the controversies and contradictions of those moments. Indigenous removal, for example, is largely associated with Jackson and not always understood as a process that spanned several presidencies and generations. It is often reduced to the infamous Trail of Tears, which occludes the number of Indigenous nations that were subjected to removal. The arguments of those who fought removal and opposed national expansion become less important. When history is reduced to single individuals and singular events, much is glossed over.

Second, this singular focus allows us to subsume individual and collective choices—the series of decisions concerning Indigenous dispossession and national expansion, for instance, —are often presented as inevitable, as the result of "history" rather than of human judgments.[5] Events become understood as the product of an "age" or a political moment, not as a series of collective decisions that were contested in their own time. This tends to absolve the citizenry and the nation of responsibility for those events, which in turn makes it more difficult to argue for restorative justice, since no one was "really" responsible for doing harm.

Third, memorializing collectives like "the founders" has an accumulated weight. There are so many of them, in so many places, and their stories are so often told that their collective meaning is inescapable. The origin story of the founding has become largely monolithic and unchangeable. Even when it evolves by, for instance, the replacement of "the founding fathers" with "the founders" and then "the founding generation," in a series of moves designed to render that moment understood more inclusively, these additions and emendations are not deeply transformative.

Fourth, it allows people to read present interpretations of national values back into history, as if those interpretations were always the dominant ones. So it is easy to think that the US Revolution was based on a universal idea of human equality much as that idea is understood and debated in the present, and not as it might have been understood and debated in its original context. But ideas about equality have in fact changed and adapted over time, and those changes affect institutional structures and political practices.

All of these moves facilitate belief in a nation that has always been dedicated to specific ideals and is always in the process of enacting them, a version of national identity that entails advantages for those who are always celebrated in these moments and places and costs for those whose experiences run counter to it. They are made more powerful by the interpretive contexts in which they are found; every iteration of rendering space into place has implications for national identity.

Space, Place, and National Identity

Whenever we assign meaning to geographical space, we engage in "placemaking." When we label a house a "home," for example, we give it a sense of belonging that it previously lacked. Whenever we assign meaning to a space, we select some aspects of it to emphasize and others to ignore or minimize. Referring to part of the United States as "the West," for example, emphasizes one set of symbolic meanings, evoking images of frontiers, pioneers, cowboys, and befeathered "Indians." Such references also deemphasize other symbolic meanings—for example, the location of "the West" as south of Canada or north of Mexico; its histories as they occur without reference to US American expansion; its connections to, rather than separation from, the rest of the United States and the Americas more generally.[6] These differences are consequential for how we think about, experience, and share any particular place, and they influence our understanding of communal identity.

But because of the ways place is made out of space, these elements of place appear natural and inevitable rather than created and constructed. So "of course" we would preserve this house or that battlefield. These places assume historic importance by the fact of having been already preserved. For example, Plymouth Rock is protected, and is offered to tourists as the site of the first landing of the *Mayflower*, the ship that brought Pilgrims to the New World.[7] In choosing this rock, on this place, someone also decided that it was the arrival of the *Mayflower*, and not, for instance, any of the earlier visits from Europe or elsewhere to the North American shores, that were worth commemorating, thus privileging these particular colonists. It also reinforces the idea that the Americas were somehow "new" and lacked history prior to the arrival of the Pilgrims. These choices make sense given the perspective of white settlers and their history that followed. But they erase the histories and perspectives of those who were already living in, and had a different set of names for, the region that is now called "Plymouth." That is exactly the point: we collectively commemorate the past to naturalize and render inevitable a history that was neither natural nor inevitable at its own moment and that privileges one perspective above other possible perspectives. While Thanksgiving originated in Abraham Lincoln's desire to offer gratitude for the Union defeat of the Confederacy, that holiday is not celebrated by mass burnings of the Confederate flag, but with turkeys and "Pilgrim hats." It is worth asking why that might be the case; whose version of national identity is facilitated in that version, and whose might be privileged in other possible versions?[8]

In the United States, there is a canon of symbolically important events and places.[9] Like Plymouth Rock, places like Bunker Hill, Gettysburg, and the Alamo have a recognizable stature. They are sites of patriotic pilgrimages, where citizens and other visitors go to learn and to teach their children about US history and citizenship. These places are real, of course, at least to some extent, and the events that took place at these places mattered for national history. But these places and the narratives of those events are also creations—they are presented and managed with the tourist audience in mind and often with the specific intention of promulgating a nationalistic ideology.[10] They are well able to do this because their rhetorical work is accomplished almost invisibly.[11] Certainly, in the US American case, places associated with the Revolutionary era—like Yorktown, Lexington, Concord, and Bunker Hill—are emblematic of the Revolutionary story. In part, this is because of how the stories associated with that era have traditionally focused on the nation's promise of future inclusion rather than its contemporaneous or continuing exclusions.[12] Those stories are treated as being uniform across the nation, presenting the nation itself as a seamless whole.[13] One way of managing national differences is to tell stories of national unity, which define those differences as minor, and emphasize those things members of the nation presumably have in common.

Even as they are generalized, however, those stories are emplaced. Because something happened *here*, the place is marked as historically important. At the same time, the fact of the place, the *here*, lends credence to the history. It is a mutually reinforcing cycle that wields collective memory in the service of situated national identity.[14] These sites thus have a preferred, dominant meaning. When visitors tour Boston's Freedom Trail, for example, the various sites along the way offer a unified story of revolutionary patriotism. But these sites are necessarily vulnerable to alternative readings. Even visitors exposed only to the seamless story of patriotism might understand those commemorated in Boston as patriots, or as traitors, or as capitalists looking to make money, or as white supremacists committed to maintaining racial hierarchies whatever the cost, or as a complicated combination of all these things.

I argue here that the context of memorial emplacement can tilt readings in one or more of these directions.[15] Memorials like the Jefferson statue in the Capitol rotunda place Jefferson in a particular historical frame, one that emphasizes the nation as it pivoted from its status as a colony to independence, seeming to place continental colonization safely in the past. In Independence National Historical

Park (INHP), the context emphasizes the pivot from war to the establishment of a new government. That set of memorials is in Philadelphia, the site of the nation's first capitol, and memories of Jefferson are subsumed into and affected by that larger context. Finally, at Mount Rushmore, Jefferson is one of the four presidents whose faces are carved into the sacred territory of the Oceti Sakowin, the Seven Council Fires of the Great Sioux Nation. His presence there both marks and erases the conflicts over western land, a marking and an erasure that is foundational to national identity.[16] In all of these cases, because the form of memorialization is collective, individual actions, traits, and flaws are submerged into a celebration of "national ideas," the vagueness of which makes them easy to celebrate and difficult to criticize or counter. And yet, sometimes, the surrounding context creates cracks in that narrative in interesting and important ways, all of which influences the nature of national identity.

Laying Claim: The Capitol Jefferson

The Capitol itself stands on Capitol Hill, immediately in front of the Library of Congress, and on the other end of the National Mall from the Washington Monument and, more distantly, the Lincoln Memorial. The two sides of the Capitol, one for each of the houses of Congress, meet in the rotunda.[17] The Capitol dome, underneath which the original designers hoped Washington would be buried (he is not), is decorated with an allegorical painting of the "Apotheosis of Washington," which depicts him ascending to the heavens, rising from a seat between Liberty and Authority on one side and Victory and Fame on the other. Washington is surrounded by the arts and sciences, the sea, mechanics, architecture, and other elements of the national good life, representing hopes for the progress of the new nation.

Beneath the dome, the rotunda has eight enormous oil paintings on its walls, four of which depict discovery and colonization: the landing of Columbus, the "discovery" of the Mississippi, the baptism of Pocahontas, and the Pilgrims on deck of the *Speedwell*, the ship that carried them to England, where they boarded the *Mayflower*. These four paintings all contextualize Jefferson and the others memorialized in the space as the heirs of Christian conquest, exploration, and settlement, and together make the argument for a nation based on certain values and striving to attain them. It is notable that two of these paintings represent acts of military incursion and the other two depict religion. The Pilgrims are engaged in worship, and Pocahontas, representing Indigenous people, is assimilating into the Christian church. The implicit idea here is that colonial settlement brought western civilization to the Americas, that the Indigenous people were assimilated willingly into that civilization, and that even the violence of colonization served a worthy purpose.

The other four paintings are connected to the Revolution, depicting the presentation of the Declaration of Independence to John Hancock, president of the Continental Congress, General John Burgoyne's surrender at Saratoga, Lord Charles Cornwallis's surrender at Yorktown, and George Washington resigning his military commission. These four portray important military and ideological moments for the new republic. Military victories, of course, but also a statement of ideals in the Declaration and an enactment of them, as Washington's decision to resign his commission was widely understood as an action that privileged civilian authority over the military, an important democratic principle. The nation, these pictures suggest, was founded in war, but immediately became dedicated to democratic values.

Equally revealing are the relief sculptures. Four are portraits of early explorers: John Cabot, Christopher Columbus, Sir Walter Raleigh, and Sieur de La Salle. The relief panels above the entrances to the rotunda are scenes that represent a specific narrative of US history: the "Landing of the Pilgrims," the "Preservation of John Smith by Pocahontas," William Penn's treaty with Indigenous people, and Daniel Boone battling Indigenous people. All of these underline in various ways the US American right to the land and presume Indigenous acknowledgment of that right. This acknowledgment is portrayed as the product of warfare and also Indigenous choices: Boone battles with

Indigenous people, Pocohontas decided to rescue John Smith, other Indigenous people decided to sign the treaty with Penn. In all cases, the white US American presence replaces Indigenous ones.

Jefferson's statue is on Washington's right (Jefferson's nemesis Alexander Hamilton is on Washington's left) and depicts Jefferson standing, holding a quill in one hand and a copy of the Declaration of Independence in the other. At his feet are two books and a wreath, vaguely referencing both his dedication to learning and victory. He is commemorated here, as he is in most of his statues, as the primary author of the Declaration and as a member of the founding genera-tion more generally. Less usual is the fact that the statue was cast in bronze—marble was much more often used in statuary at the time. Little specific attention is given to this particular statue. Jefferson takes his place here among others, and his individual meaning is subsumed into the general meaning of the place as a whole, which is crowded with statuary. Rather than bearing any particular meaning, Jefferson here is significant largely because he is included among other notables who contributed something to US American democracy.

The nature of these individual contributions is unclear at best. Other statues and sculptures in the rotunda span the entirety of US history and include George Washington, Alexander Hamilton, An-drew Jackson, Ulysses S. Grant, Abraham Lincoln, James A. Garfield, Dwight D. Eisenhower, Ronald Reagan, Gerald Ford, Harry Truman, and a group that commemorates women's suffrage. There are busts of military ally the Marquis de Lafayette, Washington, Martin Luther King Jr., and, as I noted, of early explorers (Cabot, Columbus, Raleigh, and La Salle). The rotunda is a crowded but uncomplicated paeon to the nation based in colonial conquest and a virtuous war for in-dependence, which led inexorably to an arc of increasing democratic inclusion. Placed within this context, it is clear that however mobile Jefferson's statue has been, its inclusion here isn't especially interesting or treated as interesting in its own right. It is best understood as part of a collectivity that authorizes the creation and maintenance of the US American republic on Indigenous land. Collectively, the rotunda makes an argument that "the colonial period" references the US relationship with Great Britian, and not with its own possessions or actions on the continent.

There are other examples of this kind of collective commemoration, which serve similar ideological purposes. At the entrance to the state capitol grounds in Richmond, Virginia, for instance, there is an enormous statue of a mounted George Washington, dedicated on Washington's birthday in 1850.[18] According to the interpretive literature at the site,

> This monument was conceived to honor Washington and to glorify Virginia's contribution to our nation's independence. Virginia's role in the Revolution is represented by bronze statues of six soldiers and statesmen, which surround the mounted figure of General Washington at the top of the granite monument. Smaller allegorical figures below the six standing statues are inscribed with themes reflecting each patriot's contribution: Andrew Lewis, Colonial Times; Patrick Henry, Revolution; George Mason, Bill of Rights; Thomas Jefferson, Independence; Thomas Nelson, Jr., Finance; and John Marshall, Justice.[19]

Here, Washington is the primary focus. Jefferson is one of several secondary figures, treated as equal to lesser-known figures such as Thomas Nelson, all of whom support and amplify Washington and the state of Virginia. As at the national Capitol, here the commemoration is both collective and thematic. In both examples, Washington literally rises above all, and the others exist to elaborate on the themes of democratic conquest and republican revolutionary virtue. These statues are arguments for independence as a break from a colonial past, portraying the new nation as something different from and more principled than colonization. As in the Capitol, this statue tells an origin story that defines and legitimates a specific version of national identity. A similar argument is made and is complicated by the context of the nation's primary site of revolutionary commemoration, Independence National Historical Park, in Philadelphia, Pennsylvania.

A Complicated Legacy: Independence National Historical Park

Independence National Historical Park sits on fifty-five acres of land in the middle of urban Philadelphia. It consists of twenty-one individual sites and is connected to four additional National Park Service (NPS) affiliated sites. INHP includes, among other buildings, Independence Hall, Congress Hall, Old City Hall, the First and Second National Banks, and the Liberty Bell. The National Constitution Center, a private museum dedicated to the Constitution, is located across the street from the building housing the Liberty Bell, and nearby attractions include the Weizman National Museum of Jewish History, the National Liberty Museum, and the Museum of the American Revolution. According to the INHP's foundation document, the park "was created to protect the historic places associated with the birth of the American republic, standing as icons of freedom and democratic ideals for people around the world."[20] Note here that the site explicitly connects the nation's creation with the ideals of freedom and democracy. It is thus no surprise that the NPS would consider Independence Hall the site's "centerpiece," as it is where the Continental Congress met, where the Declaration of Independence was debated, edited, and signed, and where the Constitution was debated.[21] The NPS calls Independence Hall "the birthplace of America," by which it means the country, and not the continent.[22]

INHP represents the transition from war to government. As the site of the nation's first governments, buildings at INHP not only housed governmental institutions under the Articles of Confederation and the Constitution, but INHP was also the place where the nation's first peaceful transition of power—often considered to be an important hallmark of democratic governance—occurred. The NPS also underlines the ongoing nature of that governance, explicitly stating that the site is significant because it represents the "paradox of freedom and slavery," and the tensions between preserving an urban site and the unevenly distributed costs of urban renewal.[23] For the NPS at least, INHP represents both history and its continuing legacies.[24] Interpretation there concentrates on the events of the US Revolution, but also endeavors to bring the impact of those events forward. The interpretive themes include, What was "Revolutionary" about the American Revolution; Liberty: Promise and Paradoxes; E Pluribus Unum: Out of Many, One; and Benjamin Franklin.[25] Some of these are confined to a specific historical moment while other elements reach into the present.

For the NPS, the historical park is important because it is a place where significant things happened and because it is a repository of specific artifacts like the Liberty Bell, which have come to symbolize foundational ideas. As the National Park Foundation puts it, "Few ideas so capture the imagination of mankind that they imbue physical objects with universal meaning. For [US] Americans, indeed for all people, there are no more potent symbols of individual freedom than Independence Hall and the Liberty Bell."[26] Much of the commemoration at INHP seems to be an unabashed celebration of the US American founding, and it tends to globalize the significance of that moment, arguing both implicitly and explicitly that the founding of the United States provided a universal model of democratic governance and democratic virtue.[27]

In part, this explains the exceptionally heavy law enforcement presence throughout the site. It is located inside a major city, and its ideological importance marks it as a possible target for those unfriendly to the United States. In addition to law enforcement officers and rangers, a number of interpretive rangers are on-site. During my most recent visit, those interpretive rangers spent considerable time correcting errors. Visitors bring many misconceptions to the site—some believed that Bibles were placed on the desk of every delegate to the Continental Congress, that women were present for and participated in the debates, that "all the founders hated the idea of a strong federal government," or that none of the delegates brought enslaved people with them, for example. Rangers corrected all these misconceptions: no Bibles were ever distributed—indeed, many members of the founding generation would have found such a practice to be counter to their ideals; women were excluded from public debates; there was considerable disagreement concerning important philosophical and practical questions among the delegates; Thomas Jefferson's labor on the Declaration of Independence was eased by the unacknowledged work of his enslaved valet; and George Washington housed enslaved people in the nation's first executive mansion, adjacent to the current site of the Liberty Bell.

These links to slavery are the most interesting thing about INHP for my purposes in this chapter, because how Jefferson is remembered in the park reflects the context of that remembrance. Jefferson is remembered at INHP for his authorship of the Declaration, as a member of a Continental Congress, and as Washington's first secretary of state. He is also remembered as being among those founders who supported and participated in the system of chattel slavery. Rangers make available a small card bearing the image of Jefferson on one side, noting that "Jefferson is remembered today as a Virginia politician and plantation owner, an author and architect," along with one of his more famous quotations: "I cannot live without books." It's an interesting list, noting his political activities, his commitment to slavery, and some of his many talents and interests.

Jefferson is mostly present in INHP as the primary author of the Declaration of Independence. There is no question but that the writing, signing, and circulation of the Declaration were consequential acts, worthy of the attention they receive.[28] The Declaration is thought to give voice to national ideals, and the document itself is both "a sacred text and an icon."[29] As a sacred text, it outlined the broad principles of democratic governance as well as defending the colonists' decision to declare their status as an independent nation.[30] The Declaration of Independence was neither an entirely original document, nor did it express entirely original ideas. Similar documents and the ideas themselves had been circulating for some time in North America and in Europe.[31] But its originality was not the point. The Declaration served both practical and ideological purposes. It was an official statement announcing the colonists' view of their political situation, and it laid out a more general statement about the nature of the relationship between citizens and their governments.

In essence, it transformed claims to the rights of Englishmen into the rights of humankind.[32] Not especially central to its contemporary moment, it became the ideological foundation of the nation.[33] The more central the Declaration became to how the nation understood itself, the more central Jefferson, as its author, became. While elsewhere (such as on his gravestone) Jefferson is lauded as *the* author of the Declaration, here in INHP, it is made abundantly clear that Jefferson shared his duties with the Committee of Five and with the Continental Congress as a whole. The Declaration is treated as one event among many. The focus is on the pivots from colony to nation and from war to governance. The scope of interpretation is broad, and the focus is therefore wider than just the Declaration. Jefferson appears more as a member of a collective than specifically as an individual.

Jefferson's activities and preferences are underlined and celebrated in some places (like tours of Independence Hall) and shadowed in others (the presence and interpretation of the Liberty Bell, the notation that he was a "plantation owner," and the archeological exhibit at the site of the first executive mansion that shows the quarters of the enslaved people who worked there). The Liberty Bell was originally rung to celebrate major events and holidays. Repaired at least once, it received its final crack on Washington's birthday in 1846 and has not been rung since. Adopted as a symbol by the abolitionist movement, the bell has amassed a complicated set of meanings—originally used to celebrate the freedom of white men, then wielded in support of expanding that freedom to enslaved people, it has traveled the nation, served as a symbol of freedom during the Cold War, and now resides in a building located between Independence Hall and the much smaller exhibit dedicated to the enslaved people who worked and lived in the President's House.

As we will see in detail in the next chapter, slavery, like other elements of the nation's painful past, is hard to commemorate appropriately.[34] In this particular case, controversy erupted just as a $314 million renovation of INHP and the building housing the Liberty Bell was being completed in 2002.[35] That controversy centered on the fact that the site where the bell is displayed was first owned by

Philadelphia's largest slave owner, and when George Washington lived there it became the "President's House."[36] In Pennsylvania at the time, enslaved people held in the commonwealth for more than six months were freed. Washington, seeking to avoid such an eventuality, rotated his enslaved labor force to and from his plantation, Mount Vernon.[37] In that context, the meaning of the founding ideals, and the meaning of the bell, became subjects of heated debate, concerning the history of how we commemorate the founding generation, the historical absence of slavery in those commemorations, and the ways that commemoration influences national identity, so the stakes of the debate were far greater than might first appear.[38]

In general, memory practices have long separated the veneration of the founders from the remembrances of slavery. Including both in the same geographical location tends to blur the traditional narratives, and there is as yet no satisfactory single narrative that can encompass both (although there are an increasing number of sites that stress the complicated nature of the founding).[39] Trying to convey that complicated message across the variety of sites at INHP is challenging. Some rangers on guided tours stress these complexities whereas others do not even mention slavery. But for those who care to attend to these matters, the slave quarters of the President's House are on very accessible display. And while the immediate focus is on Washington as an enslaver, other members of the founding generation, such as Jefferson, are also implicated in the practices that are detailed in this small exhibit.

The curious thing about this archeological site is that it is very visible and all but invisible at the same time. Approaching the Liberty Bell from one side, visitors must pass through this exhibit, which consists of a structure meant to imply the presence of a house, a plexiglass protected archeological site and interpretive signage. It is visible from the street, and those passing on foot or in cars can easily see that the site is there; whether they ponder its meaning is of course unknowable. The exhibit of the Liberty Bell itself makes the tensions between freedom and slavery clear. The signage there does not offer a triumphalist narrative, but seeks to complicate the celebratory tone of

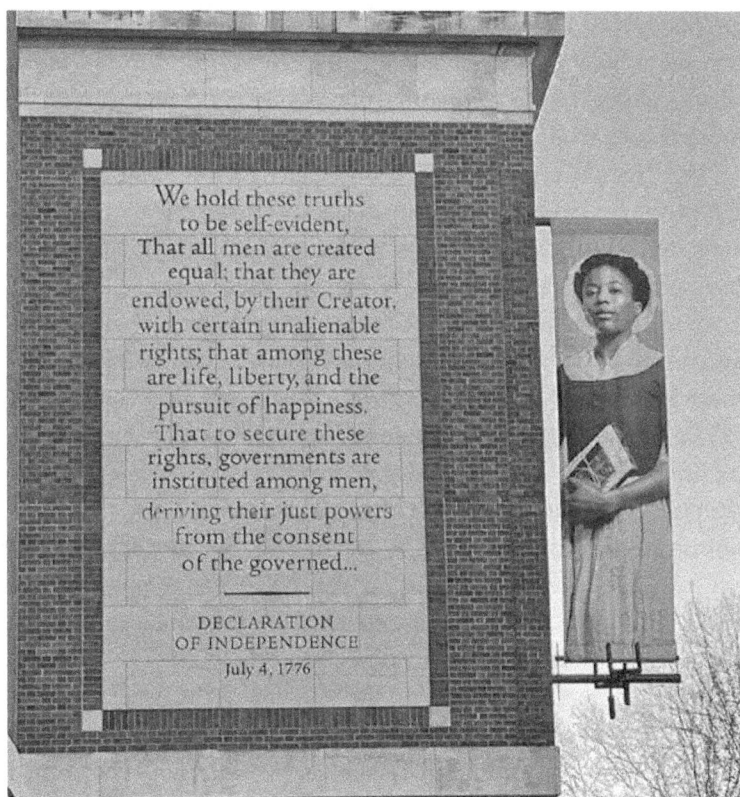

We hold these truths
to be self-evident,
That all men are created
equal; that they are
endowed, by their Creator,
with certain unalienable
rights; that among these
are life, liberty, and the
pursuit of happiness.
That to secure these
rights, governments are
instituted among men,
deriving their just powers
from the consent
of the governed...

DECLARATION
OF INDEPENDENCE
July 4, 1776

At Independence National Historical Park, Jefferson and the other
founders are treated collectively, and the larger context of the site includes a
diverse and multilayered view of national history. Photo by the author.

INHP in general. These complications are there for those who look
for them; they are probably easily overlooked by those seeking an uncomplicated story of US American dedication to founding principles.
But it is notable that the Liberty Bell receives many more visitors
than does Independence Hall, even though they are very close together, and both are free to the public.[40] This is partly the difference
between viewing a sacred relic and a historic site[41] and partly due to
the fact that visitors to Independence Hall must do so as part of a
(free) tour, while it is possible to view the Liberty Bell without prior

arrangement. The Liberty Bell, cracked as it is, serves as a reminder that democracy itself is "fragile and imperfect,"[42] and to the extent that its presence inflects interpretation of the founding, that message impacts how the founders are viewed as well.

The NPS, like museums and other interpretive entities such as the privately managed Museum of the American Revolution, generally has begun doing more to complicate the interpretation of sites like INHP, explicitly acknowledging complexities and telling more nuanced stories.[43] In part, this impetus has come from those in local and national communities who have demanded more inclusive—and more accurate—interpretations.[44] INHP is a rich and complicated site, in which visitors can spend considerable time exploring the complexities of the founding moment and its legacies or simply pop into the building housing the Liberty Bell and be on their way. Even those wanting only a brief visit pass by exhibits on the colonists' relationships with Indigenous peoples, on slavery, on the complex history of the Liberty Bell. As they access the site, they are also likely to encounter posters and banners announcing the presence of exhibits dedicated to "Black Founders," at the Museum of the American Revolution, to see posters and signage that remind them of the contemporaneous presence of Black US Americans, Indigenous people, and women. All of these contextual elements influence how Jefferson and the founders are remembered. At INHP, that remembrance celebrates and also complicates and enriches public understanding of the founding years. This makes it especially interesting to move to places where such complexities are present to a much lesser degree, such as Mount Rushmore, in South Dakota.

Invisible Imperialism: Mount Rushmore

A bronze statue of Thomas Jefferson is placed among those of forty-three of the nation's forty-seven presidents (Grover Cleveland—until Donald Trump's reelection in 2024 the only president to serve two nonconsecutive terms—is only there once, and presumably, more recent presidents will eventually be included) in downtown

Rapid City, South Dakota. Rapid City bills itself both as "the most patriotic city in America" and as the "City of Presidents," two labels that support and amplify one another. Jefferson's statue is fairly non-descript, as are all the others. He stands, with a slight smile on his face, leaning on a desk, quill in hand, presumably drafting the Declaration of Independence. Jefferson's statue is appropriately across from one representing his friend James Madison, and also across from Bill Clinton and diagonal to Gerald Ford.

These statues are worth noting not only because they presumably present a draw for those visiting the area, and/or serve as a source of amusement there—the city's Self-Guided Walking Tour not only includes directions to the various presidential statues but also advertises a scavenger hunt. Visitors who correctly identify pieces of ten statues earn a prize.[45] All that is required of these visitors is that they be able to recognize a shoe or other details of the statues. Information about the presidents is not required to earn the reward. It is not even available (although there is a web page with one-paragraph summaries of the various presidential administrations).[46] The "City of Presidents" advertises its patriotism by emplacing statues of the nation's leaders. It does not do so by offering even the most basic information about them. Here at least, claims to patriotism do not require civic knowledge but rely on a vague display of those who presumably embody some kind of civic presence. Visitors have no way to know which of these presidents may have owned slaves (twelve of them did), which of them may have endorsed or opposed women's suffrage (Woodrow Wilson, for example, did both), or who may have been implicated in Indigenous removal (this depends on how you count). Visitors have, in short, no way to measure, to understand, or to judge these presidents. They are told it is patriotic merely to position them on the street.

These statues are innocuous enough. One can easily drive around Rapid City without really attending to them. Much harder to ignore, because it is visible from so much of the surrounding area, is Mount Rushmore National Monument.[47] That monument consists of the gigantic heads of four presidents, carved into one of the sacred mountains of the Paha Sapa (Black Hills) in what is now called South Dakota. Along with the surrounding area, the land was taken illegally from Native people, who continue to refuse the settlement mandated by the US Supreme Court in 1980, insisting that the only legitimate remedy is the return of the land.[48] Yet even in the unlikely event that the US government would agree to repatriate the land to its rightful owners, it cannot be returned to its original state; the damage is too extensive. The NPS has made some minor efforts to include an Indigenous presence at the site—there is a very small "village" located at the base of the mountain—but there is no discussion at the site of the fact that it is sacred land, no engagement with the ongoing controversies, no mention of the various protests that have occurred there, and no recognition of continued inequities, national and local, concerning Indigenous people. These absences continue, despite both arguments by local Native people for more inclusion of these issues, and more national pressure for return of Indigenous lands in both the United States and Canada.[49]

These absences are all the more striking because of the physical context of the site. Western landscapes and western culture are key elements of South Dakota's tourism industry. Black Elk Peak (as Harney Peak was renamed in 2016) is less than fifty miles from Mount Rushmore. There are nine distinct Indian reservations in South Dakota, which is home to nearly seventy thousand Indigenous people, roughly 8.5 percent of the state's population. The *mako sica* (badlands) are just outside of Rapid City. Both Wind Cave and Badlands National Parks, each within seventy-five miles of Mount Rushmore, make a point of including Native history and Native people in their interpretative materials and displays, and certainly, the nearby Custer State Park would call up images of the "Indian Wars" to even the least attentive visitors. In addition, less than twenty miles down the road from Mount Rushmore there is a site claiming to be in honor of Indigenous peoples, featuring an enormous in-progress carving of Crazy Horse, although no actual images of him exist, so any likeness to him is improbable.[50] Journalist Brooke Jarvis deftly captures this larger context, writing,

Western expansion and settler colonialism join in a jolly, jumbled fantasia: visitors can tour a mine and pan for gold, visit Cowboy Gulch and a replica of Philadelphia's Independence Hall (shoot a musket! Exit here!), and stop by the National Presidential Wax Museum, which sells a tank top featuring a buff Abraham Lincoln above the slogan, "Abolish Slavery." In a town named for George Armstrong Custer, an army officer known for using Native women and children as human shields, tourist shops sell a t-shirt that shows Chief Joseph, Sitting Bull, Geronimo, and Red Cloud, and labels them, "The Original Founding Fathers," and also one that reads, in star-spangled letters, "Welcome to America. Now Speak English."[51]

The context in which Mount Rushmore is emplaced is a buffet of meanings, challenging and reinforcing simple notions of patriotism. Yet, emplaced on Indigenous land, surrounded by tourist sites that specifically recognize the presence of Indigenous people and by those people themselves, Mount Rushmore itself remains curiously aloof from Native people and curiously resistant to recognition of Native claims upon either the land or visitors' attention. Except that it isn't really curious or unexpected at all. Mount Rushmore remains resistant to Native claims not only because of the legal tangle involving the land, but also because of the symbolic heft of the monument itself.[52]

Mount Rushmore National Monument, which attracts nearly three million visitors annually, comprises 1,278 acres, most of which is undeveloped back country. The carvings are a total of sixty feet high and 365 feet across, and the presidential heads emerge improbably from the mountain face. According to the NPS, "The purpose of Mount Rushmore National Memorial is to commemorate the founding, expansion, preservation, and unification of the United States by preserving, protecting, and interpreting the mountain sculpture in its historic, cultural, and natural setting while providing for the education, enjoyment, and inspiration of the public."[53] The NPS considers the site an "internationally recognized symbol,"[54] representing "freedom and democracy and a special place for all people and cultures."[55] It is not surprising that many visitors find it a place of technical curiosity ("How did they do that?"; "Isn't it cool?") and uncomplicated patriotism—national and state flags wave in the breeze, and the site is full of markers of what Michael Billig has called "banal nationalism," a vague and essentially empty loyalty to ubiquitous symbols of the nation.[56]

The carving began as a private enterprise by Gutzon Borglum, an avowed white supremacist who had worked on the notorious sculpture commemorating Confederates on Stone Mountain, Georgia.[57] His nativist and white supremacist views were integral to his conception of the project and to the contemporaneous public reception of it.[58] That it was on illegally taken Indigenous land was not considered either relevant or important. That it defiled sacred land by carving into it images of some of those who had been ardent supporters of Indigenous removal was also not a matter upon which white citizens of the 1930s were terribly concerned. That it commemorated "the" national story as one of creation, expansion, preservation, and unity would also have likely seemed to them both natural and appropriate. And rather than positioning these things as a matter for contemplation or even rectification, interpretation at the site continues to avoid even the most cursory discussion of them.

That interpretation, as Carole Blair and Neil Michael have documented, elides politics almost entirely.[59] Examples of their point abound. The Junior Ranger Handbook, for example, completely ignores politics and the presidents. Activities offered to potential junior rangers concern the carving, they are asked to complete a crossword, and they are given the opportunity to place their home state in relation to the memorial. There is little about the lives, activities, or administrations of the four presidents whose heads dominate the site.[60] The movie that provides an overview of Mount Rushmore (there is another specifically dedicated to Borglum) is narrated by former news anchor and author of *The Greatest Generation*, Tom Brokaw, a choice that underlines the uncritical patriotism that pervades the monument.

The film's narration explicitly connects the monument to "1776," although the actual connection being referred to is not entirely clear, and viewers are told that the original plan called for commemoration of a pantheon of "western heroes." Borglum, visitors are told, wanted to represent "our entire national experience," a claim that is unavoidably exclusionary given that the men portrayed on the mountain were all white supremacists who failed to consider women as even potential political equals to men. The movie then informs viewers that these presidents were chosen by Borglum for specific reasons: Jefferson "articulated the central idea of American democracy" and authorized the Louisiana Purchase; Washington represents the best of the US American character and ideals; Lincoln was the "Great Emancipator" and "prophet of American permanence"; and Theodore Roosevelt advocated economic freedom and is associated with the Panama Canal. Mount Rushmore, the film concludes, is "uniquely American" because it expresses "bold ideals" and "big aspirations" and represents "the hope democratic society offers the future." The very vagueness of these claims avoids not only partisan politics (as do all NPS sites), but also the content of "politics" at all, because it presents these values as universally shared and obvious in their meaning, and does so without attaching them to any actual referents or outcomes. It is perfectly possible, for example, to argue that none of these presidents were unambiguously dedicated to "democracy," depending on how one understands that word.

But politics are essential to and deeply embedded at Mount Rushmore. The project, as Borglum designed it, was intended—and was widely understood as intended—to be a monument to US American continental conquest.[61] The fact that national expansion is featured (Jefferson's head was intended to be first in line, and was moved behind Washington's only when the original location proved unsuitable for carving) and national permanence underlined both go to the idea that the nation was meant to be continental in scope, and that Indigenous dispossession was both natural and morally right. As Blair and Michael note, the museum actively distracts from the discussion of these ideas by focusing attention on the technological processes and technical prowess of the carvers.[62] It is also notable that while Mount Rushmore has been the site of various political protests, no information about them is publicly displayed.

Leaving the film and museum, visitors are able to walk past the out-door amphitheater and travel the short (0.6 mile) Presidential Trail, which offers various vistas of the carvings (access to the mountain itself is no longer allowed because of protests that go unmentioned at the site). The signage along the trail offers facts about the presidents, but does nothing to complicate the film's narrative of benign national expansion. The presidential faces loom over visitors, and the limited signage offers uncritical overviews of the four presidents: the sign dedicated to Washington portrays him on a horse, with some enslaved people as a farmer at Mount Vernon, and quotes the famous Farewell Address. Jefferson's consists of two portraits and a (poor) visual of the Indigenous artifacts on display on the entry hall at Monticello, underlining the facts of Native dispossession and appropriation. The focus of Lincoln's is his stovepipe hat. Theodore Roosevelt gets three images, one with arms outstretched, presumably giving a speech, an-other with his large family, and a third on a bulldozer at the Panama Canal. All of the signs offer brief biographical facts and unreflective quotations from and about the individual presidents. These signs are, as one youthful visitor mentioned to me as he passed by, "very easy to ignore." If they choose, visitors can pause at the carvers' studio, ascend to the secret vault that Borglum had (foolishly) hoped would house foundational national documents like the Declaration of Inde-pendence and the Constitution, and take in views of the spectacular surrounding area.

However vaguely formed, Mount Rushmore offers a preferred nar-rative and a preferred understanding of national identity, and does so by including a collectivity of presidents who are used as individ-ual points on the narrative's arc. Presidents in general and these men in particular are treated as unquestionably the nation's dominant ac-tors, its most important people. They give voice (Roosevelt is actu-ally pictured speaking, and one of Washington's speeches is quoted) to national aspirations, which entail expansion and (eventually) im-perialistic unity (Roosevelt is shown at, and lauded for, his role in completing the Panama Canal).[63] Jefferson is included on Mount Rushmore specifically because of his association with national growth in the form of the Louisiana Purchase and the Lewis and Clark Expedition.

Garry Wills has it right when he argues that the Louisiana Purchase had two separate parts: acquiring territory and then settling it.[64] In doing the first, Jefferson bought from France the right to acquire Indigenous land, either through negotiation or warfare.[65] Despite Jefferson's often eloquent and impassioned defenses of the principle of consent of the governed, it is worth noting that this action put large numbers of people—Indigenous, French, Spanish, and US American—under the control of the executive branch without giving them the opportunity to offer or to withhold their consent.[66] Jefferson's vision, with all its contradictions, entailed claiming the land in order to establish on it a republican empire that would eclipse the empires of Europe both in its scale and in its commitments to a specific understanding of democracy.[67] This vision did not include Black US Americans, and it demanded the assimilation and/or removal of Indigenous peoples and their replacement with white US American yeoman farmers.[68] The first step in that process was to obtain the right to the land from France. The second was to obtain it from Indigenous peoples. To do that, the land first had to be mapped and claimed. So Jefferson sent Merriwether Lewis and William Clark, along with the other members of the Corps of Discovery, to accomplish those goals.

The Corps of Discovery is, of course, something of a misnomer, as the land was perfectly well known to its Indigenous inhabitants and to others who traveled within and through the area.[69] But by "discovering" the land, US Americans were also erasing those people and laying claim to the land. The tendency of the expedition members to plant flags and otherwise mark their presence was not merely the kind of egoism we associate with teenagers scrawling their names on walls, but was understood by Europeans and US Americans as an act of labeling and claiming land.[70]

Expansion was integral to Jefferson's view of the nation, a perspective that was unusual among members of the founding generation, most of whom were content to focus on the territory already belonging to the United States.[71] It is also notable that Jefferson's goal was specifically *white* expansion.[72] He was relatively unconcerned with Indigenous survival, and he was one of the nation's first architects of Indian removal.[73] As one of his biographers writes in a notable understatement, "Jefferson did great harms to Indigenous peoples."[74] National expansion and Indigenous dispossession are two halves of the same whole.[75] The decision to focus on one half without the other is not a passive choice. It is both intentional and consequential.[76] It is made possible at Mount Rushmore by including expansion and dispossession in an overall narrative of national development that makes these acts appear to be natural and inevitable steps along the way. Because this history did happen, it is assumed to having had to happen, and the fact of individual and collective choices is submerged by celebration of the unified and glorious outcome, manifested by fireworks and laser shows. As Blair and Michael put it, "Rushmore does more than just remember; it advocates."[77]

My point here is not to argue that the NPS should turn Mount Rushmore into a site of contemplation, although it certainly could do that. It is to note that when we take one aspect of national history, such as national expansion, and offer it as part of an overarching, predetermined, narrative, it becomes extremely difficult to even imagine other kinds of historical possibilities or to perceive the vast range of consequences of the history being thus told. Grand historical arcs are by definition reductionist. They necessarily omit some things by focusing on others. When it comes to national identity, the consequences of such impartial and misleading memory practices are significant.

Conclusion

The physical context of monuments and memorials influences the interpretations of those monuments and memorials. Placing Jefferson alongside others reduces his own complexities and facilitates a celebratory narrative of the founding. In the Capitol rotunda he becomes a small piece of an encompassing narrative of a nation dedicated to democratic inclusion. As a member of the Continental Congress and

part of the first government under the Constitution, Jefferson's individual significance is reduced, and so is his ability to represent the
complicated ideologies at play at the moment. As one of the presidential faces on Indigenous sacred land, Jefferson's visage underlines in as
stark a way as possible the fact of conquest. Other contexts—placing
him among those he enslaved, or surrounded by depictions of the Indigenous dead, for instance—would convey very different messages.
These imaginary versions would also be partial and would occlude
certain elements of his legacy; I am not arguing that they would necessarily be "better," but I do want to point out that the versions of
Jefferson (and others) that we have are not the only available ones,
and that we should consider what it means that these versions exist as
they do and where they do.

Jefferson is remembered as an individual, of course, even at places
like the Capitol rotunda, Independence National Historical Park, and
Mount Rushmore. But when he is remembered in a crowd, as part
of a collectivity, he becomes both more and less than an individual;
he becomes a piece of a larger whole. Whenever individuals are remembered as part of the whole, differences among and between them
disappear. In this case, "the founders" become unified, as if they did
not have passionate and long-lasting disagreements over matters both
large and small.[78] Politicians, pundits, and the public reference "the
founders" not only as if they were a source of unquestionable wisdom,
but as if that wisdom was unanimous.[79] When that happens, contemporary interlocutors are cut off from the vast, complicated set of
decisions that comprised the founding and the early republic, and are
rendered less able to understand the legacies left by those decisions.

Jefferson himself is partially responsible for this state of affairs,
and that too was by design. Noting, in his first inaugural, after a particularly nasty presidential campaign, that "we are all Republicans,
we are all Federalists," Jefferson not only ignored the chasm that di-
vided the politics of the two emergent political parties but encouraged
his audience to do so as well.[80] To argue that "the founders" agreed
on anything is to empty the political values and practices that ani-
mated their moment of meaning. When Jefferson is remembered as a

member of a collectivity, then, he becomes important symbolically as a pivot point—between British colonization and US American independence, between independence and governance, and between the establishment and expansion of the nation. These combine to provide a clear and misleading narrative of national origins.

The misleading nature of this unified narrative matters for several reasons when it comes to national identity. First, it omits the perspectives of those whose experiences and histories would nuance or change the contours of that narrative, effectively excluding them from the national story and making their participation on an equal basis in national politics more difficult. It also allows some among us to harden their views on the nature of national identity, as they claim to be tracing their specific perspective back to a sacred and inviolable past.[81] Recognizing a more complicated version of that past allows people to consider the present as contingent, as flexible, and as at least potentially welcoming.

Moreover, a misleading national sense of identity has policy consequences as well. When we glorify the abstraction of "the founding," for example, we overlook the fact that ten of the nation's first twelve presidents were enslavers.[82] We ignore the disproportionate influence the Constitution's design provided to the slave states, and the consequences that had and has for policy. Making those legacies more obvious when interpreting the past makes it more possible to consider them as important aspects of the present.

Joseph Ellis reminds us that the goal of the US Revolution was not nationhood.[83] But it was very much about "peoplehood." The Declaration declared that "Americans" had become distinct from the British; that the temporary "political bonds" that had held these two peoples had to be dissolved—had indeed already dissolved. The Constitution then amplified that sense of national identity, claiming as it does to act for "we, the people." But the "people" were larger, more diverse, and more complicated than the founding generation was willing to recognize, and calling back to them hinders our capacity to understand who exactly "the people" are now.

4

The Popular Jefferson

Thomas Jefferson opens the second act of the enormously successful Broadway musical (and now film) *Hamilton: An American Musical*. Prancing—there really is no other word for it—around the stage, dressed in bright purple, beribboned and belaced, Lin-Manuel Miranda's Jefferson is something of a dandy. The costume reveals much about Miranda's dramatic perspective on Jefferson: witty, sharp, and a bit sly, the Jefferson of this play is as ambitious as Alexander Hamilton and his nemesis Aaron Burr, but more artfully so than either of the two main protagonists. This Jefferson is not a particularly nice person. He is scheming, superficial, vindictive, and arrogant. Although a cabinet battle on the subject of slavery—and Jefferson's willing participation in that institution—was deleted from the show, a couple of nods in that direction remain.[1] Jefferson makes principled arguments on behalf of the "common people," but that aside, there is little in this portrayal of Jefferson to commend, and the legions of adults and young people who learned something of the founding era from this wildly popular musical would not have found much in him to admire.

This is interesting for a couple of reasons. It is certainly one more step in the dance between Hamilton and Jefferson that has had one of them gaining popularity at the expense of the other over the entirety of US American history, and it therefore tells us that we are perhaps more in a "Hamilton" moment than a "Jeffersonian" one. But it is also more than that. Because it isn't Jefferson's ambition that sets him apart in this play. All of the male characters are ambitious. It isn't his willingness to engage in intrigue, although he is happy to be so engaged. Again, all of the main characters (excepting George Washington) are so engaged. It isn't just his eloquence, although the pace of Daveed Diggs's rapping, which enabled the writing for the character, was surely remarkable, Hamilton's eloquence was the show's main focus. Like the main protagonists, Hamilton and Burr, Jefferson is complicated. He makes principled arguments on behalf of democracy, and he owns enslaved persons. He is public spirited and self-interested. As we saw in previous chapters, commemorative considerations of the founding tend to put members of the founding generation beyond contestation. In popular culture, in contrast, that contestation is much more possible. Rather than being rendered larger than life, monumental in scale, popular culture depictions tend to bring out the humanity in its characters. When their humanity is the focus, so are their complexities, complications, and flaws. Depictions of the founders and the founding moment in popular culture, therefore, help us examine the complexities, complications, and flaws in national history, and that has consequences for national identity.

Of these complications, none is more important than the question of slavery and of racialism more broadly understood, and so that is the primary focus of this chapter. I want to be clear, though: Jefferson was personally an enslaver, and he fathered children with one of those he enslaved. But he was also a public man, influencing and making public decisions about public policies, including slavery. I do not mean to slight the very real importance of those public policies, or of Jefferson's hand in making them, when I place slavery in the context of his private life. Instead, I am turning our attention to how popular culture uses the private Jefferson as a way of negotiating those very public questions.

In making this argument, I first offer a brief discussion of the potential of tourist sites and popular culture narratives as sites of conscience and moral reflection. Then I offer a quick history of Jefferson's relationships to slavery before turning to three kinds of narratives found in popular sites and biographies: Jefferson as a romantic figure, as a complicated figure, and as one who is embedded in the context of slavery. I conclude with some thoughts on what this tells us about how questions of race and racial hierarchies continue to form and unsettle US American national identity.

Popular Culture and Moral Reasoning

There are many reasons for travel: business, family, and recreation can all call people away from home. All travel is in some way educative. We are told that "travel broadens the mind" and that we "learn about ourselves by leaving home." Tourist sites, as we have seen, are specifically created to attract visitors. One way they do so is by marking places as historically significant; the United States has a canon of such places.[2] Many of these places contain or are primarily dedicated to monuments or other forms of public commemoration, and are meant, as we have seen, to invoke a kind of civic piety.[3] These places are designed as "theaters of ideology," intended to create reverence for the nation.[4] The "nation" thus becomes unified through the telling of a single narrative that binds its various components together, and the founding moment has a singularly important place in forging that narrative.[5] This chapter adds a crucial piece to that argument, underlining the fact that these are also narratives of belonging. To feel as if they are part of a community, people need to be able to see themselves in that community's narratives, to find themselves in those places.[6] There is thus a "distinctly moral element" to these narratives, because they inform people of their place in the world and guide them toward correct actions in it.[7] Visiting these tourist sites is one way of inculcating these narratives and their moral lessons, while indicating who is and who is not part of the community.

But there are others as well, and here I want to combine conversations about places—like Monticello—with other kinds of narratives, which can accomplish some of the same ends as tourism sites. Consider the kinds of ephemera one can amass at such sites, for example. Visitors to places associated with Jefferson have the opportunity to buy glassware, paperweights, socks, books, coffee cups, puzzles, Lego kits, T-shirts, finger puppets, scarves, dish sets, hats, jewelry, plants, dog dishes, and various other relics of their visits. These are trivial, of course, but they also carry meaning: this place was important enough for someone to purchase (often at considerable expense) a piece of it.

Or consider stories about those places. One can visit Johnny Tremain's Boston, or Jefferson's Paris, or George Washington's Valley Forge. I use these examples intentionally. Johnny Tremain is the titular character of a Newberry Award–winning children's book written in 1943 about the onset of the Revolutionary War. Young readers may well have learned something about the places and people associated with that event through that fictional account. Others may have learned something about the French Revolution by following Jefferson to Paris by watching the 1995 movie *Jefferson in Paris*. And many more have learned something by watching the stage (2015) or film (2020) productions of *Hamilton: An American Musical*. These narratives can also induce powerful senses of belonging and national reverence, but unlike national parks and monuments, popular culture narratives and sites maintained by private entities move and change as popular tastes move and change. They do so more rapidly and with greater ease than governmental memorials and monuments can. Johnny Tremain's Boston has been replaced by Hamilton's New York as a site of nation building in the popular imagination, and the entirely virtuous founding fathers have been generally replaced by more nuanced versions of the founding generation. As with tourist sites, these narratives are not neutral, but offer, within the context of the story, moral judgments about events and the characters who participate in them.

Which is to say that popular culture intersects with political culture and affects public understandings of political events, past and present.[8] These effects can come from television shows, films, and music;[9] can affect and reflect mass understandings of gender, race, sexuality, and identity;[10] and can impact public opinion on issues like the environment, religion, sports, domestic violence, and abortion.[11] Certainly overtly political texts—like *Hamilton*, *Veep*, *Designated Survivor*, and *The West Wing*—have the most obvious impact on shared understandings of politics and political actors.[12] The stories we tell about Jefferson, in other words, the ways he circulates across the mass culture, are also stories about US American citizens and the public culture they inhabit.[13] To the extent that Jefferson is representative of the nation, when audiences make moral judgments about Jefferson, they are making decisions about the kind of nation they want, and the identities they want to claim. And from his day to ours, there have been a lot of stories told about Jefferson.

Jefferson, Slavery, and His Biographers

Jefferson was an interesting figure to historians and biographers even while he was still alive, and that interest has not significantly waned since. The historiography is well-established; the first generation of Jefferson biographers generally had personal connections to him and were able to rely on his family papers.[14] The narrative that these generally friendly biographers offered was largely accepted by those who followed them. While historians and biographers took varying positions on Jefferson's public life, they remained unified on the question of Sally Hemings, differing only in the degree to which they refused to credit the possibility that Jefferson had fathered her children and the reasoning for this belief. This unanimity reflected not only the consensus about Jefferson but also the prevailing (white) consensus about slavery and race relations more generally.[15] Which is another way of saying that this treatment of Jefferson and his relations with Hemings rested on deeply embedded racism. For most of national history, historians and biographers privileged the testimony of his white family and relations and denigrated or ignored the testimony of Black US Americans, both enslaved and free. Thus, while rumors concerning his relations with Hemings had circulated at least since Jefferson's first administration, they were treated as rumors, scurrilous attempts to discredit Jefferson.

Until 1974, when Fawn Brodie published *Jefferson: An Intimate History*, the first biography to treat Jefferson's private life as more than an appendage of his public one.[16] In crafting her narrative, she took the words of previously ignored Black US American interlocutors seriously.[17] Highly controversial in its own time, Brodie's book argued for a romantic relationship between Hemings and Jefferson.[18] While there is no extant evidence for how either of them felt about the other, and while a case can easily be made that romance is impossible between an enslaved person and someone who owns them, Brodie's work put the relationship between Hemings and Jefferson at its center, and thus created an image of him in the public mind with which biographers, historians, and those who managed his home at Monticello had to contend. They initially did so by dismissing Brodie and her work, until in 1997, Annette Gordon-Reed published *Thomas Jefferson and Sally Hemings: An American Controversy*.[19] An attorney herself, Gordon-Reed took a forensic approach to the controversy and produced a careful and detailed analysis of the evidence for and against the possibility of Jefferson's paternity of Hemings's children, describing the systematic bias that underpinned the historical treatment of the question. In 1998 DNA evidence confirmed the relationship between Jefferson and his unacknowledged and enslaved Black family. In 2000 Monticello conceded the point, and generally speaking, so has everyone else.

This widespread recognition has changed the way Jefferson is viewed in biographies, histories, and other forums. It has become virtually impossible to discuss Jefferson without also discussing Hemings, and it is impossible to discuss Hemings absent the broader context of slavery. So it is to the question of slavery, and Jefferson's relationship to it, that I now turn.

Jefferson, Race, and Slavery

Thomas Jefferson was born into a slaveholding, privileged family, and both the privilege and the slavery that made it possible remained central to his life.[20] Famous for his imaginative capacities, Jefferson was unable to envision a conflict-free multiracial society or one that was a successful republic that included a large and perpetual underclass.[21] I want to quickly tease out these two strands in Jefferson: his commitment to white supremacy on the one hand, and his dedication to a kind of broad economic opportunity on the other. The second is rather easily dealt with. Jefferson idealized the yeoman farmer, and abhorred a commercial state. His view of the nation entailed widely available land, settled by white farmers, who would remain economically and politically independent from large commercial centers, and who would therefore maintain both their frontier virtue and a democratic republic.[22] These yeoman farmers would get that land from Indigenous people who would either assimilate or face removal. They were male, of course, and they were white.[23]

There is no question but that Jefferson believed in the natural superiority of white people, especially when contrasted to either free or enslaved Black US Americans or to Indigenous peoples. Both had admirable qualities; neither were the intellectual, artistic, or moral equals of white people.[24] He dismissed the poetry of Phillis Wheatley, for example, and denigrated the capacities of Benjamin Banneker. Even his most accomplished Black contemporaries were treated by him as unworthy of notice. This belief was so deeply entrenched that it rendered him incapable of seeing, even given the circumstances of his own home, that his own racial distinctions, like race itself, were fragile categories.[25]

Like many white US Americans of his time, Jefferson was aware of the immorality of slavery and the plantation system. But the wealth generated by this system was foundational to the overall national economy, to the economy of the South, and to Jefferson's own life.[26] So on the one hand, he was, especially while in France, happy to claim that he abhorred slavery, and had even worked to end it; but on the other hand, he was unwilling to actually put any of his political or financial capital behind any such effort.[27] Moreover, he was more than willing to not only allow, but to endorse, the expansion of slavery into western territories as part of his "empire of liberty," which he saw as the nation's moral destiny.[28] Even his creation of the University of Virginia, one of his proudest legacies, was based on his desire to keep Southern gentlemen at home, away from the abolitionist teachings and practices of the North.[29] And of course the actual physical structures of the university were built by enslaved laborers.

The conundrum bequeathed by Jefferson and his contemporaries

—the concurrent dedication to human rights as universal and the maintenance of very clear, legally instantiated, racial hierarchies—has long been understood as central to the US American nation and the identities of its citizens.[30] There are at least three ways of parsing that foundational contradiction. The first is to argue that for the members of the founding generation, liberty was understood as the exclusive right of white men.[31] This was the interpretation preferred by secessionists, for example, and the white supremacists who continue to follow them. The argument here is that the Declaration was never intended to include the enslaved.[32] It is also the judgment of many more recent biographers and historians, who increasingly note the various ways that white supremacy and racial hierarchies were built into the nation's founding.[33] These two groups make very different conclusions about these interpretations. Secessionists and their heirs argue that white supremacy is the "true" legacy of the founding, and most others see this as a flaw that must be addressed.

The second way to parse the contradiction between claims to universal rights and support for slavery is to acknowledge, as Garry Wills does, that "My Jefferson is a giant, but a giant trammeled in a net, and obliged (he thought) to keep repairing and strengthening the coils of that net."[34] In this understanding of Jefferson and his contemporaries, slavery was a trap that they saw, understood as a trap, and were unable to free themselves from. This, of course, sidesteps the fact that others of that generation did free themselves—and also those they enslaved. The commitment to slavery was a commitment to the maintenance of hierarchies from which they profited; they all understood this. Some people made choices that others did not.[35]

The third way to parse the contradiction is to argue with historian Jon Meacham that "Jefferson offered a bold vision when he declared that all men are created equal. We know that neither Jefferson, nor the Founders, nor we fully live up to that principle, but the standard that Jefferson articulated was inspirational and aspirational. It has been used for centuries as a touchstone for people seeking freedom and demanding their own voice in the political process."[36] This "flawed founder" perspective has been used by Abraham Lincoln and many others to argue that Jefferson and his contemporaries were wise enough to articulate important universal principles and weak enough to be unable to live up to them. Here, the argument is that Jefferson and his contemporaries made public statements on the evils of slavery, thought that abolition was both inevitable and beneficial, and yet were unable to disentangle themselves from slavery. It differs from the perspective offered by Wills in emphasizing the obligation of those who followed the founders to make good on their promises and enact their ideals. This is the interpretation Jefferson himself seems to have ascribed to, aware of the judgments of history and the potential taint on his own legacy.[37]

This interpretation often hinges on the fact that without the slave-holding states, neither independence nor the new nation would have been possible. Concessions to what would increasingly come to be known as "the slave power" were required—slave states demanded the deletion of the Declaration's charge against King George for starting the slave trade, and slave states required the three-fifths compromise and other concessions in the Constitution. Slavery was the price of national union.[38] The majority of those involved in the decision-making found these concessions tolerable, if not palatable. There is no evidence that they disturbed Jefferson, who, in all of his many public capacities, and despite a very few feeble efforts to end slavery and a limited number of comments condemning it, proved a loyal representative of slave-owning interests.[39]

His loyalty to the slave system did not preclude him from criticizing it or from making a few tepid efforts to dismantle it. These actions are often discussed by historians and biographers, and so I will review them briefly here. First, in 1769, as a member of the House of Burgesses, he cosponsored a bill allowing for gradual emancipation. Second, as a young attorney, Jefferson defended some people of color in suits against their owners. Third, in both his *Summary View* and the draft of the Declaration, he blamed the British monarch for instituting the slave trade in the colonies. Fourth, his draft of a constitution for Virginia included emancipation. Fifth, commenting on slavery in his *Notes on the State of Virginia*, he wrote, "I tremble for my country when I reflect that God is just; and that His justice cannot sleep forever."[40] And finally, in a letter written to John Holmes during the Missouri Crisis, he wrote, "We have the wolf by the ear, and we can neither hold him, nor safely let him go."[41] Always, his advocacy for abolition or emancipation came with the understanding that expatriation would be required. Jefferson could not imagine a democratic republic in which white and Black citizens lived peaceably together.[42] It is also worth noting that Jefferson's advocacy of emancipation came only at moments when the political power of the slaveocracy was not at stake.[43] This is a thin record upon which to hang any defense of Jefferson as a dedicated opponent of slavery. Of course, no one now tries to argue that Jefferson was, in fact, a dedicated opponent of slavery, although there are a number of people who try in a number of ways to defend him on this issue. Defend him or damn him, it is now increasingly impossible to address anything about Jefferson without also dealing with the question of slavery. Putting Jefferson and slavery in conversation inevitably also means offering up a version of national history and national identity.

Three Jeffersons

Like any other public figure, although more frequently than most of his contemporaries, Thomas Jefferson has appeared in popular culture as a character in political cartoons or as a semi-fictionalized character in books, plays, and films. In the present moment, in addition to the various monuments and commemorations already discussed, he appears, for instance, as one of the animatrons in Walt Disney World's Hall of Presidents, in which he calls the presidency "a splendid misery," somewhat dampening the show's intended optimistic theme.[44] Some of these depictions, like the Hall of the Presidents, fall into the category of the "Collective Jefferson" and serve many of the same functions, so I do not need to detail those again here.

The collective Jefferson aside, there are three main ways that Jefferson gets portrayed in relation to slavery: as a romantic figure, as a complicated figure, and as a figure deeply embedded in the structures and institutions of slavery. These each have different kinds of

consequences for how US Americans understand themselves in relation to slavery, and thus how they understand themselves as a nation.

The Romantic Jefferson

Jefferson appears in politically based films, of course, playing both
major and minor roles. But he also appears as a protagonist in a love
story featuring Sally Hemings. The earliest of these depictions, *Jefferson in Paris* (1995), treats Jefferson's relations with various women
in his life: his daughter Martha, his friend (and maybe more) Maria
Cosway, and Sally Hemings. The film takes Jefferson's paternity of
Hemings's children as its premise, and backtracks from the testimony
of one of his previously enslaved sons to the story of his parentage.
The film presents the liaison between Jefferson and Hemings as a romance; she is flirtatious, he is entranced. There are tensions, to be sure.
Jefferson tries to prevent either Hemings or her brother from learning
that since slavery is illegal in France they can declare themselves free;
both of them require concessions from Jefferson to remain with him
when he returns home. Less connected to the actual historical record
are the personal tensions. There is an implication that Martha's desire
to become a nun is related to her reaction to her father's relationship
with Hemings, to whom she is noticeably unkind. The film also implies that Jefferson's relationship with Cosway ends as a result of his
attraction to Hemings. The film ends with Hemings's pregnancy, the
families' return to Virginia, and his promise to free any of her children
when he dies, a promise he also requires of Martha.

The film was neither a critical nor a commercial success, but my
concern here isn't with its quality so much as it is with its portrayal of
the relationship between Jefferson and Hemings as a romance. Critic
Roger Ebert found the film cold. He referred to Jefferson as "remote"
and claimed that "the filmmakers seem to have few ideas about the
nature of their feelings."[45] The *Washington Post*'s critic Eve Zibart
considered,

> Most bizarrely, the movie nearly ignores the crucial paradox, that of
> the liberal icon Jefferson's purportedly taking teenaged slave Sally
> Hemings (Thandie Newton) as mistress. Poor Sally's problematical

existence is presumably the excuse for the story.... But this Sally is a simple-minded and sometimes sly flirt (the word "pickaninny" painfully comes to mind) incapable of inspiring such personally taboo passion. The resonance of Sally's being half-sister to Jefferson's sainted dead wife is unexplored. The drama this movie so obviously avoids— the rivalry of two intelligent, conventionally unacceptable women (the married Cosway and the black Hemings) for Jefferson's soul—is the only one that might have mattered.[46]

Given that the film focuses on the romance between Jefferson and Hemings, both of these reviews unsurprisingly focus on the question of how Jefferson and Hemings were presumed to have felt. But as Zibart notices, the film ignores the question of how a man dedicated to Jefferson's principles could also have maintained a sexual relationship with an enslaved teenager. Viewing the relationship between the two as a matter of romance, however improbably portrayed, erases the very real questions about slavery and its entailments. Even Zibart finds the really interesting question that the film misses to be one of rivals for Jefferson's soul. The question of slavery apparently did not affect that soul's status.

A few years later, Sally Hemings again found herself in Paris, this time as the titular character in *Sally Hemings: An American Scandal*, a two-part television miniseries.[47] This story centers on Hemings rather than Jefferson, and is replete with historical inaccuracies. Like *Jefferson in Paris*, *Sally Hemings* assumes both a romance between Jefferson and Hemings and his parentage of her children. It also features Martha as something of a villain, disapproving and resentful of her father's commitment to Hemings. The show assigns considerable agency to Hemings, who is prone to argue with Jefferson, sometimes in inflammatory ways, challenging him on his treatment of her, on the gap between his professed ideals and his status as an enslaver, and on his relationships with other women. She is shown as traveling in the presidential carriage to and from the nation's capital, challenging Martha's treatment of her, and behaving in ways it is impossible to imagine any enslaved person, or any dependent woman, being able to act.

As the film progresses, Jefferson becomes increasingly aware of the disconnect between his opinions on African Americans as expressed in his *Notes*, and his attraction to and respect for Hemings. As they argue over precisely this question, in fact, a tortured Jefferson admits to being wrong, and regrets his previous racism. Jefferson fully recognizes the error of his ideological ways but changes nothing about his material practices. He retires from public office, and he and Sally enjoy a happy retirement at Monticello. There they mourn together his mounting debt and the subsequent sale of most of the enslaved people on the plantation. The news that the plantation itself is lost is portrayed as the proximate cause of his death.

Unlike *Jefferson in Paris*, this film treats not only the onset of the romance but also its long consummation, and treats that as a spousal relationship. Jefferson and Hemings suffer many of the same tensions as many married people, and are indeed married in all but name. The question of her enslavement comes up sporadically, and she occasionally rages against the system of slavery and its injustices, but her loyalty to him remains unwavering. Slavery, in other words, did not really come between two devoted hearts. The distortions of this telling are manifold. Much of the history is simply wrong well beyond any reasonable allowance for artistic license. Moreover, while there are depictions of the brutal realities of enslavement, they are undercut by Hemings's relative privilege and commitment to maintaining her relationship with Jefferson. While it is important to understand that enslaved people did exercise agency, and did create lives of their own even within the confines of the system, they likely did not have the power to physically assault white men, probably were unable to accuse them of rape, and were generally unlikely to be able to tell them to leave their homes.[48] They were unlikely to verbally challenge their owners, physically assault their owners' friends or relatives, or travel without their owners' knowledge.

My concern here is less with the historical inaccuracies and more with the ideological commitments that they enable. Depicting life at Monticello such that Hemings was a willing participant in a romantic relationship with Jefferson and that this relationship became a committed one on both their parts, in which power and affection seemed to be equal on both sides, is to allow its audience to imagine a kind of benign slavery, governed by mutuality and not oppressive power. Slavery here has only some negative consequences. Resistors to the system are brutally punished, to be sure, but those who do not disrupt it seem unharmed. Sally is victorious over Martha both in Jefferson's affections and in matters of household arrangements. The final scene between the two women is an argument that there is nothing that needs redress; no reparations are required. Following Jefferson's death they simply go their separate ways, each to their own families.

In both these films, by framing Jefferson's relations with Hemings as a love affair, a romantic view of slavery itself can't help but become part of the story.[49] In this, these films are akin to many plantation sites that are now open to visitation.[50] Like the Jefferson of *Sally Hemings*, these sites prefer the word "servant" to "slave," and commit the same kind of what Perry E. Carter, David Butler, and Owen Dyer call "racial erasure."[51] Like these plantation sites, these films sell a version of a "big house" story.[52] By softening Jefferson's feelings for Hemings, the very idea of slavery is also softened. And in softening slavery, claims concerning its continuing, unequal, and pernicious legacies are weakened. White US Americans become not people who owe something to those who were enslaved, but their affectionate partners. Differences in the power accruing now to the descendants of the enslaved and enslavers are naturalized rather than contested or viewed as a distorted legacy of a pernicious system. Complicated matters of race and racial relationships become blurred in a romantic haze. Those complexities, however, remain. And sometimes they become the focus of the story.

The Complicated Jefferson

Jefferson was a famously complicated man, and this often becomes one of the points in telling stories about him. He is one of the main characters, for example, in *1776*, the Broadway play that premiered in 1969 and was made into a film in 1972. Very much a product of its time, *1776* tells the story of John Adams's efforts to convince members of the Continental Congress to sign the Declaration and commit to independence.[53] Jefferson is depicted as fairly aloof, yearning for his home and family, and eventually arguing that they collectively needed to abolish slavery, claiming that he has resolved to emancipate his own slaves. This depiction, of course, takes liberties with the truth. While Jefferson's initial draft did include a charge against King George for his role in foisting the slave trade on the colonies, and while that charge was deleted from the Declaration before it was signed, there is no evidence that Jefferson was among those who ever considered emancipating most of those he enslaved.[54] However inaccurate, portrayals of "Jefferson as opponent of slavery" have circulated since his death.

More interesting is that *1776* takes the opportunity to explain the connections between molasses, rum, and enslaved persons. The unpleasant realities of the global economy are discussed, and the characters make clear the Northern complicity in the economic realities that made slavery seem indispensable to those who were involved in the fight for independence. The film explicitly labels the clause condemning the slave trade "a luxury we can't afford." Slavery here becomes a necessity, its abolition a luxury. John Adams declares that "history will never forgive us," and is encouraged to remember "first things first" by Benjamin Franklin. The clause is removed, the last obstacle is overcome, and the Declaration is signed. It is thus clear that the founders collectively understood the devil's bargain that lies at the root of the founding. It is one of the many portrayals of Jefferson that put racial issues at the heart of national identity, label those issues "a dilemma," or "a paradox," and that then place Jefferson at the heart of the national racial dilemma.[55]

In a more recent example, Ken Burns released his film *Thomas Jefferson* in 1997. In Burns's hands, Jefferson appears complicated rather than hypocritical. Very early in the film, viewers are given an extensive list of his various contradictions, near the end of which is:

He distilled a century of Enlightenment thinking into one remarkable sentence which began . . . "We hold these truths to be self-evident, that all men are created equal," yet he owned more than 200 human beings and never saw fit to free them. "Thomas Jefferson was a shadow man," said John Adams. "His character was like the great rivers whose bottoms we cannot see and make no noise." He remained a puzzle to those who thought they knew him best, embodied contradictions common to the country whose independence it fell to him to proclaim in words whose precise meaning Americans have debated ever since.[56]

This is a noteworthy introduction. It presents Jefferson as a person of manifold contradictions, only one of which dealt with his views on slavery. And, as in so many more contemporary views of Jefferson, it positions him as embodying the manifold contradictions of US American national identity.

As is typical of Burns's films, the overall ambience is often wistful. There is commentary by a number of noted historians who refer to Jefferson's centrality to the US American psyche, with some of them pointing to the gap between his vision and practices. The film details Jefferson's life in fairly conventional terms, but also tends to elide the pervasive nature of slavery in that life. The narrator, for example, informs viewers that "alone in a rented room, Jefferson went to work" on the Declaration of Independence. But he was not, in fact, alone. As Nikole Hannah-Jones reminds us, "As Jefferson composed his inspiring words, however, a teenage boy who would enjoy none of those rights and liberties waited nearby to serve at his master's beck and call. . . . Jefferson, who would later hold in slavery his own children by Heming's sister Sally, had chosen Robert Hemings from among about 130 enslaved people who worked on the forced-labor camp he called Monticello to accompany him to Philadelphia and ensure his every comfort as he drafted the text making the case for a new republican union based on the individual rights of men."[57] Burns ignores that aspect of the writing of the Declaration, preferring instead the image of the great man toiling in solitude. While the narration that follows touches on the tensions caused by the "sufficiently abstract" ideals in the Declaration, "the essential words of the American creed," according to historian Joseph Ellis, and their unattainable nature, those tensions are treated as being "like Jefferson's personality; wishing to be above it all and concealing the contradictions." Rather than delve into the question of how a person—and a country—could argue for human equality while enslaving other humans, Burns rather quickly moves on.

Partly, of course, this is because Jefferson is a capacious individual; his story has to be told economically if it is to be told at all, and this is a story about Jefferson, not one on the history of slavery. But I dwell on this because it is characteristic of so many of the biographies of Jefferson. Burns and many biographies either ignore or excuse Jefferson's status as an enslaver. There is a tendency to throw up one's hands and say, as does historian Clay Jenkinson in the film, that "Jefferson is right at the heart of this national paradox." I do not criticize this very reasonable conclusion. I do want to point out, however, that it has consequences in terms of national identity. When Jefferson's complications and the nation's get conflated, both Jefferson and the nation are absolved of responsibility. The people who managed the contradiction by deciding to emancipate those they enslaved, those who objected to slavery and fought to end it, those who rebelled against their own enslavement, those who escaped it, those who suffered under it, all these people and their choices get erased. They didn't argue that slavery was complicated; they argued that it was wrong. Sometimes they acted on these arguments. And sometimes they paid tremendously for doing so. This was all very much part of the fabric of Jefferson's moment and tends not to get much sustained attention here (or in many treatments of Jefferson).

In fairness, this film does not entirely evade the issues of race and slavery. Burns's Jefferson "wrestled with the question of race," and the various historians quoted in the film do note that his very comfortable life required enslaved labor. They also note that he "considered himself a good slaveholder," which admits the possibility that there is such a thing, but that even so, he didn't want his name publicly associated with human trafficking. All of those interviewed express their disappointment in this aspect of Jefferson. John Hope Franklin graciously says, "I'm a forgiving man, therefore I forgive him for what he did. But I remember that what he did was a transgression against mankind." Franklin's judgment, while merciful and kind, is still clear.

The film also takes up the topic of Sally Hemings, and here it must be remembered that the film predates the DNA evidence, and so Jefferson's parentage of her children is presented as a controversy rather than as a fact. Burns gives the last word on that controversy, however, to John Hope Franklin, who says, "It doesn't really matter whether he slept with her or not. After all, he owned her. She was subject to his exploitation in every conceivable way." We know such things happened, Franklin said, "And I see no reason why Thomas Jefferson should be excused from that." So here, Burns implicitly argues through Franklin that neither Jefferson nor the rest of us should be excused from either the history or the perpetuation of historical hierarchies in our own day.

And this is important because I want to contrast it to the romantic version of this story that we find in *Jefferson in Paris* and *Sally Hemings*. Some of the difference here is a matter of genre—Burns is a documentarian; the other films are fiction. Yet presenting Jefferson as a man in love who is faced with the complication of happening to enslave the object of his affections also presents slavery as one of the obstacles that come with romantic tales. Presenting slavery as one of the many complications of a complex man allows consideration of the inconsistencies that inhere in national history. It opens the door to the possibility that past injustice need not continue into the present and that it may demand redress. Burns offers Jefferson as a model of a continuing contradiction still in need of resolution.

With this in mind, consider the dominant depiction of Jefferson circulating at this moment: Lin-Manuel Miranda's *Hamilton*, in which Jefferson is a relatively minor foil for the musical's eponymous character. On several occasions in the show, Jefferson makes principled arguments both for his vision of an economy driven by yeomen farmers and for a foreign policy that favors France in its perennial wars with Great Britain. Miranda notes that Jefferson's ideological disputes with Hamilton were both deeply personal and importantly political.[58] Jefferson is positioned in those disputes as both principled and self-interested. Miranda has Hamilton argue against Jefferson's preferred economic policies in similar terms:

A civics lesson from a slaver. Hey neighbor,
Your debts are paid because you don't pay for labor.
"We plant seeds in the ground, we create." Yeah keep ranting.
We know who's really doing the planting.[59]

Here, Jefferson's principled policy arguments are submerged in
Hamilton's criticism of his motives and actions.[60] Jefferson's preference for a nation of yeoman farmers is placed in the context of his
preference for the system of chattel slavery. Moreover, Jefferson reacts
petulantly when he loses an argument on foreign policy to Hamilton, although again, he is impelled by a complex mixture of the personal (loyalty to Lafayette), the political (desire to prevent Hamilton's
ascendency), and the principled (political philosophy). These things
combine to motivate Miranda's Jefferson, who is quite willing to use
Hamilton's private life against him politically.

Miranda's Jefferson is depicted as aristocratic, witty, eloquent, and
popular. He is also slyly malicious and petty. He is, in fact, "an arrogant, preening, self-congratulatory jerk."[61] There is no question but
that in Miranda's vision of the founding moment, focused on Hamilton as it is, Washington, and to a lesser extent, Hamilton, not Jefferson, are the models for citizenship.[62] Treating citizenship as a complex
matter in which the personal, the political, and the moral are often
at odds creates possibilities for a nuanced rather than an exclusively
celebratory version of national identity. That understanding is made
even more visible when Jefferson appears within the context of the
system of slavery. And that is most easily done when he is seen at his
home, the plantation of Monticello.

The Enmeshed Jefferson

Monticello sits high upon a hill near Charlotteville, Virgina. With
its palatial residence, carefully tended garden, and extensive grounds,
Monticello was Jefferson's beloved home—and also home to hundreds of those he enslaved. Jefferson was deeply in debt when he died,
and both his Monticello plantation and nearly all of its enslaved people were sold to pay those debts. The house was purchased by private owners and eventually sold to the Thomas Jefferson Foundation,

created in the early 1920s, which manages it today as a private enterprise, open to the public.[63] For much of its history as a tourist attraction, Monticello had a lot in common with other plantation sites across the South. Its narratives tended to erase the history of the enslaved people who lived there in favor of the private lives of the white family; the experiences of the enslaved, when they were mentioned, were often trivialized and deflected; the lives of the enslaved and their owners were treated as distinct, rather than as a way of complicating and nuancing the overall story of life on plantations.[64] In other words, as commemorative landscapes, Southern plantations like Monticello tend to romanticize the antebellum era and marginalize the experiences of those whose enslaved labor produced the wealth so prominently on display.[65] There are reasons for this, of course. These are for-profit sites, and the impulse is to create narratives that offer the best chance of attracting visitors to them.[66] It is hard to imagine large numbers of people rushing to host weddings at sites portrayed as forced labor concentration camps.[67]

Yet there are good reasons to include narratives of all those who lived in these spaces. Including these narratives provides more accurate histories of the sites, those who lived there, and the eras they purport to portray. Moreover, enslaved people created identities and lives for themselves even in horrendous circumstances; these are stories worth telling.[68] And, there is increasing interest in including slavery in more general histories.[69] Including complete histories of such places is thus both ethically compelling and potentially profitable.[70] As a plantation, Monticello thus offers important stories. It was also deeply important to Jefferson himself, and is thus offered to the public as one way of understanding both the man and his times.[71] So I want to do a brief visit to Monticello as tourists see it to discuss what Monticello's Jefferson can tell us about contemporary US American national identity.

The Jefferson Foundation sees its mission as both preservation and education.[72] Monticello is listed among the "Sites of Conscience," an international coalition of "historic sites, museums and memory initiatives—that activate the power of places of memory to engage the public with a deeper understanding of the past and inspire action to shape a just future."[73] In other words, Monticello takes seriously its obligation to remember the past as a way of shaping a future, and at Monticello, depictions of slavery are an important part of that obligation. This was not always the case.[74] The Jefferson Foundation spent considerable time and resources arguing against the idea that Jefferson may have fathered children with Hemings; it did little to narrate the lives of those he enslaved; and Mulberry Row, where many of the enslaved persons worked and lived, was neglected. Much has changed. There are now tours that feature slavery and the lives of the enslaved; information about the Hemings family and other enslaved families is available on the website and is included in the tours; and the fact of slavery at Monticello is made abundantly clear.

Visitors might first visit Monticello's website, where they will find the usual information about location, hours, and so on, and also links to the site's introductory film, *Thomas Jefferson's World*, a virtual tour that includes sites specific to slavery, his presidency, "Slavery at Monticello," and "The Paradox of Liberty," which is about the daily lives of those whom Jefferson enslaved.[75] The information available here is neutral in tone. There are very few adjectives, for example, and the site clearly endeavors to offer information rather than judgment. Even apart from the website, unlike many Southern plantations Monticello offers a wealth of detail on the enslaved people who lived there. The introductory film, for example, notes that Monticello was "home to the Jeffersons and the families of free and enslaved workers including as many as 140 enslaved African American men, women, and children," and that "within the confines" of slavery, "enslaved people developed strong family ties and a dynamic community of their own, independent of Jefferson." These kinds of statements emphasize the humanity of enslaved people and avoid the kind of dehumanization or erasure that are often associated with these sites. Whenever possible, the enslaved laborers at Monticello are given names and the details of their lives are provided. This is true even in the general tours, which are not specifically about slavery.

A word about the available tours is important here.[76] Visitors can select a variety of tours, including "Highlights," which is the general tour, "Behind the Scenes," which takes visitors to parts of the house not seen on the "Highlights" tour, specialty tours, like "Archeology at Monticello," tours dedicated to young children, "Slavery," or "From Freedom to Slavery," which is a 2.5-hour tour that extends the "Highlights" tour into areas of the plantation where enslaved people lived, worked, and were buried. All tours allow visitors access to a docent-guided tour of the first floor of the house; "Meet Thomas Jefferson," a reenactor who tells stories and answers visitors' questions; the grounds and gardens; the visitors' center; the orientation film; shops; and restaurants. The foundation is in the process of renovating the visitors' center in time for the 2026 celebration of the 250th anniversary of the signing of the Declaration of Independence (there are delays, and the renovations may or may not meet this deadline). Visitors will all have to pass through the new visitors' center (it is currently optional, and most of the material there is about the various renovations to the house), so they will receive an orientation to the site. I was told by several docents that at least part of the motivation for this renovation is to systematize the site's interpretive material on slavery—much of that interpretive work is currently the responsibility of individual guides, and not all of them have the same expertise and interest. In other words, those in charge of interpretation at Monticello want to integrate its treatment of slavery with the overall treatment of the site, rather than maintaining it as an "add-on."

This is important, because the role of docents and guides is pivotal to both visitor experiences and the educative capacities of historical sites.[77] Docents at Monticello receive extensive training and exercise significant discretion over the material they cover. All of the docents on the tours I participated in ("Highlights," "Slavery," and "From Slavery to Freedom") made slavery part of the tour. On my "Highlights" tour, for example, when the docent pointed out an (inaccurate) map of Africa hanging in the entry hall, they noted that the parts of Africa that were accurately portrayed were also those that white US Americans knew well because of the transcontinental slave trade. They asked visitors to reflect on how Burwell Colbert, the enslaved butler who spent considerable time in that room, might have felt when he looked at that map. This kind of commentary assigns intelligence and humanity to enslaved persons, and asks visitors to consider their experiences in that light, encouraging them to empathize with those who were enslaved, not only with the white family. This is not a tour that focused only on the experiences of the white family or that erased the experiences of the enslaved people who lived there. It is one that asked visitors to consider the lives of the enslaved and their owners as pieces of the same whole.

Similarly, both iterations of tours emphasizing slavery end at the enslaved persons' cemetery, and as in the opening of Gayle Jessup White's lovely book, visitors are called to contemplate the differences between the white and Black descendants' grave sites.[78] Such calls underline the ongoing nature of the inequalities that can be traced back to slavery. Moreover, such calls to contemplation have important implications, because they ask visitors to internalize the experience of Monticello and to consider the site from a variety of perspectives. A site itself can only do so much. Only a very few of the visitors to Monticello participate in the slavery-specific tours. Most purchase the much cheaper grounds passes or the "Highlights" tour, with limited opportunities to learn about slavery in any detail.[79]

Other than the tours, visitors are able to view the sites' orientation film, *Thomas Jefferson's World*, which treats Monticello as a metaphor for Jefferson and for the nation, "always a work in progress." It goes further than many treatments of Jefferson as complicated, however. The film explicitly calls slavery "cruel," names many of the enslaved families, and notes the variety and skill of the labor they accomplished for Jefferson. It states that the ideals he outlined were contradicted in his life and at this place. This narration marks the humanity of the enslaved and concretizes rather than abstracting the conflict between ideals and practices. It is clear that this contradiction has real consequences for real human beings, and that those consequences played out in the space visitors are about to encounter. It ends by noting that the contradiction continues and that the rights Jefferson detailed still have not been fully achieved.

It is certainly possible to visit Monticello and to experience it primarily as a way to learn something about Thomas Jefferson. It is also possible to visit Monticello and to learn that Jefferson lived his life embedded in a context that relied on the enslavement of other human beings. Those other human beings are named; many of them have narratives of rich lives, full of relationships with others. They are stories of resilience and survivance. And they are stories of oppression. It is clear that there are no "good slaveowners," despite many enslavers' pretensions to the contrary. The Jefferson of Monticello, then, is a collective Jefferson, but the company of the "founding generation" is here expanded to include those the "founders" enslaved. It is hard to get around the complexities that this creates, or to extricate Jefferson from the web created by the fact of slavery.[80]

This is an important way to think about how we might remember Jefferson and what consequences that might have for national identity. To see him as a romantic figure softens and blurs slavery, and does not require contemporary audiences to contend with it. Slavery is rendered safe and placed safely in the past. To think of him as a complicated figure allows contemporary audiences to recognize the complexities and contradictions baked into the US American nation. To think of him as inextricably bound up with slavery requires audiences to contend with the ways that we continue to be inextricably bound up with its legacies. These forms of remembrance bring with them different entailments who for US Americans are and want to be.

Conclusion

Popular culture allows us to envision and to contend with important issues at any given moment. When we focus on a person like Jefferson, who appears in popular culture in a variety of ways across time, we can see whether and how the nation has changed in its understanding of those issues. Jefferson is an interesting example for a few reasons. First, all popular culture texts enable consideration of important cultural questions through fiction—*MASH*, for example, was a consideration of Vietnam, although placed in Korea; and Aaron

Sorkin's *The American President* was a romanticized reflection on the US presidency that reached fuller expression in *The West Wing*. When those texts focus on a particular issue (like slavery or war), a single institution (the presidency), or a specific person (like Jefferson), they are attempts at achieving an understanding of those events through narrative.

Second, Jefferson was an actual person, who often becomes fictionalized. Some critics object to fictional treatments of real events, especially because of the ways that audiences may be encouraged to confuse the fiction with historical fact.[81] Those treatments may instead be lauded for their capacity to encourage audiences to further investigate the people or events in question. In either case, fictionalizing historical characters offers opportunities and constraints that purely fictional characters do not. Because the setting is presumed to reflect a historical reality, it allows audiences to envision a context different from their own; it allows them to see out of the eyes of those who made important decisions and played important roles in national history. It also limits the imaginative possibilities, however, because some things (like Sally Hemings traveling in the presidential carriage) simply strain credulity and undermine the narrative and therefore its capacities to imagine things otherwise.

This chapter has dealt with Jefferson as he is treated in popular culture—in film, on the stage, and in his own home. In this capacity, he is often depicted alongside those he enslaved. This is important. The nation continues to grapple with its ongoing history of racial oppression, from slavery into the present day, and with the legacies of the various forms that oppression has taken over the years. White US Americans have accepted, hidden, denied, and deflected that history and its legacies by turns over the centuries. The nation has never come to a shared understanding of them. Jefferson is useful to all of the ways US Americans seek to reconcile themselves to the past. There are, for example, traces of a valorous Jefferson, who needs to be forgiven for his complicity in the system of chattel slavery. In forgiving him, it becomes possible (although not inevitable) for the lingering entailments of that system to be elided or ignored. There are also those who yearn for a romantic Jefferson, in which the South as a site of white nostalgia tends to figure prominently. The costuming is often lush, the genteel plantation is evoked, and slavery becomes domesticated into a family circle of reciprocal relationships. This erases the violence of slavery even as it sometimes seems to acknowledge it. There is also what may seem to be an emergent consensus about the role of slavery in national life, which appears to come down to something like, "it's complicated." And, of course, so was Jefferson.

If, as William Jeremiah Moses suggested, Monticello is treated as a metaphor for Jeffersonian democracy, always in process, never quite coherent, never quite finished, it is useful to think of it not as Jefferson's home, but as the home of those whom he enslaved—those who, after all, spent much more time there over the years than he did.[82] Monticello, then, becomes one important site for reflecting on the legacies of democracy and inequality can coinhabit the same terrain. The Jefferson who was embedded in that home and in that system is the Jefferson that holds the most potential for holding him up to an accounting—to require an assessment of him that does not neglect the system of slavery in favor of the democratic system he is credited with helping to create. This is as close as we seem to come to requiring something like a full accounting for the stain of slavery.

In this regard, it is interesting that both popular and scholarly discussions of Jefferson and slavery tend to rely on the same very few pieces of actual evidence of his views on slavery and those he enslaved. Jefferson, it should be remembered, maintained an active public life for decades. He left tens of thousands of documents. And yet the material on his positions on slavery can barely be called minimal. This suggests that he did not want those opinions known at the time or included in any lasting public record. And there is only one reason for that. He knew those opinions were wrong and would be condemned, if not in how own time, certainly in the future.

The white people of the US American nation remain in much the same position. Believing in Jefferson's claim that all of us are created equal, white US Americans do not know how to live up to that belief any more than he did, at least in part because doing so requires giving up some of the privilege gained by the fact of racial hierarchies. Jefferson was unwilling to, and seems to have understood himself as unable to emancipate his slaves, to reduce the scale of his own luxuries, to accommodate his own theoretical commitments. Many white US Americans see themselves similarly trapped. That trap is one of Jefferson's legacies: unable to envision a different future, and hoping that future generations would somehow see a path forward. So it is to a consideration of what Jefferson has to teach those future generations that we now turn.

5

The Children's Jefferson

The interpretive ranger at Independence National Historical Park did all the usual things during a tour of Independence Hall—explaining the building and its furnishings, detailing the events that took place there, and commenting on several of the individuals and offering quick anecdotes about them. They also told the assembled tourists that after the Declaration of Independence was signed, it was taken into the square behind the hall and read to the amassed public, which included men, indentured and free; women and children; enslaved and free Black people; the wealthy and impoverished; newly arrived immigrants; and descendants of families who had long been residents of the colonies. This depiction painted a different picture of the founding, and of the nation, than do many of the stories children have historically been told about that moment. It offered an image of a diverse crowd, standing together as they heard for the first time what would become some of the most sacred words in US American history. Yet the ranger pointed out that many of those listening in 1776 could not have helped being aware that these words did not apply to them, even as they may have hoped that their inclusion would not always be an impossibility.

The tourists listening to the ranger describe the diversity of the crowd hearing the inspirational words of the Declaration for the first time were experiencing a version of a story they had been told over and over for their whole lives. The story of Independence Day is taught to even the youngest children, who hear it from mayors and presidents, from parents and scout leaders, from teachers and from religious leaders. In big and small ways, telling the story of independence is central to how the nation celebrates July 4th. On that day, more than on any other, the nation explicitly talks about what it means to be a US American, tells its origin story, and links that story to the ongoing process of being a citizen. On that day, more than any other, the naturalization ceremonies taking place across the country make national news as thousands of people officially take the oath and become citizens of the United States.[1]

This chapter focuses on this aspect of how national identity is created, maintained, and changed, by looking at how the nation's origin story, in the person of Thomas Jefferson, is taught to children, and what that tells us about citizenship in the US American community. That is to say, teaching children about Jefferson is also teaching them about the country he helped to found, and who is included in it and why. Specifically, I argue that Jefferson in particular is defined as having certain important characteristics that matter when it comes to citizenship. When the "founders" are the center, other people are reduced to the margins. This has implications for how belonging to the nation is enacted and understood.

To make this argument, first I offer a quick discussion of the importance of children's literature to national identity. I follow that with a brief argument about citizenship and national identity, and then I turn to Jefferson himself, treating him as a role model and exemplar of US citizenship, and consider some alternative narrative possibilities. I conclude with a discussion of what we teach children tells us about national identity.

Teaching Children National Identity

Children watching the YouTube video "Thomas Jefferson for Kids" will learn several things about him: that he loved science and education, that he was the main author of the Declaration of Independence, that he was the third president of the United States, and that both he and his house are on the nickel.[2] They will be taught definitions for both "colony" and "independence." Similar videos about the founding are widely available.[3] Which is to say that US Americans teach even quite young children some basic facts about the US founding, often highlighting the role of the Declaration of Independence in that story. These origin stories are, as we have seen, central to public memory and to collective identity, and are deeply inculcated in part because we learn them as children, and they become part of the fabric of collective life, accepted without reflection because they have always been there and because the narrative so rarely changes.

Public memory, in other words, and thus national identity are both created and influenced by the stories we tell children.[4] This explains something about the manufactured controversies surrounding the teaching of race and diversity initiatives and the impulse to ban books from schools and public libraries.[5] Some people fear what is being taught to children—even "children" in colleges and universities—because they fear these teachings will challenge their own beliefs and preferences, potentially leading to a future of which they do not approve. This anxiety is a product of the fact that all children's literature is didactic. Whether in the form of film, video games, music, or the written word, especially if it is aimed at younger children, it teaches lessons about something.[6] Those lessons can be as fundamental as "we should be kind to one another," as simple as "the wheels on the bus go round and round," or as culturally specific as table manners.[7] As children age, it can also include things like the histories of institutional structures that support systemic inequities and/or facilitate greater equality. All of these things, in different ways, influence and reflect national identity, and so the stakes of what children are taught about the nation and its practices and norms are very high.[8]

The Commonwealth of Virginia, for example, which requires even its youngest citizens to be told that "people throughout Virginia's history have collaborated and compromised to achieve common goals and to be successful as good citizens," includes Jefferson (along with George Washington, Powhatan, Pocahontas, Maggie Walker, and Arthur Ashe) as an example of good citizenship.[9] The section of the commonwealth's curriculum on the Declaration notes that "in practicality, it only applied to white men," and includes information on

James Armistead Lafayette, an enslaved Black American who worked as a spy during the Revolution and then had to fight for his own freedom (which he eventually attained). Students in Jefferson's home state are thus taught that the founding moment was complicated and that the benefits of the Revolution were unequally available to those living in the new nation. These standards of learning are likely not unique to Virginia, and indicate that students are taught the parameters of citizenship from quite young ages.

It matters that these things are taught through history, and not through other avenues, such as religious texts or nonfiction. When citizenship is the product of history, it is rooted in the verifiable past, and thus has the weight of tradition behind it. It is also taught as "true"; the past is treated as incontestable. The founders, children are told, met in this place, on this day, and did this thing. It is instructive to remember that only some of those considered "founders" met in Philadelphia; that the Declaration was not, in fact, signed by most of them on July 4, 1776; and that originally, not all the delegates to the Continental Congress signed it. What children are taught as verifiable history is often inaccurate. But it is taught as "the truth" for a reason, because that "truth" grounds the national origin story, and also grounds the sense of national identity that benefits from it. To be clear, some of these inaccuracies matter more than others. It does not matter to the nation's identity what day the Declaration was signed. It matters a great deal that only white men who owned a certain amount of property were understood to be included in its statement of universal rights. But presenting the universal claim to equality and rights as timeless marks the nation as more conceivably and more intentionally inclusive than if the "timeless" element of the document lay in its exclusions.

Moreover, claims to truth are persuasive. Children, even those in the younger grades, understand the difference between fiction and nonfiction; they understand events; they grasp the consequences that adhere to those events; they distinguish between heroes and villains and between right and wrong. They can, in other words, grapple with moral choices.[10] But they often need help doing so. When writing for children, cues are important. Tone, for instance, needs to match content. For example, telling children that Thomas Jefferson owned slaves in rhyme conveys a different kind of message than explaining slavery in a somber tone. Young children especially are concrete thinkers, who need things spelled out for them in explicit ways. They do not, as a general rule, do especially well with sarcasm, so writing without irony is important.

Children's books are often heavily illustrated, which helps them concretize the material. Because pictures convey meaning and can be as persuasive as words, they should be consistent with the written text.[11] Explaining that slavery is bad, for example, while depicting Jefferson behind a plow in the fields with workers sends a confusing message about why slavery is bad and about who exactly is doing the work.[12] Depicting him on a horse overseeing the labor of others, or in his gazebo reading a book while others work outside in the hot sun, conveys a different sense of who was doing what at Monticello, and at what cost.[13]

Nuance is especially important in biographies, where children benefit from being taught about the puzzles and contradictions that characterize human life.[14] Such books not only offer chronologies but also help teach children about experiences, ideas, and motivations.[15] To explain, for example, that slavery was a common practice among wealthy white Southerners in Jefferson's time provides some context for Jefferson's choices regarding slavery. Many of the books on Jefferson do this, implying in the process that slavery was so natural as to present no actual choices for enslavers. A book that explained that some of Jefferson's acquaintances, influenced by the Declaration he wrote, chose to emancipate those they enslaved would provide a different kind of context and could lead to a different kind of understanding about Jefferson and others among the founding generation and the choices they made.[16]

We expect different things from a book written for young adults than we do from those written for six-year-olds. As children age, they can spend more time with a book, they do less with illustrations, and they can accept more nuance. But even very young children can

There are an enormous number of books aimed at juvenile audiences about Thomas Jefferson. Most tend to flatter him. Photo by the author.

process the information in illustrations, can be informed or confused by (in)consistencies between text and pictures, and can contribute to the meaning making that is reading.[17] As with all literature, authors may have preferred meanings, which are often impossible to know with any certainty. Those meanings may or may not be conveyed, and unintended meaning may be produced as well. When alphabet books do something as simple as associate the letter "I" with "Indian," for example, the picture accompanying the letter is often of a generic male Indigenous person in a headdress. The book's author may have simply meant to teach children the letter "I." They are also teaching stereotypes about Indigenous peoples. There are positive examples, as well, of course; when books depict women or people of color occupying inspirational roles, that matters too.[18]

The books and movies I use here are a scattering of the ones available at Jefferson-related sites—places like Independence National Historical Park, Fort Clatsop (in Astoria, Oregon), the National Archives and gift shops on the National Mall, and Monticello. They are aimed at a variety of ages, from the youngest children to young adult readers and viewers. In general, I chose not to rely on material prior to the 1990s because those books are less likely to continue to circulate. They are also more likely to erase difficult issues like slavery or Indigenous dispossession or to treat them in unfortunate ways.[19] I am not arguing that these texts necessarily form a representative sample of works intended for these audiences, but that they reveal an interesting set of problems, tensions, and possibilities when it comes to remembering members of the founding generation and Thomas Jefferson himself, and what that tells us about citizenship and national identity.

Citizenship and National Identity

All communities are both inclusive and exclusive. Some might be based on faith, for example, and would therefore include all believers and exclude all nonbelievers—a person of faith easily sees themselves as a "member" of their church. Communities might be formed based on shared ethnicity, or history, or as the result of geopolitical negotiations. National boundaries, in other words, are often as ideological and political as they are material. They exist because of invented commonalities and differences.[20] In the example of the United States, despite a long history of immigration laws that were often overtly and specifically exclusionary (like the 1882 Chinese Exclusion Act or the immigration quota system), the nation has prided itself on being a community of belief, arguing that everyone who ascribed to specific national values was welcome in the nation. Often, those values are traced to the founding. Ideologically, one is a member of the US American community to the extent one agrees with the founding values. Legally, it is a different matter. The oath required for naturalization, for example, is based on swearing allegiance to the Constitution, renouncing loyalty to other nations, and (since 1950) promising to bear arms in the nation's defense as required.

One can be a legal citizen, in other words, by agreeing to uphold and defend the Constitution. Adherence to national values is not required; adherence to national law is. But ideologically, one isn't really "American" without believing, to at least some extent, in things like the centrality of liberty and equality to the nation. Even young children will settle disputes, for instance, with the claim that "majority rules." But the meaning of those values changes over time.[21] It is commonplace in this political moment, for example, to cite the importance of "equal protection under the law," a phrase and a set of practices that would have astounded the framers of the Constitution, and that required an amendment (the Fourteenth) to it.[22]

Citizenship is thus both legal and social.[23] Immigrants, for example, are expected to "earn" access to citizenship that those born within a nation's territory take by right. They must meet specific legal requirements that include interviews and tests. But unlike citizenship, belonging is not a legal matter. Many legal citizens are treated as if they do not belong; they can be marginalized for religious beliefs, for their status as newly arrived, and/or for their ethnic or racial identities. In addition, because some people have always been considered more suitable as citizens than others, and because citizenship in the United States is tied to commitment to specific ideas, one way of managing inclusion has been to demand that aspirational citizens learn how to be citizens. This has historically tended to have both legal and social components.[24] Immigrants have been expected to learn both laws and social practices, and it has always been easier for many people to become a legal citizen than to be consistently recognized as equally belonging to the nation.

Citizenship as belonging, in other words, involves hierarchies among members of the community, with some being considered more central to the nation and others more marginal.[25] In the United States, some of those hierarchies are not completely stable but change over time. There were moments when one's status as an immigrant from Ireland, for example, was reason for exclusion, or when one's Italian ancestry marked one as an outsider. Other hierarchies have proven more rigid. Black and Brown US Americans continue to face formidable resistance to their claims to equality, as do women, LGBTQ+ people, the differently abled, and others.

In the United States, both these exclusions and the capacities to alter them are present in the founding and its ideals and are embedded in what we understand as civic identity.[26] Universal claims to equality have allowed the nation to pretend that it has always been more in-clusive than it has been, have facilitated charges of national hypocrisy, and have enabled arguments for greater equality and inclusion. These arguments are ongoing, and are often met with resistance from those who are already included and who often fear that their places in the national hierarchies are threatened by the inclusion of those who were previously excluded.[27] The stability and fluidity of national hierar-chies explain why, when it comes to how the national story is told to children, the controversies are so intense and the urge to control the narrative is so strong. To the extent that membership in the national community is dependent on belief in national values, and to the de-gree that those values can change over time, noting what values are considered important enough to teach children about is a useful lens into contemporary understandings of national identity.

The Model Jefferson

Children often encounter Jefferson as they learn about the basics of US history. They are usually told that he is a "founding father," the principal author of the Declaration of Independence, and the third president. He is often (incorrectly) given credit for "doubling the size of the nation" and (correctly) for authorizing the Lewis and Clark Expedition. He is frequently portrayed as continuing to influence and inspire the nation. Children who have been taken to historical sites or who are required to write a biography of a famous person as part of a school exercise may be inspired by Jefferson's inventions, his interest in fossils, or his love of words. They may desire to be an inventor or an architect like he was, or to play the violin, as he did. He is portrayed as possessing qualities worth emulating, and children are encouraged to reproduce at least some aspects of his character (his studiousness, for example, is often underlined). When it comes to books aimed at a juvenile audience, children are taught about Jefferson because he did important things, because he thought important things, and because he left important legacies. In all of these ways, they are also being taught what it means to be a citizen of the nation he helped to found.

The Active Jefferson

As with all heroes, often when Jefferson is portrayed as worth emulating, his virtues are stressed above his flaws, which are set aside
or ignored. Many of these are the kinds of hagiographic biographies
so often associated with "great men." This approach is often aimed
at the very youngest children. In *The Little President*, for example, a
picture book on the US presidents, readers (or more likely, listeners)
are told about Jefferson, "This little president / was super-smart. / He
liked buildings and inventions, / books, fossils, and art."[28] The text is
accompanied by a picture of Jefferson peering into a microscope with
parchment and a quill pen behind him. He is thus offered to children
here as the smart, science-oriented author of the Declaration of Independence. Neither he nor any of the other presidents in this delightful
little book are treated in any detail, and all are offered to children as
exemplars of one sort or another. Other books, aimed at a more so-
phisticated audience, still introduce Jefferson to children by noting his
many talents: as an architect, musician, lawyer, and so on.[29]

In these texts, Jefferson is considered admirable because of the
things he did—he authored the Declaration and lived a life of service
to his country. He is a model citizen because despite his many talents
and interests, he sacrificed his private preferences to the needs of the
nation.[30] In a typical example, the table of contents for *Presidents of
the United States: Thomas Jefferson Our Third President* indicates the
pattern I'm referring to here: "Path to Glory" is followed by "American Leader," "In Command," and "A Second Term."[31] The idea is that
Jefferson's whole life should be understood as a progression toward
fame and the presidency. In books and book series like this, children
are introduced to the basic facts of US history and the presidents associated with much of that history. It is also an approach that centers
presidents in the national history, which is of dubious accuracy, and
highlights their virtues above their complexities. Readers of this particular volume are told, for example that "Although Monticello was
the only place in the world that Jefferson truly wanted to be, he often
had to leave. After all, he was one of America's founding fathers, men

who helped establish the United States of America."[32] Unsurprisingly, the book relies on Jefferson's own preferred narrative of himself as a reluctant statesman, called to duty. It also underlines his commitment to home and hearth; Jefferson is portrayed as just the kind of "father" a nation needs.

Books like this one struggle to reconcile national ideals, which they often attribute to Jefferson, with his own practices, which are often treated as difficult to reconcile. These books tend to argue that, like the country more broadly, Jefferson himself faced conflicts between material necessity and philosophical principle. In one book, for example, children are told, "Jefferson may have struggled with the idea of slavery. But he did not think he could run his large plantation without the labor of enslaved workers."[33] Here, the national dilemma is made clear: slavery was both morally wrong and financially profitable. When children are given this information, Jefferson stands in for the founding generation, which included signers of the Declaration, declaring human freedom, and the authors of the Constitution, which embedded chattel slavery into national law. These two things, placed side by side, offer a view of the limits of national ideas, although authors who choose to valorize Jefferson tend not to dwell on these matters, preferring to envision him as the conflicted author of the Declaration of Independence and a member of the founding generation. His actions as author of the Declaration and as president are what earned him a place in history. But it was dedication to certain ideas that continues to earn him a place as an exemplar of citizenship.

Children reading these books are taught that national ideals are more important than the nation's inability to live up to them, that civic duty is central, and that admirable people make sacrifices for the greater good. They are instructed in the broad strokes of national history, generally through an optimistic lens, and may come to believe that the formal end of slavery and the civil rights movement owed something to Jefferson and the ideas he so eloquently articulated. They may also infer that equality has been more or less fully achieved. These messages may create satisfaction among privileged children and some cognitive dissonance among those who have not experienced the nation or their own place in it in this way.

The Thinking Jefferson

Books that make explicit and implicit arguments that Jefferson is a model citizen because of the things he believed, rather than chiefly because of the things he did, are often aimed at children older than those who constitute the audiences for the "great man" biographies. These books tend to emphasize Jefferson's manifold talents and interests above his institutional roles. They might, for example, focus on his love of learning and dedication to books, his interest in science and measurement, or his attention to gardening. These books offer reasons beyond the founding for admiring Jefferson, and point to the kinds of characteristics considered important for children as citizens to learn. Like "great man" histories, in doing so, these volumes often ignore or elide the more problematic elements of Jefferson's story. Frequently, it is Jefferson's love of learning that gets foregrounded in these books.[34] Children are often taught that Jefferson was fond of reading, that he owned hundreds of books, and that science especially was central to him. In these books, the tale of Jefferson and the moose is featured prominently.[35]

Briefly, that story is this: as part of a multivolume work produced between 1749 and 1804, Georges-Louis LeClerc, the Comte de Buffon, criticized the flora and fauna of the New World as inferior in size and fecundity to what was available in Europe. Jefferson took issue with this characterization, which was part of the reason for his authorship of *Notes on the State of Virginia*. That volume, among other things, defended the people, plants, and animals of the North American continent against these charges of inferiority. When it came to the plants and animals, Jefferson showed particular interest in large mammals, and, upon moving to France, and finding his descriptions of them met with disbelief, he asked a hunter to go to Maine, shoot a moose, and ship it to Paris, where he planned to display it and confound his nation's critics. Sadly, it was the wrong season, and moose with antlers were unavailable. The moose, when it finally arrived in Paris, was a sorry, moldy, and somewhat threadbare specimen. There is no record of Buffon either ever actually seeing this moose or of changing his mind regarding the Americas and its inhabitants, but the story of the moose is entertaining in its own right and flexible enough to put many of Jefferson's admirable traits on display: his creativity, his persistence, his dedication to empirical fact and science, and so on.

For example, in *Jefferson Measures a Moose*, Jefferson is depicted as a person who "loved asking questions about numbers." He is so entranced with measurement, in fact, that among other examples, "he knew how much it cost to see a monkey and how hot it was in Philadelphia on July 4, 1776."[36] He is therefore "baffled by" Buffon, who had the nerve to write about the New World without having visited there, measuring, weighing, or even seeing its animals.[37] The book then takes readers through Jefferson's move to France and his desire to obtain a moose, and notes that "when the moose arrived at last, it was a little less impressive than he'd hoped."[38] But still it was big, so surely it would convince Buffon. But, the book tells readers, "Some people have a hard time saying, 'I was wrong.' Some people would rather DIE. That's what happened to Buffon. (Of course he was quite old)."[39] Buffon, whose demise becomes a counterexample of correct behavior, falls to Jefferson's more virtuous example of the importance of accurate measurement and the need to base one's opinions on verifiable and verified facts. Because of his dedication to these principles, his fellow citizens "knew they could COUNT on Jefferson."[40] The moral here, of course, is that, like Jefferson, children who count can also be counted upon. Admirable people and good citizens are those who make judgments based on empirical facts and not blind prejudice.

Jefferson didn't just love measurement, he equally famously loved books, and thus helped create the Library of Congress. *Thomas Jefferson Builds a Library*, for example, focuses on this aspect of his character.[41] The book follows Jefferson to Philadelphia, Paris, and Washington, DC, but the narrative is always centered on his love for books.[42] Readers are given to understand that it was that love of books and not his crushing debt that motivated the sale of his individual library to the nation: "After fifty years of collecting, Tom owned more books than just about anyone in America. He couldn't let his country go without a library. Guess what he did?"[43] Books are his legacy as well. "Tom's collection never stopped growing. Two hundred years later, the Library of Congress owns more than 171 million items on over 860 million miles of shelves in 470 languages. It adds around 9,000 new items a day."[44] The text thus glosses over Jefferson's less admirable qualities like his debt and focuses on his accomplishments and contributions, but the lesson is clear: Jefferson's love of books contributed to his own success and to that of the nation as a whole, and as good citizens, children should attend to their educations, support that of others, and strive to contribute to the nation.

Jefferson's love of science is sometimes portrayed through his attention to his garden.[45] In *Thomas Jefferson Grows a Nation*, for example, readers are told that "Thomas Jefferson liked to grow things. At Monticello, his home in Virginia, he grew potatoes, peppers, pippins, peaches, juniper, larkspur, and peas."[46] The author does not note that Monticello was a plantation relying on the work of enslaved laborers, but argues that "Throughout his life, he scattered seeds, like a brisk wind, around the world."[47] These seeds are both literal and metaphorical, for—accompanied by a picture of Jefferson behind a plow (an activity he probably never engaged in)—the text reads, "After planting the seeds of freedom by writing the Declaration of Independence, Thomas had something new to nurture. And like any farmer imagining the harvest of a newly tilled field, Thomas envisioned a nation of farmers."[48] Throughout the book, Jefferson is depicted not just as valorizing famers, but as a farmer himself. The text includes his own claim that "I return to farming," and the verbs indicate that he is the one doing the activities of farming.[49] Even as president, "he dresses in his usual farmer's attire."[50] The book concludes by noting that "Thomas loved to grow things—he grew seeds and science, liberty and learning, farmers, freedom, and democracy."[51] The implication is that Jefferson's commitment to "liberty and learning" was unequivocal and that he did all of this growing alone and essentially unaided. Children following this model of Jefferson would remain humble (even if dressing as farmers was not an option for them), and would also be dedicated to "growing democracy." They might learn to associate the rural United States with national virtue, as Jefferson did.

Collectively, as with the "great man" biographies, these books often erase or elide the subject of slavery, the national treatment of Indigenous people, and both Jefferson's and the nation's moral ambiguities and inconsistencies. When it is a matter of introducing very young children to the presidents, this is perhaps understandable, although in my view children old enough to experience racism are old enough to learn about it. As children get older, it would seem reasonable to include more material on those aspects of national history, as celebratory versions of national history give way to more nuanced and complicated accounts. Generally, when those elements are included, they are contained in discussions of Jefferson's various legacies.

Jeffersonian Legacies

Many of Jefferson's legacies are discussed in books that treat him as a "great man" or that focus on his role in creating the Library of Congress, of course, and it is typical to see things in that context like, "Jefferson's ideas helped build what the United States strives to be—a democracy where the people participate in their government. In all of the positions he held, Jefferson never lost sight of this goal."[52] Here, readers are offered a celebratory view of Jefferson, the nation, and its political institutions. This view treats the universal application of national ideals as a given. As with all the other books on Jefferson, he is used to make an implicit case for the centrality of those ideals to national identity. To be a US American is to accept and enact them. Readers are also sometimes given the chance to contemplate the incomplete nature of the nation in its relationship to those ideals, to think about how they might be imperfectly realized.

So, here I want to discuss the tendency among many of the books on Jefferson to include, sometimes as afterwords or in other kinds of ancillary material, discussions of Jefferson and slavery, often doing so in relation to national ideals. In one example, the author includes an afterword titled, "Thomas Today," which notes that "owning slaves was common among Southern landowners" and tells readers that "we must decide for ourselves how slavery taints the legacy of Thomas Jefferson," which might seem to call readers to contemplate the question of how the history of slavery might impact the nation and its citizens more broadly. This possibility is undercut, however, because it is clear where the author stands on this question: "Fortunately, his words spoke louder than his actions. Slavery was finally abolished in 1865, yet Thomas's inspirational words live on and continue to affect the way we live today. From 'all men are created equal' grew the civil rights movement and the women's rights movement, and it will remain a kernel of hope in the struggle for equality in the future."[53] Jefferson did, the author continues, "much more nurturing than I could squeeze into this book," and his "resilience and optimism are important parts of the American spirit."[54] Rather than encouraging children to render their own judgments of Jefferson, this author preempts that option by offering their own understanding of how children should understand Jefferson's legacy.

Another volume, *Thomas Jefferson for Kids*, concludes, as do so many biographies of Jefferson, by referring to his complexities. When Jefferson died, the text claims, "America lost a complicated man. A man who believed in frugal government yet lived his own life burdened by debt. A man who hated kings and privileged nobles yet lived as an aristocrat himself. A man who believed passionately in freedom and liberty and yet owned slaves who toiled for his comfort."[55] The book thus lets young readers view Jefferson as worthy but also imperfect. The book concludes with the idea that "Jefferson was a complex, brilliant man—an architect, a scientist, a writer, a dreamer, the supreme believer in freedom from government."[56] Even though his flaws are listed, the last word goes to his achievements and his belief in freedom from government. Positioning Jefferson as emblematic of good citizenship is only possible if he is treated primarily as admirable and secondarily as flawed. This treatment also makes it possible for readers to understand the nation as also worthy and also imperfect.

Other books are less willing to concede his flaws, and argue that Jefferson was "committed to ending slavery," and/or that the ideals that he outlined in the Declaration have been integral to the expansion of civil rights since his own time.[57] This approach allows for criticism of the shortcomings of the founding moment and acknowledges the progress that has been made since. It can sometimes veer into implying that national ideals have been fully actualized and that citizens have no further responsibility in this regard. For example, readers of one book are told, "The poor, women, and people of color were most often left out" of consideration for the rights assigned to white men, placing inequality firmly in the past and implying that these deplorable circumstances are no longer the case.[58] This treatment of Jefferson's legacy can disable active citizenship by making it appear as if the work of improving the nation has already been completed.

Another strategy is to treat slavery and other inequities as tangential to the main narrative. It is pretty common, for example, to offer information on Indigenous dispossession or slavery in sidebars and insets. In one example, Jupiter, an enslaved person whose primary responsibility was attending to Jefferson, is the subject of a sidebar. It is important to include information about him, and notable that he is both named and given a space dedicated to him. But the treatment itself is not without problems. The text states that "the two probably played together before Jupiter became Thomas's personal slave and traveling companion. . . . Jupiter even lent Thomas money to tip his friends' slaves."[59] This framing erases the inequalities between Jefferson and those he enslaved. In fact, Jupiter appears to have more power—and certainly more money—than Jefferson.

Another inset in the same book addresses Jefferson's personal relationship to slavery: "One of the great complexities of Thomas Jefferson was that he recognized slavery as an evil and even spoke against it, yet he owned hundreds of enslaved people over his lifetime and relied on their labor for his comfort and existence."[60] The inset includes an image of an ad requesting aid in locating an escaped enslaved person and an argument for freeing someone suing for their freedom. A couple of things are worth noting here: first, and most importantly, the book problematizes Jefferson's stance on slavery, but does so in a sidebar, not in the main text of the book, relegating the question itself literally to the margins of the main discussion of Jefferson. Second, it points to slavery's complexities but does not offer readers any assistance in resolving them or in digging deeper into what it might mean that at least one of the nation's founders was committed to and profited from the institution of slavery.

"The Hemings Family" is also treated through an inset. That text reads in part,

> Betty Hemings and her 11 children became the property of Thomas Jefferson on the death of John Wayles. . . . Most likely, some of Betty's children were the half siblings of Martha Jefferson. Over the decades, Thomas Jefferson held more than 80 people related to Betty Hemings in bondage. The Hemings family held a place above all other slaves at Monticello. . . . The greatest prize—freedom—was granted to only 11 slaves at Monticello out of the 600 men and women Jefferson owned over his lifetime. All 11 were the children or grandchildren of Betty Hemings.[61]

Here, Jefferson seems to have only incidentally participated in slavery, as a result of his father-in-law's death. And the inset does not mention that some of Betty Hemings's grandchildren were his children.

Sally Hemings receives an inset (on the science of determining the paternity of her children with Jefferson) and is mentioned in the text, where the relations between she and Jefferson are treated without judgment: "Many slave owners took advantage of enslaved women and fathered children with them."[62] The unequal power relations are revealed in the phrase "took advantage of," but this does not seem to be a cause for judgment. Rather than treat Jefferson here as a window into the kinds of power relations and abuses that characterized slavery, the text instead chooses to provide factual information from which, with some effort, those things can be inferred. The author notes that Hemings "had belonged to Jefferson since she was a toddler," and that her children's births were recorded, as were those of others born into slavery, in his Farm Book, but makes no effort to reason from that to a wider context or to tease out any implications of these facts.[63]

Questions about Jefferson's legacy in relationship to slavery are similarly elided when he is placed in a context in which his beliefs and actions seems natural and reasonable.[64] *Thomas Jefferson: A Day at Monticello* begins with: "Thomas Jefferson (1743–1826) grew up in the mid-1700s at Shadwell, his father's plantation in the hills of central Virginia, one of the British colonies in North America. From his father, Peter Jefferson, he learned about surveying the land, growing tobacco, and about a society where free white people owned black slaves." Here, the ownership of slaves is treated as integral to and a natural part of his world as growing tobacco or the skill of surveying, and it is troubling that it seems to be given the same moral weight.

The book proper follows an adult Jefferson through his day at Monticello. Throughout, Jefferson is depicted as treating his enslaved workers courteously—he says good morning to Colbert, who is identified as his enslaved butler, he greets the workers on Mulberry Row, and so on. He tours the plantation with his grandson Francis, who serves as a proxy audience, for Jefferson explains the workings of the plantation to both Francis and the readers. Francis encounters an enslaved child with whom he has previously played, and expresses some dismay when he learns about the length of that child's working day.[65] Francis then has the following invented conversation with Jefferson:

> "Why is it that I have the time to study and to play with my cousins and to ride with you, sir, while Israel must run the drum carding machine from sunrise to sunset?"
>
> Jefferson sighs, looks at his grandson, and says, "There is nothing I would not give for a workable plan for ending slavery. I believe it is evil and threatens the future of our country."
>
> "Then why do we still have slaves?"
>
> "Here in the Southern states," his grandfather begins, "slavery is part of the whole system of life. Ending it will require time, patience, and dedication. I am an old man. I have lived longer than most of my

friends with whom I founded our country. The work of ending slavery is for the young—for those who can follow it up and see it through. I hope that you, Francis, and your generation will accomplish this most important work.[66]

Here, the author works hard to save Jefferson from himself. The text relies on an invented conversation and a selective and generous reading of the historical record. It naturalizes slavery as "part of the whole system of life," without interrogating in any way that this system depended on the making of continuous choices. Francis is charged with solving the knotty problem of slavery, and in doing so, Jefferson, now an old man, is absolved of responsibility for it.

I spend so much time on this example because saving Jefferson from himself also tends to absolve the polity as a whole. Slavery is depicted as an inherited system that posed a problem that white people managed as best they could until it was finally eradicated with the Civil War. No one really bears responsibility, and no compensatory actions are required. Slavery remains safely in the past, with no entailments that imply burdens on the present. Contemporary citizens are equally absolved from the need for any actions required to make the nation more inclusive.

In the wake of the DNA evidence confirming Jefferson as the father of Sally Hemings's children, and given the current political context in the United States a whole, it has become difficult, if not impossible, to write about Jefferson for any audience but the very youngest, without somehow contending with the question of his relationship to slavery. Authors of children's books must also, willingly or not, contend with the question of the nation's relationship to slavery and its legacies and entailments. They do so with greater or lesser degrees of grace. Some authors leave judgment up to the readers, arguing that they need to decide for themselves. Others offer it as one among many of Jefferson's many complexities. Still others imply or assert that Jefferson opposed slavery and did what he could to end it, while some authors literally marginalize and contain discussions of slavery by confining it to sidebars and insets. Finally, some authors place responsibility for slavery on the context, making the case that there was really nothing to be done about a system everyone found abhorrent.

All of these options offer different views of citizenship, belonging, and responsibility. If judgment is truly left up to readers, that can be empowering, encouraging even young children to exercise their own judgment on matters of political significance. Thinking about the nation as a complicated amalgam of the praiseworthy and shameful can be differently empowering, and can encourage action to encourage inclusion and tilt the balance toward justice and equity, even while understanding that neither is easily achieved. Saving Jefferson from himself would seem to absolve both the nation and its citizens from responsibility to either the past or the present. Bracketing discussions of slavery, the enslaved, and the histories of both serves to highlight these things as requiring special attention by the nation's citizens, while segregating them from the main conversation. Making slavery appear largely as a choice forced on well-meaning people by an invidious context disables citizenship and renders belonging difficult to achieve.

None of the authors I included here, or any of the others like them, are likely to have considered their narratives from the perspective I offer here. Most of them were probably concerned only with writing an entertaining and informative account of Jefferson or some aspect of him for children. But the stories we tell are who we are, and they have consequences we may not regard during the telling. With this in mind, I next discuss a few different stories: ones that have different kinds of consequences and entailments for national identity, citizenship, and belonging.

Teaching Children Hard Things

All of the books discussed here offer lessons about who Jefferson was and what that teaches children about how they might navigate the tricky terrain of national citizenship. When those lessons center the founders, one version of the nation is foregrounded. That version tends to emphasize founding ideals and national progress toward enacting them. It tends to minimize the gaps and inconsistencies between those ideals and the nation's history. This version teaches children that presidents are central to the national experience, and that they are people who should be admired. Children learn that like Jefferson, good citizens show allegiance to the nation and make sacrifices for it. They are attentive to education and especially to science, and they make good choices based on solid knowledge. Like Jefferson, they are committed to national ideals, and they can be excused from failing to live up to them. The national history of uneven privilege and inequality is generally treated as ancillary to the national story, which emphasizes progress. These are pretty standard versions of how national history has been taught and how people like Jefferson have generally appeared in those histories.

But there are other possibilities we might want to consider as we think about those histories in terms of national identity. Children can learn hard things.[67] They can learn about the national histories of inequality and their continuing consequences. Take, for example, the short video prepared by the White House Historical Association and Untold History.[68] The video begins with an essential contradiction: "Thomas Jefferson, founding father and principal author of the Declaration of Independence, envisioned an America where all men are created equal. But over the course of his life, he enslaved over 600 Black men, women, and children." The video does not bury the contradiction, nor does it seek to protect Jefferson from its entailments. Rather, it sets Jefferson aside and focuses on three of the teenagers (Ursula Granger Hughes, Edith Hern Forest, and Frances Gillette Horn) who he enslaved and who worked as his chefs. It notes the long hours they worked, their exercise of agency as they strove to make lives for themselves in the context of slavery, and the presence of a vibrant Black community in which they participated. The video actively encourages viewers to consider the implications of the opening contradiction, concluding with, "Thomas Jefferson wrote all men are created equal. What do you think he meant by those words?"

Similar possibilities appear in books about some of Jefferson's

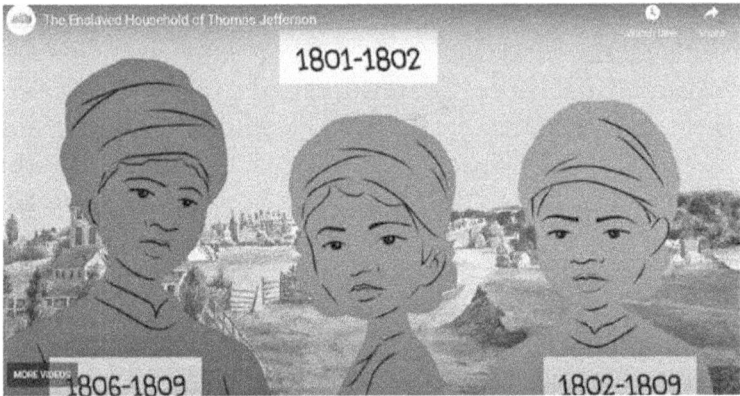

Some materials produced for children about Jefferson, like this video, focuses on the people he enslaved. Photo by the author.

contemporaries. At Fort Clatsop, in Oregon, for example, established at the Corps of Discovery's end point, visitors can purchase *The Journey of York*, which tells the story of the only enslaved person to travel with Lewis and Clark.[69] The book's preface notes that "As property, York did not have a choice in whether he would volunteer for Jefferson's dangerous mission. Slaves did not have many choices."[70] The book is clear on the constraints York faced, but also assigns him agency; the book's cover, for example, depicts an African American man alone and steering a boat. The story itself is told from York's point of view and includes his recognition that while others on the expedition happily celebrated the Fourth of July, "I did not have any independence." York identifies with Sacagawea, because "Everyone called her his [Charbonneau's] wife, but I heard how this teenage girl had been stolen from her family. Charbonneau bought Sacagawea in trade and made her his wife. I think that is why she and I became so close. She was the only other one out there who knew what it meant to be called the property of another."[71] Readers are encouraged to empathize with the loneliness and pain shared by Sacagawea and York, and to understand the national policies and practices that caused them.

York is proud when "York's Eight Islands" are named after him, and prouder still when he is allowed to vote on the site of the winter camp, since "I knew that in the United States we lived in, a slave had no right to vote. A black man never had the right to put his word up beside a white man."[72] His sorrow is also clear when at a celebration at the newly established Fort Clatsop, "Captain Lewis called out the names of those brave heroes" who had participated in the expedition, and "my name was not included. That's when it first became clear that my return home would not be celebrated as everyone's else's."[73] And indeed, York was returned to slavery, possibly eventually freed, and potentially lived out his life among the Apsáalooke (Crow) people.[74] Throughout this story, York is the focus. The story is his, and the white men and others who populate it serve his narrative.

This book, however, relies on imagined conversations and an al-most entirely invented York. We do not actually know what York looked like, how he felt, or how he reacted to events. What we know about him comes entirely from the words of others. So including peo-ple like York also requires putting words into their mouths and attrib-uting thoughts and emotions to them without even the possibility of gauging their accuracy. It is worth considering whether this does justice to the subject and whether the advantage of empathy is worth the invention of a historical record.

Yet there are cases where there is a historical record that can be used to support narratives about Jefferson's contemporaries. There are a number of available oral histories and narratives from the formerly enslaved and other kinds of historical records that can be used in constructing such stories.[75] *My Name Is James Madison Hemings*, for instance, takes one of Jefferson's enslaved sons as its subject, and relies heavily on a published interview with him about his life.[76] The flyleaf asks questions rather than making claims: "What if you were born into slavery in 1805? And what if the man who owned you . . . were also your father? And what if he were one of the most important men in America? And what if he wanted the fact that you were his son kept secret? Such was the world of James Madison Hemings. This is his story."[77] Anyone picking up this book will know what they are get-ting: a story that illuminates slavery as an institution in understand-able terms: "Slavery: when one person owns another human being," and also humanizes enslaved people: "But each enslaved person has a name, a mother, and father—and a mind, a heart, and a story."[78] Hemings's story can be taken to stand in for the stories of many other enslaved people, and through his eyes, children can experience something of what that would have been like, knowing who his father was, relatively privileged but unacknowledged: "Many days I sat outside on the grand lawn, staring at the beautiful mansion of this man. How could I be both his slave and his son?"[79]

In books like this, the abstraction of Jefferson's contradictions is given both immediacy and force. It concretizes the question of how Jefferson could argue for human equality and also own other human beings with sharp clarity. The authors are clear about how much of this remains unknowable: "And the fact that we resembled him, especially as we grew older—was he secretly proud of this? Perhaps he did not know what he felt."[80] The Hemings of the book is similarly baffled by his own feelings: "And what was I supposed to feel for my father, my 'master'? What was I supposed to feel when he was very old, lying sick and in bed, dying?"[81] Questions like this one encourage even young readers to imagine Hemings's life and to empathize with him. The book ends with this uncertainty. Hemings is aware of how little, in a material sense, he inherited from his father. He does not know how Jefferson himself negotiated any of this in his own mind; he only knows his own story.

Such books appear even more important when they are compared to other cognate books, such as *What Was the Lewis and Clark Expedition?*, also available at places like Fort Clatsop.[82] Part of an award-winning series, this book consistently includes Sacagawea, but has only one cursory mention of York, in which he is described as being so strange to Indigenous people that they tried to rub the color off of his skin.[83] Sacagawea is treated as ancillary to the expedition; she lacks agency and a real story. This encourages readers to empathize with Lewis and Clark and to distance themselves from her and her experiences.

Cognate books that include the stories of the minoritized and excluded are important, as Sara VanderHaagen argues.[84] They are often stories of pain and suffering rather than tidy examples that glorify the national history. They thus offer a fuller and more accurate version of that history, and help complete the picture told by more hagiographic stories. They are stories of heroism, resistance, and resilience that offer examples worth emulating and exemplars of moral action, often in the face of great peril. They are also stories of citizenship, highlighting in human terms the consequences of political exclusion, illustrating the sacrifices of those who contributed to the nation from positions of exclusion, and expanding the national understanding of who contributed to the national origin story.

Conclusion

All rhetoric is in some sense pedagogical; citizens receive lessons about the nation, its hierarchies, and who belongs through speeches, monuments, and throughout popular culture. Rhetoric is most obviously pedagogical when it is aimed at children, and this is why the battles over what children should be taught can be so intense. These battles are of a piece with arguments about which monuments should be taken down and which should be left in place; they are similar to arguments about the correct parameters of presidential speech; and they are akin to arguments about what is appropriate material for popular consumption. The standards for all of these things change over time. Those changes are always hotly contested because they reveal changes in ordering of national hierarchies, changes in the nature of national belonging.

We are what we remember, and we are the stories we tell. The question of how we teach children about Jefferson is also a question about how we manage national narratives and thus how we manage national identity. Whose stories we choose to tell and how we choose to tell them instruct the young in matters that go beyond the material of the stories themselves. Imagining Jefferson and his contemporaries in the past also constructs and maintains collective memory. When we remember Jefferson exclusively as a great man who did great things, we create and sustain a nation that primarily recognizes the contributions of the powerful and the privileged. These narratives emphasize certain events and actions and minimize others. Such narratives tend to stabilize long-standing national hierarchies of belonging. When we tell stories that emphasize individual talents and achievements, we help to create a nation that valorizes individualism and that singles out certain talents as more notable and worthy than others. These stories also instruct citizens in the attitudes and behaviors of good citizenship and the requirements of belonging. And when we tell stories that manage the legacies of the nation's past in whatever ways, we create a nation that may have difficulty contending with those legacies honestly. We might do better to treat those legacies as integral to the national history, and recognize them as creating inclusion for some, exclusion for others, and hierarchies from which only a few benefit.

Telling the stories of Jefferson's diverse contemporaries opens up spaces that many stories about Jefferson seem to foreclose. Stories of Jefferson are worth telling and should be told. But there are other stories, also worth telling, that can be told more often. Those stories inform children of how complicated and diverse the nation was; what kinds of hierarchies operated when and with what kinds of consequences. Those stories facilitate a more active citizenship for more people and encourage a broader sense of national belonging.

Conclusion

Thomas Jefferson remains ubiquitous. He reminds US Americans of the importance of the founding moment, provides ways to ground national identity in a long tradition while opening possibilities for adaptation and change, offers the ability to contemplate matters of inclusion and exclusion, and illuminates the ways that race and racism have been and remain central to how the nation understands itself. Images of him and references to him are everywhere because he was so complicated and multilayered that he can be purposed to suit a variety of agendas across time and ideology. Because collective memory is so strongly connected to collective identity, the way that Jefferson is remembered at any given moment reveals a great deal about how the United States understands itself in that moment.

Of course, all of the various places where I found Jefferson—in presidential speech, monuments and memorials, popular culture, and children's books and films—are experienced by different people differently. These sites all speak to people with different voices, and images appear differently in them. Some people may view Mount Rushmore, for example, with something like horror, seeing it as a desecration of sacred land. Others take a more innocently patriotic view, and find it inspiring and evocative of their love of country. But these sites also have meanings that underlie the most innocent or cynical interpretations, and it is those meanings I have tried to uncover here.

Finding Jefferson (and Rhetoric) Everywhere

I looked for Jefferson in particular kinds of places, where the rhetoricity of public communication is especially accessible. There is, for example, a very long tradition of studying public address, particularly presidential speeches. There is considerable research on monuments and memorials, and a great deal of scholarship on the politics of popular culture. While there is less on children's literature, to my mind this is an important place to look for material on collective identity because it is avowedly didactic and because it is currently so hotly contested. It is somewhat remarkable that there are so many children's books dedicated to Jefferson; many more so, it seemed to me, than are available on any other founders or presidents, with the exception of Abraham Lincoln.

Jefferson and Lincoln may be the only presidents on whom a study like this could focus, although it would be interesting to see how someone like FDR might have been repurposed by presidents—Ronald Reagan, for instance, claimed to have been an FDR liberal until becoming a conservative, and referred to him fairly often as president.[1] It would be interesting to see if Andrew Jackson attained a national level of commemoration or if his appeal was limited to the South and parts of the West. Perhaps at a great enough historical remove, Ronald Reagan may be as heavily memorialized as Jefferson. But it is hard to conceive of other public figures with a capacious enough legacy to make such an analysis possible, especially given that memorial practices, both as a private and as a public matter, are changing.[2] Monuments to specific individuals are less common in general, and so tracing histories of national identity through monuments would need a different focus if the aim is to capture that in the present.

If we are going to look for national identity in speeches, memorials of various kinds, and in popular culture, including children's literature, it is important to remember that however it is done, marking someone's life is a choice. Like all choices, it involves selecting some elements and ignoring others (labeling Jefferson the "Apostle of Democracy" entails ignoring his history as an enslaver; valorizing

Jefferson for the Louisiana Purchase means ignoring its impact on Indigenous people). Whether the heroization occurs in speeches, monuments, or characterizations, it is always an attempt to portray one aspect of a person as worthy of emulation, as foundational to the community. So it is important not only to note that someone is valorized, but also to note the terms of that valorization, for therein lies the keys to the conception of communal identity. The qualities being admired are those that delineate "good citizens." They may also appear as the opposite of good citizens; one can imagine stories of Jefferson that argue that enslavers and/or expansionists did not contribute to democracy, and that thus ignore his admirable qualities.

As those examples indicate, it is also important to remember that these choices are never neutral, even if (especially if) they appear to be so. No memorial is produced without someone dedicating time and other resources to it. It is worth inquiring why specific figures are depicted as they are: why was it important to envision George Washington as specifically honest (Parson Weems's cherry tree story)? Why did the sculptor of his statue (on display at the Smithsonian) put him in a toga?[3] Why might James Madison have attributed some characteristics to Jefferson and not others, and why might later presidents have made other choices? It is likely that any conception of any historical figure was also contested in its own time, if not in ours. It is worth asking whose interests were being served by any kind of memorial, and whose were being ignored or erased. We might ask, for instance, about the consequences of the fact that there are so few monuments to those who fomented rebellion among enslaved persons and so many to those who enslaved them.

Which is also to say that memorials and other forms of remembrance have an accumulated weight that is worth considering. The fact of so many ways to remember Jefferson marks him as being significant in a way that might well distort a sense of national history. Certainly emphasizing presidents—even those who governed at moments when Congress was more powerful politically—facilitates a misunderstanding of government and how it worked. And the sheer number of times a story—like that of the founding—is told embeds that story more deeply in national consciousness than other stories, other ways to find belonging in the nation.

The placement of physical memorials matters. The National Park Service, for example, recently added a copy of Franklin Roosevelt's famous "D-Day Prayer" to the World War II Memorial on the National Mall.[4] This is most unusual, in that it is a specifically religious artifact placed on government land. The act providing for the installation was signed into law by President Barack Obama in 2014 after considerable lobbying on the part of the Friends of the National World War II Memorial, and was funded by the Lilly Endowment.[5] The prayer's proponents argued that it deserves a place on the memorial because of its ability to unify and comfort the nation. This claim is also a claim about who among its citizens were and are most central to the nation. At a time when there are very public and intense arguments about the proper role of religion in US national politics, the memorial would seem to be taking a side. It is notable that it was decided to put the prayer installation on the Mall, and at the World War II Memorial, and not just off the Mall, at the FDR Memorial. The prayer modifies the meaning of the memorial and the Mall even as its presence there modifies the way the prayer might be interpreted.

Other kinds of physical placements matter too. The first national memorial to Jefferson was not in the nation's capital but in Missouri, where it marked the significance of the Louisiana Purchase. Placing a statue of Jefferson at Felix Schlag's grave (he designed the Jefferson nickel) elevates the meaning of that grave; placing Jefferson on the nickel elevates his stature. Placement can influence which aspects of a memorial is highlighted and which aspects might be less apparent. Contexts matter as well as physical placement. One might reasonably ask why Richard Nixon chose to rely on Jefferson as a justification for his policies on revenue sharing—someone in his speechwriters' office presumably thought this choice would prove persuasive to someone in the intended audience, even though that reasoning is not necessarily clear to us from this distance. So it is worth noting when and how a figure gets used by others and to what kinds of ends.

It is equally important to remember that these portrayals might not be working in the ways that their originators intended. When we now note that Jefferson and some of his descendants are buried high on the hill at Monticello while those he enslaved were laid to rest in what was once a neglected section of the property, that reveals much that Jefferson hagiographers might want hidden. When Jefferson comes to symbolize national histories of inequity that have yet to be repaired or eliminated, that too runs against the grain of some of his most ardent supporters. When his statues are contextualized by information about slavery and Indigenous dispossession, those actions modify the meaning of the originals.

This underlines the fact that because commemoration is social, meaning changes over time. As the removal of the statues on Monument Avenue in Richmond, Virginia, indicates, forms of memorialization that were highly regarded by some people at some moments may be differently regarded by others at later moments. Monumental stability cannot be taken for granted, and the ways that meaning shifts over time is an important factor in tracking the changing nature of communal identity. The meaning of a historical figure is created and re-created by those who wield them as a symbol, whether they do so in a public speech, as a monument, or as a character in a story. It is also created and re-created by audiences and visitors, who bring their own histories and sensibilities to the texts. Those audiences and visitors may well be siloed into distinct memory communities, and may not share any given interpretation of a text or site. It is important, then, to remember that a text's preferred meaning isn't its only meaning, may not even be its most widely shared meaning, and that these meanings and their importance are fluid and can shift over time.

Which is in turn a reminder that as much as memorializing might represent an effort to freeze politics, and using a figure like Jefferson might represent a way of authorizing one version of politics at the expense of other possibilities, politics are never static, and they are never monolithic. Efforts to make them so are always subject to leakage—from other contexts, from other interpretive possibilities, from time itself. Just as every effort to remember Jefferson is an effort to define national identity, those efforts are always incomplete.

Remembering Jefferson

Presidents have the loudest and clearest voice when it comes to national identity, and presidents have used Jefferson to authorize specific policies and also their understanding of what the nation is and what it might become. Early chief executives saw Jefferson as a spokesperson for national independence and glorified him for his participation in the founding. His views on the need for an agrarian nation with a limited government were especially attractive to those who wanted to maintain chattel slavery and the power of the southern states that accompanied and protected that system. Both the Declaration of Independence and the Virginia and Kentucky Resolutions were useful to those advocating secession, and they continue to inspire white supremacists, revealing the ways racial hierarchies were baked into the founding. The Declaration, however, Jefferson's most vaunted legacy, has been and continues to be used by those advocating increased inclusion and demanding a fuller application of human rights, in the United States and globally.

In other words, ways to upend those hierarchies were also baked into the founding, although more contemporary presidents have rarely looked for them in Jefferson. FDR found in Jefferson ways to advocate both for his New Deal, with its emphasis on using government to provide economic security for the average person, and for his belief that the United States represented the most democratic nation in the world and had a sacred mission to protect and expand global democracy. In resting these arguments on Jefferson, he relied on Jefferson's arguments in favor of expanding the economic opportunities for white US Americans while preserving much of the racial hierarchies on the 1930s. Cold War presidents largely followed Roosevelt's lead, until Ronald Reagan found in him a way to argue both the nation's global mission and a reduction in the government's role in the domestic arena. Jefferson has proven remarkably pliable, but in the wake of confirmation of his actions toward Sally Hemings and their children, his usefulness as a moral exemplar has changed. Rather than reflecting the best of national history, he has come to embody its complications, flaws, and, sometimes, its need for rectification.

These changes over time are also reflected in the ways Jefferson is memorialized. Some monuments to him, like his memorial on the Mall in Washington, reveal FDR's contortions as he edited Jefferson quotations to present him as an "Apostle of Liberty" while eliding his role in slavery and his belief in white supremacy. That Jefferson remains, but such elisions are less possible, and even stable monuments like the Jefferson Memorial may have emendations that clarify his own history in relation to that of the nation. With or without official interpretations that acknowledge Jefferson's complications, visitors will bring with them vernacular understandings of Jefferson, that often include knowledge of those complications, when they visit such sites. Other monuments have been more radically changed. Jefferson remains present at Gateway Arch National Park, and there are lingering traces of its incarnation as the Jefferson National Expansion Memorial, but those traces are increasingly dingy on the one hand and recontextualized on the other. Jefferson is no longer portrayed there as an uncomplicated advocate of western expansion, but is placed in a context that asks visitors to consider the causes and consequences of settler colonialism. Visitors can avoid these questions, and many are somewhat startled to find them emplaced at the arch, but they are there, if one chooses to look for them.

Other monuments to Jeffersonian ambitions, like his pier stone next to the Washington Monument, have become irrelevant to understanding the US American national experience. Current national identity does not need, for example, to account for a historical moment in which the United States sought to make itself central to global navigation. The nation's claims to global significance reside, both literally and metaphorically, on other grounds now. Other bits and pieces of Jefferson continue to linger, but they have the ideological significance of wallpaper, lacking any real import, and are often neglected and set aside. Jefferson remains relevant only to the extent that he can embody matters of contemporary concern.

Like Jefferson as an individual, the founding moment remains ubiquitous. It is the nation's origin story, and it is told in a variety of places, although generally in the same ways. That story is revered and protected. Even when "the founding fathers" gives way to the more inclusive "founding generation," when others are added to the story, they may nuance it, but they do not fundamentally change it. At places like Independence National Historical Park, for example, one can see the traces of slavery that were present at the founding— the foundations of the building where those Washington enslaved lived abut the building housing the Liberty Bell, and this juxtaposition is integral to the presentation of the bell itself. But the interpretation elsewhere at INHP and at other sites commemorating the founding often collapses the founders into a singular and monolithic group, especially for more casual visitors, and in doing so protects the "founding" as a moment more deserving of reverence than criticism or contemplation.

Other collectivities are even more reverential. Mount Rushmore, for instance, provides visitors with a superficial and uncomplicated patriotism that rests on stolen Indigenous land and never grapples with that fact. The presidents collected there are treated as estimable, but the grouping itself—Washington, Jefferson, Lincoln, and Theodore Roosevelt—was chosen by a white supremacist in order to commemorate and perpetuate his preferred political order. Rather than present the monument in that light, visitors are instead given few ways to interpret or analyze alternative meanings of the monument. When the nation's history is thus collectivized, it becomes very difficult to expose visitors to nuanced or complicated interpretations of that history, and the ideological heft will always tend toward the celebratory, avoiding or ignoring more complicated interpretations.

But those interpretations are increasingly part of the national self-understanding, and popular culture provides ways to allow citizens to consider their nation's history in different ways. Jefferson is a useful window into some of these ways, as his "relationship" with Sally Hemings has become increasingly foregrounded in how he is understood. Some view that relationship as a romantic one, in which Jefferson and Hemings appear as star-crossed lovers, two devoted hearts separated by the accident of slavery. These people, knowingly or not, are also promulgating a romantic view of slavery and enslavers, erasing its injustices and the suffering of the enslaved even when those form part of the story. This view of Jefferson and Hemings, and of slavery, implies that even when understood as an economic system based on human enslavement, it somehow wasn't all that bad. It also tends to view the entailments of slavery as belonging exclusively in the past, requiring no ongoing conversation, action, or rectification.

Others view Jefferson and Hemings as evidence of how complicated a man Jefferson was. In this view, Jefferson embodies the nation's complicated relationship with race and the legacies of slavery. Past citizens were responsible for slavery, but it has no real consequences. Like the romantic view, this one tends to relegate slavery to the past and to limit its entailments. Current citizens appear to bear no responsibility for slavery and owe nothing to the descendants of the enslaved, because all citizens now stand on an equal footing. Any concessions to slavery as history would not be understood as rectification but as "special privileges," which by definition run against the requirements of democracy, favoring some citizens above others. Viewing Jefferson and slavery through the lens of "it's complicated" can incapacitate the need for action on anyone's part in the present.

A more nuanced version of the complicated Jefferson argues that slavery was a trap from which he and the other founders were unable to free themselves. This can also incapacitate present action. Ignoring the manifold ways that slavery was both an institution and the product of ongoing choices made both individually and collectively, the idea of an enmeshed Jefferson posits slavery as overwhelming political reality rather than as an ongoing set of choices. The founders were, in other words, courageous enough to plan and execute a revolution against the strongest military force in the world, but were helpless in the face of an institution of their own making. This view disables action in two ways. First, if the conundrum of racial hierarchies was too difficult for even the founders to solve, citizens in the present cannot be expected to do more than that most talented generation of US Americans could. It is therefore reasonable for present citizens to throw up their hands and leave the matter for future generations to solve, just as the founders did. Second, the founders left this problem to future generations, and responsibility therefore cannot be avoided.

And yet, since slavery itself ended, that responsibility can also be understood as having ended. As this indicates, popular depictions of slavery and Jefferson's relationship to it open wedges for criticism and action, but they tend to be narrow wedges.

Those wedges may broaden when we examine how these things are explained to children, for their understanding of Jefferson and his context guides the nation into the future. Telling a national story that relies on the accomplishments of "great men" stabilizes long-standing national hierarchies and works against the possibility of increased inclusion and belonging. Relying on stories that emphasize individual talent and merit stresses certain aspects of citizenship above others, and individualize community. Stories that sideline slavery and its entailments limit the possibilities for contending with the national past and addressing contemporary inequalities.

More promising are books and films that set Jefferson aside and focus on cognate characters—those he (and others) enslaved or exploited. When there are historical records, these stories can be used to better contextualize the founding, to offer a more rounded view of who was doing what and with what consequences. Stories of the founders are often stories that depend on their courage and conviction; cognate stories are also stories of courage and conviction. They are often also stories of community, and of shared suffering, resilience, and survivance. These are stories that can inspire understanding and impel action to make the nation a more equitable place. They are stories well worth telling. And it is thus interesting that they have power largely because they sideline Jefferson and his other white contemporaries. Which brings us to the question of whether Jefferson, as ubiquitous as he has been, will continue to be so.

Interpreting Jefferson

Whenever the topic is the nation, all of the modes I've discussed here, whether they be presidential commemorations, monuments and memorials, plays, films, or children's books, make claims about national identity, whether Jefferson is invoked or not. And the modes

themselves matter. When presidents choose to speak about something, that very act marks the subject as important. Historically, citizens have given presidential speech more weight than the speech of
others. When the president speaks, that speech makes national news.
Presidents highlight events by participating in them; they focus attention on people and events by attending to them. So when presidents
begin to treat Jefferson differently, that flags changes in the how the
nation sees him. Presidents no longer find in Jefferson an uncomplicated source of inspiration. Relying on him as a warrant for national
belief and national action is now accompanied by a "but." Jefferson
believed in democracy, and he articulated important national ideals.
But. That "but" is important. It tells us that the nation, at least as far
as most of its contemporary presidents are concerned, is increasingly
willing to contend with the vexed nature of the founding.

Others are also contending with this, as Jeffersonian monuments
and memorials reveal. His statues are being removed from some
places, defended in others, and contextualized in still others. Conversations about what Jefferson means, and to which members of which
communities, are unavoidable. It is unlikely that more memorials to
him will be planned or installed, as citizens and their local and state
governments are often preferring to commemorate those who rebelled against slavery, helped further its demise, or argued in other
ways for human liberty.[6] Even as Jefferson is valorized in many examples of popular culture and children's literature, he also appears more
flawed, less admirable, and more open to criticism. The founding itself is more likely to be emended but not fundamentally altered, but
individual founders like Jefferson are more easily criticized—more
likely to be seen in less uncomplicatedly flattering ways—and that
may one day lead to a more nuanced and complicated sense of the
founding itself.

This is all for the good. A nation that sees itself as either already
perfected or as requiring no individual action to improve is a nation that is lost in nostalgia, looking smugly forward as well as back-
ward. And while presidents and politics are probably regarded these
days with more cynicism that reverence, trying to maintain a false

reverence by pretending that this cynicism is not present would be a mistake. Mount Rushmore is increasingly probably something of an anachronism for some. Historian Jon Meacham has argued that "Americans have never quite let Jefferson go."[7] If this is true, it will be a different Jefferson who moves forward with the nation. Sites like the Jefferson Memorial will always be part of the national landscape, to be sure, but Jefferson himself may one day become detritus in the national imagination, unless Jeffersonian stories can continue to be useful to understanding evolving national community and national identity. His usefulness as a marker of the nation's complicated relationship with race and the legacies of slavery indicates to me that he is likely to remain relevant, if not necessarily in the ways he might have preferred.

This points to another fact about how we remember Jefferson, and it gets to the question of who "we" are. I suspect that the audience for Mount Rushmore and for slavery tours at Monticello are not the same. National politics are often siloed, and so are national audiences for Jefferson commemorations. Ken Burns noted, "We are all in some way or another the descendants of Thomas Jefferson, for good or for ill."[8] He is probably right. But we are not all the same descendants. Different sections of the national audience can understand Jefferson in vastly different ways and with vastly different kinds of implications for national identity. Judgments of Jefferson may become exclusively salutatory to one audience and exclusively condemnatory to another. Either would, from his point of view, possibly be better than being consigned to ideological irrelevance.

More optimistically, both for Jefferson and the nation, there is the possibility that as the nation approaches the 250th anniversary of the signing of the Declaration of Independence, Jefferson will continue to serve, as he always has, as a national lightning rod.[9] His contradictions and conflicts, if not his example, can continue to provoke and inspire, as he always has.[10] Abraham Lincoln found in the founding not a set of fixed ideas, but a set of principles. He saw the Declaration in particular as a living document, whose meaning could continue to transform the nation and the lives of its citizens. To the extent that citizens continue to care about the language of the Declaration and the ideas embedded in it, Jefferson and his complicated, contradictory legacies will continue to be relevant.[11] The nation might continue to remember Jefferson, and in doing so, will continue to define itself.

Notes

Introduction

1. On his politics, see, among many others, John Boles, *Jefferson: Architect of American Liberty* (New York: Basic Books, 2017); Joseph Ellis, *American Sphinx: The Character of Thomas Jefferson* (New York: Alfred A. Knopf, 1997); Jon Meacham, *Thomas Jefferson: The Art of Power* (New York: Random House, 2013); Dumas Malone, *Jefferson and His Time*, 6 vols. (Boston: Little, Brown, 1948); Merrill J. Peterson, *Thomas Jefferson and the New Nation: A Biography* (New York: Oxford, 1975); Merrill J. Peterson, *The Jefferson Image in the American Mind* (Charlottesville: University Press of Virginia, 1998). On his rhetoric, see Stephen H. Browne, "'The Circle of Our Felicities': Thomas Jefferson's First Inaugural Address and the Rhetoric of Nationhood," *Rhetoric & Public Affairs* 5, no. 3 (2002): 409–438; Stephen H. Browne, *Jefferson's Call for Nationhood* (College Station: Texas A&M University Press, 2003); Jeremy Engels, "Disciplining Jefferson: The Man within the Breast and the Rhetorical Norms of Producing Order," *Rhetoric & Public Affairs* 9, no. 3 (2006): 411–435; James L. Golden and Alan L. Golden, *Thomas Jefferson and the Rhetoric of Virtue* (Lanham, MD: Rowman & Littlefield, 2002); Mark Sturges, "Founding Farmers: Jefferson, Washington, and the Rhetoric of Agricultural Reform," *Early American Literature* 50, no. 3 (2015): 681–709.

2. Thomas B. Farrell, "The Weight of Rhetoric: Studies in Cultural Delirium," *Philosophy & Rhetoric* 41, no. 4 (2008): 467–487.

3. In a similar vein, although they do not focus on the presidency, Celeste Condit and John Lucaites have studied the use of equality over time. See Celeste Michelle Condit and John Louis Lucaites, *Crafting Equality: America's Anglo-African Word* (Chicago: University of Chicago Press, 1993). See also Eric Foner, *The Story of American Freedom* (New York: Norton, 1999).

4. Throughout this book I treat commemorating and memorializing as essentially the same, although because it necessarily involves shared rituals, the former is much more obviously social and communal than the latter. See Edward S. Casey, *Remembering: A Phenomenological Study*. (Bloomington: Indiana University Press, 2000).

5. It is telling in this regard that on March 27, 2025, Donald Trump signed an executive order titled "Restoring Truth and Sanity to American History," which calls for the reevaluation of how US history is presented at various sites and museums funded by the government. See https://www.whitehouse.gov/presidential-actions/2025/03/restoring-truth-and-sanity-to-american-history/.

6. See, for example, Megan Irene Fitzmaurice, "Commemorative Privilege in National Statuary Hall: Spatial Constructions of Racial Citizenship," *Southern Communication Journal* 81, no. 4 (2016): 252–262.

7. Casey, *Remembering*, 216.

8. National Park Service, "National Park Service Sites Related to Thomas Jefferson," last updated March 4, 2018, https://www.nps.gov/thje/learn/historycultu re/national-park-service-sites-related-to-thomas-jefferson.htm.

9. Matthew Smith, "The Most and Least Popular US Presidents, According to Americans," July 27, 2021, https://today.yougov.com/topics/politics/ar ticles-reports/2021/07/27/most-and-least-popular-us-presidents-according -ame?utm_campaign=wp_th_5_minutefix&utm_medium=email&utm_source =newsletter&wpisrc=nl_fix&fbclid=IwAR2NPdDa5asnUbucNL3N_p52 VUr9-DvsxMy5ZkrxxdoCDTeiF1q-79upaxA&mibextid=iloqvq&fs=e&s=cl.

10. See, among many others, Winston Groom, *The Patriots: Alexander Hamilton, Thomas Jefferson, John Adams, and the Making of America* (Washington, DC: National Geographic, 2020).

11. A quick search of Amazon.com for biographies yielded more than a thousand results; a search for books only on his presidency yielded 163 results, while searches for his politics tallied at 773, and for his private life the number was close to 200. Even accounting for the inevitable overlap between these categories, it is safe to say that there are a lot of books dedicated to Jefferson. Andrew Burstein notes that "in the first decades of the twenty-first century, more books were published on Jefferson than on any of the other celebrated founders, including Washington and Adams. In fact, there were more books about Jefferson than about the American Revolution itself." Andrew Burstein, *Democracy's Muse: How Thomas Jefferson Became an FDR Liberal, a Reagan Republican, and a Tea Party Fanatic, All the While Being Dead* (Charlottesville: University of Virginia Press, 2015), 111.

12. Jon Meacham, "Introduction," ix–xxi, in Jon Meacham, ed., *In the Hands of the People: Thomas Jefferson on Equality, Faith, Freedom, and the Art of Citizenship* (New York: Random House, 2020), xiii.

13. Francis D. Cogliano, *Thomas Jefferson: Reputation and Legacy* (Charlottesville: University of Virginia Press, 2006); Leonard Levy, "Jefferson and Civil Liberties: The Darker Side," 396–417, in Peter S. Onuf, ed., *Jeffersonian Legacies* (Charlottesville: University of Virginia Press, 1993), 398; Meacham, "Introduction," xiv; Peterson, *Jefferson Image*; Bradford J. Vivian, "Jefferson's Other," *Quarterly Journal of Speech* 88, no. 3 (2002): 284–302.

14. See, among many others, Allen Jayne, *Jefferson's Declaration of Independence: Origins, Philosophy, and Theology* (Lexington: University Press of Kentucky, 1998); Peter S. Onuf, *Jefferson's Empire: The Language of American Nationhood* (Charlottesville, VA: University of Virginia Press, 2000); Jean H. Yarborough, *American

Virtues: Thomas Jefferson on the Character of a Free Republic (Lawrence: University Press of Kansas, 1998).

15. See, for example, Burstein, *Democracy's Muse.*

16. Christopher Lasch, "Foreword," vii–xxiii, in Richard Hofstadter, *The American Political Tradition: And the Men Who Made It* (New York: Vintage, [1948] 1973), xii–xiii.

17. Joyce Appleby, "Introduction: Jefferson and His Complex Legacy," 1–16, in Onuf, *Jefferson's Legacies*, 1.

18. Burstein, *Democracy's Muse*, ix; Gordon S. Wood, "The Trials and Tribulations of Thomas Jefferson," 395–417, in Onuf, *Jeffersonian Legacies*, 395.

19. Barbara Oberg, for instance, concludes that despite all the scholarship on him, "Jefferson remains a mystery." Barbara Oberg, "Introduction," 1–21, in Robert M. S. McDonald, ed., *Thomas Jefferson Lives: Biographers and the Battle for History* (Charlottesville: University of Virginia Press, 2019), 2.

20. Hofstadter, *The American Political Tradition*, 32.

21. Dumas Malone, "Foreword," 8, in Editors of American Heritage, *Thomas Jefferson and His World* (New York: Golden Press, 1960), 8.

22. Groom, *The Patriots*, 117. For other examples of lists, see Thomas J. Craughwell, *Thomas Jefferson's Crème Brûlée: How a Founding Father and His Slave James Hemings Brought French Cuisine to America* (Philadelphia: Quirk Books, 2012), 2; Meacham, *Thomas Jefferson*, xxii; National Park Service, "Thomas Jefferson Memorial," last updated August 30, 2022, https://www.nps.gov/thje/learn/his toryculture/index.htm; Keith Thompson, *Jefferson's Shadow: The Story of His Science* (New Haven, CT: Yale University Press, 2012), 1; Simon Winchester, *The Men Who United the States* (New York: Harper Perennial, 2013), 6.

23. Thompson, *Jefferson's Shadow*, 120. For other examples of Jefferson's contradictions, see, among many others, Fawn M. Brodie, *Thomas Jefferson: An Intimate History* (New York: Norton, 1974), 448.

24. Oberg, "Introduction," 3.

25. On constitutive rhetoric, see, among many others, Maurice Charland, "Constitutive Rhetoric," 616–619, in Thomas O. Sloane, ed., *Encyclopedia of Rhetoric* (New York: Oxford University Press, 2001); Alan G. Gross, "Lincoln's Use of Constitutive Metaphors," *Rhetoric & Public Affairs* 7, no. 2 (2004): 173–189; Ryan Neville-Shepard, "Reclaiming the Center: Constitutive Rhetoric and the 'Moderate Ethos' in Crossover Endorsements for Joe Biden," 223–238, in Benjamin R. Warner et al., eds., *Democracy Disrupted: Communication in the Volatile 2020 Presidential Election* (New York: Praeger, 2022); Mary E. Stuckey, "One Nation (Pretty Darn) Divisible: National Identity in the 2004 Conventions," *Rhetoric & Public Affairs* 8, no. 4 (2005): 639–656; Derek Sweet and Margret McCue-Enser, "Constituting 'the People' as Rhetorical Interruption: Barack Obama and the Unfinished Hopes of an Imperfect People," *Communication Studies* 61, no. 5 (2010): 602–622; Andrew Taylor, "Barry Goldwater: Insurgent Conservatism as Constitutive Rhetoric," *Journal of Political Ideologies* 21, no. 3 (2016): 242–260.

26. On the connection between constitutive rhetoric and national identity, see Vanessa B. Beasley, *You, the People: American National Identity in Presidential*

Rhetoric (College Station: Texas A&M University Press, 2011); Mary E. Stuckey, *Defining Americans: The Presidency and National Identity* (Lawrence: University Press of Kansas, 2023).

27. There are arguments that this doesn't have to be the case. See John A. Powell and Stephen Menendian, *Belonging without Othering: How We Save Ourselves and the World* (Stanford, CA: Stanford University Press, 2024).

28. Stephen H. Browne, "Reading Public Memory in Daniel Webster's *Plymouth Rock Oration*," *Western Journal of Communication* 57, no. 4 (1993): 464–477, esp. 464.

29. For good reviews of the vast literature on public and collective memory, see Carole Blair, "Collective Memory," 51–59, in Gregory J. Shepherd, Jeffrey St. John, and Ted Striphas, eds., *Communication as . . . : Perspectives on Theory* (Thousand Oaks, CA: Sage, 2006); Michael Kammen, *Mystic Chords of Memory: The Transformation of Tradition in American Culture* (New York: Vintage, 1993).

30. Stephen H. Browne, "On the Borders of Memory," 17–32, in G. Mitchell Reyes, ed., *Public Memory, Race, and Ethnicity* (New York: Cambridge Scholars Publishing, 2010), 17.

31. Carole Blair, Greg Dickinson, and Brian L. Ott, "Introduction," 1–55, in Greg Dickinson, Carole Blair, and Brian L. Ott, eds., *Places of Public Memory: The Rhetoric of Museums and Memorials* (Tuscaloosa: University of Alabama Press, 2010), 6; Kammen, *Mystic Chords of Memory*, 5.

32. Maurice Halbwachs, *On Collective Memory*, edited, translated, and with an introduction by Lewis A. Coser (Chicago: University of Chicago Press, 1992), 38; Barbie Zelizer, *Remembering to Forget: Holocaust Memory through the Camera's Eye* (Chicago: University of Chicago Press, 1998), 3; Barbie Zelizer, "Competing Memories: Reading the Past against the Grain: The Shape of Memory Studies," *Critical Studies in Media Communication* 12, no. 2 (1995): 213–239, esp. 213.

33. John R. Gillis, "Memory and Identity: the History of a Relationship," 3–24, in John R. Gillis, ed., *Commemoration: The Politics of National Identity* (Princeton, NJ: Princeton University Press, 1994), 3.

34. For different perspectives on this point, see Derek H. Alderman and Joshua F. J. Inwood, "Landscapes of Memory and Socially Just Futures," 186–197, in Nuata C. Johnson, Richard H. Schein, and Jamie Winders, eds, *The Wiley-Blackwell Companion to Cultural Geography* (New York: John Wiley & Sons, 2013); Barbara A. Biesecker, "Remembering World War II: The Rhetoric and Politics of National Commemoration of the 21st Century," *Quarterly Journal of Speech* 88, no. 4 (2002): 393–409; Victoria Gallagher, "Memory and Reconciliation in the Birmingham Civil Rights Institute," *Rhetoric & Public Affairs* 2, no. 2 (1999): 303–320, esp. 307; Sydney Goggins, "Reshaping Public Memory in the *1619 Project*: Rhetorical Interventions Against Selective Forgetting," *Museums and Social Issues* 14, no. 102 (2019): 60–73, esp. 62; Ekatarina Haskins, *Popular Memories: Participatory Culture and Democratic Citizenship* (Columbia: University of South Carolina Press, 2015), 9; Faber McAlister, "An Uncanny Architope: Impossible Ghosts of Empire at the Bronte Parsonage Museum," *Quarterly Journal of Speech* 109, no. 3 (2023): 230–253; Iwona Irwin-Zarecka, *Frames of Remembrance: The Dynamics of Collective Memory* (New Brunswick, ME: Transaction, 1994), 9.

35. See National Museum of African American History and Culture, https://nmaahc.si.edu/explore/stories/historical-legacy-juneteenth.

36. Barbara Biesecker, "Renovating the National Imaginary: A Prolegomenon on Contemporary Paregoric Rhetoric," 212–249, in Kendall R. Phillips, ed., *Framing Public Memory* (Tuscaloosa: University of Alabama Press, 2004); Cheryl Jorgensen-Earp and Lori Lanziotti, "Public Memory and Private Grief: The Construction of Shrines at the Sites of Public Tragedy," *Quarterly Journal of Speech* 84 no. 2 (1998): 150–170; Goggins, "Reshaping Public Memory"; James W. Loewen, *Lies Across America: What Our Historic Sites Get Wrong*, 20th anniversary ed. (New York: New Press, 2009), 13; Ryan Erik McGeough, Catherine Helen Palczewski, and Randall A. Lake, "Oppositional Memory Practices: US Memorial Spaces as Arguments over Public Memory," *Argumentation and Advocacy* 51 no. 4 (2015): 231–254; Kirk Savage, *Standing Soldiers, Kneeling Slaves: Race, War, and Monument in Nineteenth Century America* (Princeton, NJ: Princeton University Press, 1997), 4.

37. Alon Confino, "Collective Memory and Cultural History: Problems of Method," *American Historical Review* 102, no. 5 (1997) 1386–1403, esp. 1399.

38. Marita Sturken, *Tangled Memories: The Vietnam War, the AIDS Epidemic, and the Politics of Remembering* (Berkeley: University of California Press, 1997), 2.

39. On the issue of making judgments between assessments of the past, see V. William Balthrop, Carole Blair, and Neil Michael, "The Presence of the Present: Hijacking 'the Good War'?," *Western Journal of Communication* 74, no. 2 (2010): 170–207, esp. 172.

40. Gail Bederman, *Manliness and Civilization: A Cultural History of Gender and Race in the United States, 1880–1917* (Chicago: University of Chicago Press, 1995), xi.

41. John Bodnar, *Remaking American Public Memory: Commemoration and Patriotism in the Twentieth Century* (Princeton, NJ: Princeton University Press, 1992), 13. See also Stephen. H. Browne, "Reading Public Memory in Daniel Webster's *Plymouth Rock Oration*," *Western Journal of Communication* 57, no. 4 (1993): 464–477; Browne, "Remembering Crispus Attucks: Race, Rhetoric, and the Politics of Commemoration," *Quarterly Journal of Speech* 85, no. 2 (1999): 169–187; Katharyne Mitchell, "Monuments, Memorials, and the Politics of Memory," *Urban Geography* 24, no. 5 (2003): 442–459, esp. 443.

42. Zelizer, "Competing Memories," 216.

43. Roger C. Aden et al., , "Re-Collection: A Proposal for Refining the Study of Collective Memory and Its Places," *Communication Theory* 19, no. 3 (2009): 219–350, esp. 312. See also Michael Rothburg, *Multidirectional Memory: Remembering the Holocaust in the Age of Decolonization* (Stanford, CA: Stanford University Press, 2009), 5.

44. Mitchell, "Monuments, Memorials, and the Politics of Memory," 443.

45. Karen L. Cox, *No Common Ground: Confederate Monuments and the Ongoing Fight for Racial Justice* (Chapel Hill: University of North Carolina, 2021), 3.

46. Gallagher, "Memory and Reconciliation," 307.

47. Bodnar, *Remaking American Public Memory*, 16; Bradford J. Vivian, *Public*

Forgetting: The Rhetoric and Politics of Beginning Again (University Park: Penn State Press, 2011), 1; Zelizer, *Remembering to Forget*, 3.

48. G. Mitchell Reyes, "Introduction: Public Memory, Race, and Ethnicity, 1–16, in Reyes, *Public Memory, Race, and Ethnicity*, 2.

49. Stephen J. Hartnett, Patrick Shaou-Whea Dodge, and Lisa B. Keranen, "Postcolonial Remembering in Taiwan: 228 and Transitional Justice as 'The End of Fear,'" *Journal of International and Intercultural Communication* 13, no. 3 (2020): 238–256.

50. See In Literature, "6 Stops in Washington Irving's Sleepy Hollow," accessed February 20, 2025, as an example of the kind of available tours I'm referencing: https://www.inliterature.net/travels/2018/10/6-stops-washington-irving -sleepy-hollow-day-trip.html.

51. For details, see Historical Marker Database, "Andre Captors Monument," accessed February 20, 2025, https://www.hmdb.org/m.asp?m=8608.

52. Tim Gruenwald, *Curating America's Painful Past: Memory, Museums, and the National Imagination* (Lawrence: University Press of Kansas, 2021); Nicholas Paliewicz and Marouf Hasian Jr., "Mourning Absences: Melancholic Commemoration and the Contested Public Memories of the National September 11 Memorial and Museum," *Western Journal of Communication* 80, no. 2 (2016): 140–162, esp. 144.

53. On this kind of forgetting, see Kristen Hoerl, "Selective Amnesia and Racial Transcendence in News Coverage of President Obama's Inauguration," *Quarterly Journal of Speech* 98, no. 2 (2012): 178–202; Vivian, *Public Forgetting*.

54. See Kieran O'Keefe, "Monuments to the American Revolution," *Journal of the American Revolution*, September 17, 2019, https://allthingsliberty.com/2019/09 /monuments-to-the-american-revolution/.

55. Nikole Hannah-Jones, "Preface: Origins," xvii–xxxii, in Nikole Hannah-Jones et al., eds., *The 1619 Project: A New American Origin Story* (London: W. H. Allen, 2021), xxx.

56. Nikole Hannah-Jones, "Democracy," 7–36, in Hannah-Jones et al., *The 1619 Project*, 11.

57. Peterson, *Jefferson Image*, 457. See also Ellis, *American Sphinx*, 5.

58. Burstein, *Democracy's Muse*, ix; Ellis, *American Sphinx*, x–xi; Hofstadter, *American Political Tradition*, 25.

59. Burstein, *Democracy's Muse*, ix.

60. Vivian, "Jefferson's Other," 284; Thompson, *Jefferson's Shadow*, 1.

61. G. S. Wilson, *Jefferson on Display: Attire, Etiquette, and the Art of Presentation* (Charlottesville: University of Virginia Press, 2018), 2; Wilson Jeremiah Moses, *Thomas Jefferson: A Modern Prometheus* (New York: Cambridge University Press, 2019), 3.

62. Cogliano, *Thomas Jefferson*; Peterson, *Jefferson Image*.

63. See Britannica, "Louisiana Purchase," accessed February 20, 2025, https:// www.britannica.com/event/Louisiana-Purchase; Ellis, *American Sphinx*, 212; Robert J. Miller, "The Doctrine of Discovery, Manifest Destiny, and American Indians," 87–100, in Susan Sleeper-Smith et al., eds., *Why You Can't Teach History*

without American Indians (Chapel Hill: University of North Carolina Press, 2015), 95–96; Thompson, *Jefferson's Shadow*, 217; Garry Wills, *"Negro President": Jefferson and the Slave Power* (Boston: Houghton Mifflin, 2003), xiii.

64. In this I follow Barbie Zelizer. See Barbie Zelizer, "The Voice of the Visual in Public Memory," 157–186, in Phillips, *Framing Public Memory*, 158.

65. For relatively recent examples, see Groom, *The Patriots*; Jon Meacham, *Thomas Jefferson: President and Philosopher* (New York: Crown, 2014); Jon Meacham, *Thomas Jefferson*.

66. Groom, *The Patriots*, 139–140; Meacham, *Thomas Jefferson*, 121–124.

67. For details, see Meacham, *Thomas Jefferson*, 133–138.

68. I use the word "relationship" here for lack of a better term. There is no question that he fathered children with Hemings. Scholars have considered their relationship to fall in various places on a wide continuum from rape to romance. If either of them ever committed their views on this to paper, they have not been discovered.

69. On Jefferson's time in France, see Lawrence S. Kaplan, *Thomas Jefferson: Westward the Course of Empire* (Wilmington, DE: Scholarly Resources, 1998), 50; Meacham, *Thomas Jefferson*, 189.

70. Ellis, *American Sphinx*, 161; Onuf, *Jefferson's Empire*, 7; Meacham, *Thomas Jefferson*, 241. For further discussion of the disagreements among the founders, see, among many others, David Sehat, *The Jefferson Rule: How the Founding Fathers Became Infallible and Our Politics Inflexible* (New York: Simon & Schuster, 2015); Joanne B. Freeman, "Punching the Ticket: Hamilton's Biographers and the Sins of Thomas Jefferson, 149–174, in McDonald, *Thomas Jefferson Lives*, 150.

71. Mel Laracey, *Informing a Nation: The Newspaper Presidency of Thomas Jefferson* (Ann Arbor: University of Michigan Press, 2021).

72. Sehat, *The Jefferson Rule*, 27.

73. Browne, *Jefferson's Call for Nationhood*, 28; Sehat, *The Jefferson Rule*, 29–30. On the 1800 election, see Mary E. Stuckey, *Deplorable: The Worst Presidential Campaigns from Jefferson to Trump* (Lawrence: University Press of Kansas, 2021), 28–41; Meacham, *Thomas Jefferson*, 322; Wills, *"Negro President*, 3.

74. Joanne B. Freeman and Johann N. Neem rightly argue that this is better understood as an example of what happens when theory meets political practice than as an instance of simple hypocrisy. See their "Introduction," 1–14, in Joanne B. Freeman and Johann N. Neem, *Jeffersonians in Power: The Rhetoric of Opposition Meets the Realities of Governing* (Charlottesville: University of Virginia Press, 2019), 2.

75. Miller, "Doctrine of Discovery," 92.

76. See Kaplan, *Thomas Jefferson*.

77. Kaplan, *Thomas Jefferson*, 127–129.

78. Wills, "Negro President," 42–43.

79. Kaplan, *Thomas Jefferson*, 165–171.

80. For more on this trial, see R. Kent Newmyer, *The Treason Trial of Aaron Burr: Law, Politics, and the Character Wars of the New Nation* (New York: Cambridge University Press, 2012).

81. Onuf, *Jefferson's Empire*, 19–20. See also Cogliano, *Thomas Jefferson*, 12–13; Ronald Takaki, *A Different Mirror: A History of Multicultural America* (Boston: Little, Brown, 1993), 48. On Jefferson as an advocate of what we would now call eugenics and ethnic cleansing, see Moses, *Thomas Jefferson*, 62, 271–272, 364–368. For a detailed history of Jefferson's policy toward Indigenous peoples, see Robert M. Owens, *Mr. Jefferson's Hammer: William Henry Harrison and the Origins of American Indian Policy* (Norman: University of Oklahoma Press, 2007).

82. Here, of course, the presidency is like the Supreme Court, but its precedents are less formal. Probably the only other president who receives as much attention from their successors is Abraham Lincoln. It would be interesting to see of other historical figures play a role—even if a temporary one—in presidential speech. I would guess that to play such a role, the figure in question would have to be understood as somehow defining their historical moment. Likely candidates would be either Theodore or Franklin Roosevelt, or, in more recent history, Ronald Reagan.

83. Scholars wanting to examine the larger political uses of monuments and memorials can do so by choosing a particular moment—say, the decade before 1860—and seeing what kinds of memorials became important at that moment. They can also delve into the conversations surrounding a given monument or memorial—asking who advocated for it, and on what grounds. Or they can focus on a particular individual or event, as I do here, that spans several historical moments or geographic locations and interrogate the usefulness of those depictions in those locations.

84. "Popular culture" is such a broad category that it is difficult to capture any one figure in it. I do not, for instance, analyze Jefferson ephemera—the scarves, coffee cups, finger puppets, trivets, busts, bookends, and so on that are available at so many sites. Jefferson is interesting in that he (and again, probably also only Lincoln) is so ubiquitous. He is also interesting in that he is an actual historical figure who often appears in fictionalized contexts. It is one thing to study, say, depictions of Superman over time, and to see how those depictions of a US icon reflects changes understandings of national identity (as they surely do). It is another to focus on a real person, if only because one would initially think that the historical record would impose at least some constraints on the narrative. They don't, necessarily—consider, for example, Seth Grahame-Smith, *Abraham Lincoln, Vampire Hunter* (London: Hackett, 2010).

85. For an important exception, see Sara VanderHaagen, "Political Truths: Black Feminist Agency and Public Memory in Biographies of Children," *Women's Studies in Communication* 35, no. 1 (2012): 18–41; Sara VanderHaagen, *Children's Biographies of African American Women: Rhetoric, Public Memory, and Agency* (Columbia: University of South Caroline Press, 2018).

Chapter 1: The Presidential Jefferson

1. Daniel Webster, "Eulogy," Faneuil Hall, Boston, August 2, 1826, https://babel.hathitrust.org/cgi/pt?id=mou.010506634929&seq=4.

2. On the idea that communities are constructed, see Benedict Anderson,

Imagined Communities (London: Verso Books, 2016); Maurice Charland, "Constitutive Rhetoric: The Case of the *Peuple Quebecois*," *Quarterly Journal of Speech* 73, no. 2 (1987): 133–150; James Boyd White, *Heracles' Bow: Essays on the Rhetoric and Poetics of the Law* (Madison: University of Wisconsin Press, 1985).

3. The most cogent discussion of constitutive rhetoric and its intellectual history is James Jasinski, "Constitutive Rhetoric," *Sourcebook on Rhetoric: Key Concepts in Rhetorical Studies* (Thousand Oaks, CA: Sage, 2001), 106–108.

4. J. Hector St. John de Crèvecoeur, *Letters from an American Farmer and Sketches of Eighteenth-Century America* (New York: Penguin, 1981).

5. Kenneth Burke, *Language as Symbolic Action* (Berkeley: University of California Press, 1966), 15–16.

6. For an example of the kind of rhetoric I'm referring to here, see Richard Nixon, "Proclamation 4022—Bill of Rights Day," December 7, 1970, Online by Gerhard Peters and John T. Woolley, American Presidency Project, https://www.presidency.ucsb.edu/node/ 210278. Hereinafter, all cites to the American Presidency Project will read as "APP, node number."

7. There are, of course, moments upon which and ways in which presidents might do exactly this. On the requirements of genre, see Karlyn Kohrs Campbell and Kathleen Hall Jamieson, *Presidents Creating the Presidency: Deeds Done in Words* (Chicago: University of Chicago Press, 2008).

8. For a further discussion of this point, see Mary E. Stuckey, "The Donner Party and the Rhetoric of Westward Expansion," *Rhetoric & Public Affairs* 14, no. 2 (2011): 229–260.

9. Julie Homchick Crowe, "Correction to: Contagion, Quarantine and Constitutive Rhetoric: Embodiment, Identity and the "Potential Victim" of Infectious Disease," *Journal of Medical Humanities* 43, no. 3 (2022): 529–530; Charles Goehring and George N. Dionisopoulos, "Identification by Antithesis: *The Turner Diaries* as Constitutive Rhetoric," *Southern Communication Journal* 78, no. 5 (2013): 369–386.

10. David Zarefsky, "Presidential Rhetoric and the Power of Definition." *Presidential Studies Quarterly* 34, no. 3 (2004): 607–619.

11. On presidential visions of national identity, see, among many others, Vanessa Beasley, "The Rhetoric of Ideological Consensus in the United States: American Principles and American Pose in Presidential Inaugurals," *Communication Monographs* 68, no. 2 (2001): 169–183; Vanessa B. Beasley, *You, the People: American National Identity in Presidential Rhetoric* (College Station: Texas A&M University Press, 2011); Alan G. Gross, "Lincoln's Use of Constitutive Metaphors," *Rhetoric & Public Affairs* 7, no. 2 (2004): 173–189; Ryan Neville-Shepard, "Reclaiming the Center: Constitutive Rhetoric and the "Moderate Ethos" in Crossover Endorsements for Joe Biden, 223–238, in Benjamin R. Warner et al., eds., *Democracy Disrupted: Communication in the Volatile 2020 Presidential Election* (New York: Praeger, 2022); Mary E. Stuckey, *Defining Americans: The Presidency and National Identity* (Lawrence: University Press of Kansas, 2023); Mary E. Stuckey, "One Nation (Pretty Darn) Divisible: National Identity in the 2004 Conventions," *Rhetoric & Public Affairs* 8, no. 4 (2005): 639–656; Derek Sweet and

Margret McCue-Enser, "Constituting "the People" as Rhetorical Interruption: Barack Obama and the Unfinished Hopes of an Imperfect People," *Communication Studies* 61, no. 5 (2010): 602–622; Andrew Taylor, "Barry Goldwater: Insurgent Conservatism as Constitutive Rhetoric," *Journal of Political Ideologies* 21, no. 3 (2016): 242–260.

12. For commentary on and a copy of the speech, see EDSITEment, "Frederick Douglass's 'What to the Slave Is the Fourth of July?,'" https://edsitement.neh .gov/student-activities/frederick-douglasss-what-slave-fourth-july.

13. Maurice Charland, "The Rhetoricians' Identity," *Rhetor: The Journal of the Canadian Society for the Study of Rhetoric* 8 no. 1 (2021): 26–32.

14. Merrill J. Peterson, *The Jefferson Image in the American Mind* (Charlottesville: University Press of Virginia, 1998); Francis D. Cogliano, *Thomas Jefferson: Reputation and Legacy* (Charlottesville: University of Virginia Press, 2006).

15. For a discussion of these as acts of constitutive rhetoric, see James Jasinski and Jennifer R. Mercieca, "The Constitutive Approach to Effect and the Alien and Sedition Acts," 313–341, in Shawn J. Parry-Giles and J. Michael Hogan, eds., *Rhetoric and Public Address in the Twenty-First Century: A Handbook* (Malden, MA: Wiley-Blackwell, 2010).

16. See David Armitage, *The Declaration of Independence: A Global History* (Cambridge, MA: Harvard University Press, 2007); Howard K. Bush Jr., *American Declarations: Rebellion and Resistance in American Cultural History* (Champaign-Urbana: University of Illinois Press, 1999); Michael J. Lee and R. Jarrod Atchison, *We Are Not One People: Secession and Separatism in American Politics Since 1776* (New York: Oxford, 2022), 42; Aleksandar A. Pavković and Peter Radan, eds., *The Ashgate Research Companion to Secession* (Burlington, VT: Ashgate, 2011).

17. Lee and Atchison, *We Are Not One People*, 39–44.

18. Mary E. Stuckey, "The Antebellum Declaration: Abolition, Secession, and Revolution," in Mary E. Stuckey, ed., *Used, Abused, and Sidelined: Debating the Declaration* (University Park: Penn State University Press, forthcoming).

19. Wilson Jeremiah Moses, *Thomas Jefferson: A Modern Prometheus* (New York: Cambridge University Press, 2019), 29–31.

20. For more on these and other uses of the Declaration, see Stuckey, *Used, Abused, and Sidelined*.

21. For an example of Roosevelt's early attachment to Jefferson, see Franklin D. Roosevelt, "Review of Claude G. Bowers, *Jefferson and Hamilton*, November 19, 1925, Roosevelt, Franklin D., Family, Business, and Personal Papers, Writing and Statement File, Press Statement 3/10/20-Draft of *Whither Bound?* 5/18/26, Box 41, "Review of Claude G. Bowers, *Jefferson and Hamilton*, November 19, 1925, Franklin D. Roosevelt Presidential Library (hereafter, FDRL), 5.

22. On the complicated relationship between Jefferson and the New Deal, see especially Peterson, *The Jefferson Image in the American Mind*, 355–376. See also Andrew Burstein, *Democracy's Muse: How Thomas Jefferson Became an FDR Liberal, a Reagan Republican, and a Tea Party Fanatic, All the While Being Dead* (Charlotteville: University of Virginia Press, 2015), 4.

23. His interest in Jefferson was well known enough that he was asked to join the Thomas Jefferson Memorial Association in 1921; he declined because, "I have been engaged in an interesting tussle with infantile paralysis." See Franklin D. Roosevelt, "Letter to JS Murphy," September 27, 1921, Roosevelt, Franklin D., Family, Business, and Personal Papers: Subject File Taconic State Park Commission Correspondence-Trips to the Lorcoco Tams and King, Box 35, "Thomas Jefferson Memorial association," FDRL.

24. Franklin D. Roosevelt, "Message to Thomas Jefferson Memorial Foundation," April 7, 1925, Roosevelt, Franklin D., Family, Business, and Personal Papers: Subject File Taconic State Park Commission Correspondence-Trips to the Lorcoco Tams and King, Box 35, "Thomas Jefferson Memorial Association," FDRL.

25. See, for example, Roosevelt, "Review of Claude G. Bowers."

26. Josephus Daniels, Letter to Franklin D. Roosevelt, January 11, 1934, President's Personal File, 86 (1932–40) Container 1, FDRL.

27. Theodore Fred Kuper, "Telegram to Franklin D. Roosevelt," December 1, 1933, President's Personal File, 1068–1092, "PPF 1075, Jeffersonians of America," FDRL.

28. Declining to speak at one of the partisan Jefferson and Jackson Day dinners, FDR wrote, "Our strongest plea to the country in this particular year of grace is that the recovery and reconstruction program is being accomplished by men and women of all parties—that I have repeatedly appealed to Republicans as much as Democrats to do their part. . . . I think you will agree with me that much as we love Thomas Jefferson we should not celebrate him in a partisan way." Franklin D. Roosevelt, "Letter to Colonel EM House," March 10, 1934, President's Personal File, 255–268, "PPF 259, Jefferson, Thomas, 1938–1942," FDRL.

29. Franklin D. Roosevelt, "Address at the Cornerstone Laying of the Jefferson Memorial," Washington, DC, November 15, 1939, APP 210278.

30. See also, among many other examples, Franklin D. Roosevelt, "Address at Jackson Day Dinner," January 8, 1940, APP 209474. On FDR's tendency to equate himself with Jefferson, see, for example, Franklin D. Roosevelt, "Address at the Home of Thomas Jefferson, Monticello, Virginia," July 4, 1936, APP 208929; Franklin D. Roosevelt, "Proclamation 2276—Thomas Jefferson's Birthday," March 21, 1938, APP 209532.

31. See Franklin D. Roosevelt, "Letter to Stuart Gibboney," May 15, 1941, OF 1505 Box 2, Thomas Jefferson Memorial Commission Miscellaneous, "Thomas Jefferson Memorial Commission, 1941–1945," FDRL.

32. See, for example, Franklin D. Roosevelt, "Address at the Groundbreaking for the Thomas Jefferson Memorial," Washington, DC, December 15, 1938, APP 209401.

33. Franklin D. Roosevelt, "Address at the Dedication of the Thomas Jefferson Memorial," April 13, 1945, APP 209959.

34. Roosevelt, "Address at the Dedication of the Thomas Jefferson Memorial."

35. For more on FDR's understanding of the war, see Ronald R. Krebs, "Tell Me a Story: FDR, Narrative, and the Making of the Second World War." *Security*

Studies 24, no. 1 (2015): 131–170; Mary E. Stuckey, *The Good Neighbor: Franklin D. Roosevelt and the Rhetoric of American Power* (East Lansing: Michigan State University Press, 2013).

36. Burstein, *Democracy's Muse*, 28.

37. Dwight D. Eisenhower, "Address in New Orleans at the Ceremony Marking the 150th Anniversary of the Louisiana Purchase," October 17, 1953, APP 232205.

38. John F. Kennedy, "Remarks at a Dinner Honoring Nobel Prize Winners of the Western Hemisphere," April 29, 1962, APP 236492.

39. Burstein, *Democracy's Muse*, 63.

40. Gerald R. Ford, "Proclamation 4430—Thomas Jefferson Day, 1976," April 13, 1976, APP 268003.

41. Gerald R. Ford, "Remarks Upon Signing Bills Commemorating the Birth of Thomas Jefferson," April 13, 1976, APP 257171.

42. Ford, "Remarks Upon Signing Bills Commemorating the Birth of Thomas Jefferson."

43. David Sehat, *The Jefferson Rule: How the Founding Fathers Became Infallible and Our Politics Inflexible* (New York: Simon & Schuster, 2015), 171.

44. Burstein, *Democracy's Muse*, 69.

45. Burstein, *Democracy's Muse*, 77.

46. Ronald Reagan, "Remarks in Atlanta, Georgia, at the Annual Convention of State Legislatures," July 30, 1981, APP 246722.

47. Ronald Reagan, "Address Before a Joint Session of the Alabama State Legislature in Montgomery," March 15, 1982, APP 245688.

48. See, for example, William J. Clinton, "Remarks on the Economic Program in Hyde Park, New York," February 19, 1993, APP 219751.

49. William J. Clinton, "Inaugural Address," January 20, 1993. See also William J. Clinton, "Remarks Announcing the Report of the National Performance Review and an Exchange with Reporters," September 7, 1993, APP 217435.

50. Burstein, *Democracy's Muse*, 87. See also Justin D. Garrison, *An Empire of Ideals: The Chimeric Imagination of Ronald Reagan* (New York: Routledge, 2013).

51. Burstein, *Democracy's Muse*, 103.

52. Dwight D. Eisenhower, "Statement by the President: Human Rights Day in Light of Recent Events in Hungary," December 10, 1956, APP 233941.

53. John F. Kennedy, "Remarks of Welcome to President Nkrumah of Ghana at the Washington National Airport," March 8, 1961, APP 236126.

54. Lyndon B. Johnson, "Annual Message on the State of the Union," January 10, 1967, APP 238176.

55. Lyndon B. Johnson, "The Veterans Day Tour of Military Installations," November 10, 1967, APP 238336.

56. See, among many other examples, Richard Nixon, "Remarks at the 80th Continental Congress of the Daughters of the American Revolution," April 19, 1971, APP 239874.

57. Martin J. Medhurst et al., *Cold War Rhetoric: Strategy, Metaphor, and Ideology* (East Lansing: Michigan State University Press, 1997).

58. Richard Nixon, ""Annual Message to Congress on the State of the Union," January 22, 1970, APP 241063.

59. George W. Bush, "The President's News Conference," July 30, 2003, APP 212750.

60. George W. Bush, "Remarks at the American Legion National Convention," August 31, 2006, APP 267898.

61. George W. Bush, "Remarks at an Independence Day Celebration and Naturalization Ceremony in Charlottesville, Virginia," July 4, 2008, APP 277872.

62. Donald J. Trump, "Remarks at the Asia-Pacific Economic Cooperation Summit in Danang, Vietnam," November 10, 2017, 331585.

63. Dwight D. Eisenhower, "Address at Byrd Field, Richmond, Virginia," October 29, 1956, APP 233778.

64. See, for example, Jimmy Carter, "Atlanta, Georgia, Remarks to Members of the Southern Baptist Brotherhood Commission," June 16, 19978, APP 248736.

65. Herbert Hoover, "Message on the Birthday of Thomas Jefferson and Its Celebration on Religious Holy Days," April 11, 1930, APP 210602.

66. William J. Clinton, "Remarks at the B'nai B'rith 150th Anniversary Havdalah Service," October 23, 1993, APP 219666.

67. Barack Obama, "Remarks at the Iftar Dinner," August 13, 2010, APP 288935.

68. Donald J. Trump, "Remarks on Signing a Proclamation in the National Day of Prayer and Executive Order Promoting Free Speech and Religious Liberty," May 4, 2017, PP 330917.

69. See, for example, John F. Kennedy, "Address in Miami at the Opening of the AFL-CIO Convention," December 7, 1961, APP 235753; Lyndon B. Johnson, "Remarks at the Coliseum in Denver," October 12, 1964, APP 242333; Nixon, "Remarks at the 80th Continental Congress"; Gerald R. Ford, "Remarks at the Annual Convention of the National Association of Secondary School Principals," February 16, 1976, APP 257764; Jimmy Carter, "Department of Education, Remarks at Ceremony Marking the Inauguration of the Department," May 7, 1980, APP 250129; Ronald Reagan, "Radio Address to the Nation on Education," March 12, 1983, APP 262978; George Bush, "Remarks at the Education Summit Welcoming Ceremony at the University of Virginia in Charlottesville," September 27, 1989, APP 263470; Barack Obama, "Commencement Address at Hampton University in Hampton, Virginia," May 9, 2010, APP 288829.

70. Lyndon Johson, "Remarks on Signing the Military Pay Bill," August 12, 1964, APP 242018.

71. On revenue sharing, see Richard Nixon, "Statement About the General Revenue Sharing Bill," October 20, 1972, APP 255247; Richard Nixon, "Radio Address on Urban Affairs," November 1, 1972, APP 255549. On campaign finance reform, see Richard Nixon, "Radio Address About a Special Message to Congress Proposing Campaign Reform Legislation," March 8, 1974, APP 256455.

72. Gerald R. Ford, "Remarks at the Swearing-In of Two Department of Health, Education, and Welfare Officials," July 1, 1975, APP 257238.

73. On economics, see Ronald Reagan, "Remarks About Federal Tax Reduction Legislation at a Meeting with State Legislators and Local Government

Officials," July 23, 1981, APP 246627; Remarks at the New York City Partnership Luncheon in New York," January 14, 1942, APP 244799; Remarks at a Reagan-Bush Rally in Gulfport, Mississippi," October 1, 1984, APP 261799. On school prayer, see Ronald Reagan, "Remarks at a White House Ceremony in Observance of National Day of Prayer," May 6, 1982, APP 245616.

74. George Bush, "Remarks on Signing the Executive Order on Employee Rights Concerning Union Dues," April 13, 1992, APP 266662; William J. Clinton, "Remarks on the National Service Initiative at the University of New Orleans," April 30, 1993, 220258.

75. George W. Bush, "The President's News Conference," July 30, 2003.

76. Barack Obama, "Remarks on the America's Great Outdoors Initiative," February 16, 2011, APP 289421.

77. Donald J. Trump, "Remarks at a 'Make America Great Again' Rally, in Melbourne, Florida," February 18, 2017.

78. Lyndon B. Johnson, "Address at the Centennial Commencement of Swarthmore College," June 8, 1964, APP 239486.

79. Gerald R. Ford, "Remarks in Philadelphia," July 4, 1976, APP 257839; Ronald Reagan, "Remarks in New York City on Receiving the Charles Evan Hughes Gold Medal of the National Conference of Christians and Jews," March 23, 1982, APP 245920. Bill Clinton also treated Jefferson as a model and democracy as a quest. See William J. Clinton, "Remarks at a Reception for Members of the Diplomatic Corps," June 15, 1993, APP 220383.

80. William J. Clinton, "Remarks Following a Screening of Excerpts from the Film, 'Thomas Jefferson,'" February 11, 1997, APP 223570.

81. Gerald R. Ford, "Proclamation 4430—Thomas Jefferson Day," April 12, 1976, APP 368003.

82. Gerald R. Ford, "Remarks at a Bicentennial Ceremony at the National Archives," July 2, 1976, APP 257788. The United States as a work in progress is a trope that appears quite often in discussions of civil rights in particular. See, for example, Jimmy Carter, "Miami, Florida, Remarks to the NAACP," July 4, 1980, APP 250548.

83. William J. Clinton, "Remarks at Cooper Union for the Advancement of Science and Art in New York City," May 12, 1993, APP 220589.

84. Gerald R. Ford, "Remarks at a Naturalization Ceremonies at Monticello, Virginia," July 5, 1976, APP 257870. See also Ronald Reagan, "Toasts of the President and Prime Minister Margaret Thatcher of the United Kingdom at the State Dinner," February 6, 1981, APP 246823.

85. Ronald Reagan, "Statement on the 239th Anniversary of the Birth of Thomas Jefferson," April 13, 1982, APP 244951.

86. George Bush, "Remarks at a Luncheon Hosted by the Catholic Lawyers Guild in Boston, Massachusetts," September 23, 1989, APP 263366.

87. William J. Clinton, Proclamation 6669—251st Anniversary of the Birth of Thomas Jefferson," April 13, 1994, APP 219015. See also William J. Clinton, "Remarks to the Democratic Leadership Council," November 15, 1995, APP 220762.

88. George W. Bush, "Remarks on Signing a Proclamation Commemorating the Birth of Thomas Jefferson," April 12, 2001, APP 213474.

89. Barack Obama, "Remarks with President Francios Hollande of France at Monticello in Charlottesville, Virginia," February 10, 2014, APP 305032.

90. Joseph R. Biden, "Remarks at the 10th Anniversary of the Dedication of the Martin Luther King, Jr., Memorial," October 21, 2021, APP 353068.

91. Donald J. Trump, "Remarks at an Independence Day Celebration," July 4, 2020, APP 343034.

92. Abraham Lincoln, "Remarks in Response to a Serenade," July 7, 1863, APP 342174.

93. Ronald Reagan, "Address to the Nation on Independence Day," July 4, 1986, APP 259223.

94. Ronald Reagan, "Remarks Announcing America's Economic Bill of Rights," July 3, 1987, APP 253231.

95. George Bush, "Remarks at the Dedication Ceremony of the Mount Rushmore National Memorial in South Dakota," July 3, 1991, APP 268258.

96. It is, of course, possible to do any of these things by focusing on an institution like the US Supreme Court, which is also driven by precedent, or even in congressional debates on specific issues.

Chapter 2: The Monumental Jefferson

1. Jefferson Monticello, "Jefferson's Grave and Tombstone," accessed February 28, 2025, https://www.monticello.org/research-education/thomas-jefferson-encyclopedia/jeffersons-gravestone/.

2. See John Hamilton Works Jr., "Thomas Jefferson's Original Graveside Monument at the University of Missouri," Thomas Jefferson Heritage Society, https://www.tjheritage.org/thomas-jeffersons-originial-graveyard-monument-university-of-missouri.

3. University of Missouri Libraries, "Thomas Jefferson Statue," accessed February 28, 2025, https://libraryguides.missouri.edu/jeffersonstatue.

4. Quoted in Galen Bacharier, "MU Refuses to Remove Thomas Jefferson Statue Despite Student Pressure," *Columbia Missourian*, June 12, 2020, https://www.columbiamissourian.com/news/higher_education/mu-refuses-to-remove-thomas-jefferson-statue-despite-student-pressure/article_1e92133c-abf9-11ea-8243-07819153e060.html.

5. Bacharier, "MU Refuses to Remove Thomas Jefferson Statue."

6. Rudi Keller, "Protestor Splashes Jefferson Statue on University of Missouri Campus," *Columbia Daily Tribune*, September 25, 2020, https://www.columbiatribune.com/story/news/education/2020/09/25/protester-splashes-jefferson-statue-on-university-of-missouri-campus/42691511/.

7. University of Missouri Libraries, "Thomas Jefferson Statue."

8. For a discussion of the importance of who has authority over place-making, see Brooke Covington, "Unpacking the Vernacular Camouflage of Virginia Tech's April 16th Memorial," *Western Journal of Communication* (2022): 1–21; Theresa

Ann Donofrio, "Ground Zero and Place-Making Authority: The Conservative Metaphors in 9/11 Families' 'Take Back the Memorial' Rhetoric," *Western Journal of Communication* 74, no. 2 (2010): 150–169.

9. Two schools changed their names in the wake of the events of 2020, one in Virginia and one in New Jersey.

10. Roadside Presidents app.

11. Edward S. Casey, *Remembering: A Phenomenological Study* (Bloomington: Indiana University Press, 2000), 225.

12. Pierre Nora, "Between History and Memory: Les Lieux de Mémoire." *Representations* 26, no. 9 (1989): 7–25.

13. Roger C. Aden, "Haunting, Public Memories, and the National Mall," 3–14, in Roger C. Aden, ed., *Rhetorics Haunting the National Mall: Displaced and Ephemeral Public Memories* (Lanham, MA: Lexington Books, 2018), 4; Kirk Savage, *Standing Soldiers, Kneeling Slaves: Race, War, and Monument in Nineteenth Century America* (Princeton, NJ: Princeton University Press, 1997), 4; Kirk Savage, *Monumental Wars: Washington DC, the National Mall, and the Transformation of the Memorial Landscape* (Berkeley: University of California Press, 2005), 10; Cari Whittenburg, "The Oklahoma City National Memorial and Museum: Materiality, Trauma, and the Comfort of Catharsis," *Western Journal of Communication* 88, no. 4 (2024): 782–801, esp. 785.

14. On the performance of civic identity and citizenship, see Robert Asen, "A Discourse Theory of Citizenship," *Quarterly Journal of Speech* 90, no. 2 (2004): 189–211; Josue David Cisneros, "(Re)Bordering the Civic Imaginary: Rhetoric, Hybridity, and Citizenship in *La Gran Marcha*," *Quarterly Journal of Speech* 97, no. 1 (2011): 26–49; Richard D. Pineda and Stacey K. Sowards, "Flag Waving as Visual Argument 2006: Immigration Demonstrations and Cultural Citizenship," *Argumentation and Advocacy* 43, no. 3–4 (2007): 164–174; on historical tourism and national identity, see Marguerite S. Shaffer, *See America First: Tourism and National Identity, 1880–1940* (Washington, DC: Smithsonian Books, 2001), 2.

15. Shaffer, *See America First*, 5. See also Gregory Clark, *Rhetorical Landscapes in America: Variations on a Theme from Kenneth Burke* (Columbia: University of South Carolina Press, 2004), 4; Leanne White, "Commercial Nationalism: Mapping the Landscape," 3–22, in Leanne White, ed., *Commercial Nationalism and Tourism: Selling the National Story* (Bristol, UK: Channel View Publications, 2017), 7.

16. Carole Blair, Marsha S. Jepperson, and Enrico Pucci Jr., "Public Memorializing in Postmodernity: The Vietnam Veterans' Memorial as Prototype," *Quarterly Journal of Speech* 77, no. 3 (1991): 263–288, esp. 263.

17. Michael Pretes, "Tourism and Nationalism," *Annals of Tourism Research* 30, no. 1(2003): 125–142, esp. 125–127. See also James Chase Sanchez and Kristen R. Moore, "Reappropriating Public Memory: Racism, Resistance, and Erasure of the Confederate Defenders of Charleston Monument," *Present Tense* 5, no. 2 (2015): 1–9, esp. 1.

18. Marita Sturken, *Tourists of History: Memory, Kitsch, and Consumerism from Oklahoma City to Ground Zero* (Durham, NC: Duke University Press, 2007), 11.

19. Blair, Jepperson, and Pucci, "Public Memorializing in Postmodernity," 263.

20. Many of these practices fall under the rubrics of what scholars have variously called "commercial" and "banal" nationalism. See White, "Commercial Nationalism," 3; Michael Billig, *Banal Nationalism* (London: Sage, 1995), 74.

21. Paul A. Sheckel, *Memory in Black and White: Race, Commemoration, and the Post-Bellum Landscape* (Walnut Creek, CA: Alta Mira, 2003), xvi, 2.

22. James Oliver Horton, "Slavery in American History: An Uncomfortable National Dialogue," 35–55, in James Oliver Horton and Lois E. Horton, eds., *Slavery and Public History: The Tough Stuff of American Memory* (New York: New Press, 2006), 44. For details on other kinds of pushback against the inclusion of slavery at parks sites, see Dwight T. Pitcaithley, "'A Cosmic Threat': The National Park Service Addresses the Causes of the Civil War," 169–186, in Horton and Horton, *Slavery and Public History*, 175.

23. Barbara Kirshenblatt-Gimblett, *Destination Culture: Tourism, Museums, and Heritage* (Berkeley: University of California Press, 1998), 7. David Lowenthal argues that "heritage is immune to reappraisal because it is not erudition but catechism." David Lowenthal, *Possessed by the Past: The Heritage Crusade and the Spirit of History* (New York: Free Press, 1996), 121.

24. Charles W. Mills, "White Ignorance," in Shannon Sullivan and Nancy Tuana, *Race and the Epistemologies of Ignorance* (New York: SUNY Press, 2007), 28.

25. Robert C. Aden, *Upon the Ruins of Liberty: The President's House at Independence National Historical Park and Public Memory* (Philadelphia: Temple University Press, 2015), 15–18.

26. On this kind of leakage, see J. David Maxson, "'Second Line to Bury White Supremacy': Take 'Em Down NOLA,' Monument Removal, and Residual Memory," *Quarterly Journal of Speech* 106, no. 1 (2020): 48–71, esp. 52.

27. Robert O'Meally and Genevieve Fabre, "Introduction," 3–17, in Genevieve Fabre and Robert O'Meally, eds., *History and Memory in American Culture* (New York: Oxford University Press, 1994), 3; Whittenburg, "Oklahoma City National Memorial," 785.

28. Sturken, *Tourists of History*, 6–9.

29. Karen L. Cox, *No Common Ground: Confederate Monuments and the Ongoing Fight for Racial Justice* (Chapel Hill: University of North Carolina press, 2021), 23.

30. Sheckel, *Memory in Black and White*, 11.

31. See "Restoring Truth and Sanity to American History," accessed April 15, 2025, https://www.whitehouse.gov/presidential-actions/2025/03/restoring-truth-and-sanity-to-american-history/.

32. Whittenburg, "Oklahoma City National Memorial," 783.

33. Annie Gowan, "As Statues of Founders Topple, Debate Rages over Where Protestors Should Draw the Line," *Washington Post*, July 7, 2020, https://www.washingtonpost.com/national/as-statues-of-founding-fathers-topple-debate-rages-over-where-protesters-should-draw-the-line/2020/07/07/5de7c956-bfb7-11ea-b4f6-cb39cd8940fb_story.html.

34. Visvajit Sriramrajan, "Hofstra University Moves Statue Amid Outcries,"

LI Herald, July 20, 2020, https://www.liherald.com/stories/hofstra-moves-jeffer son-statue-amid-outcries,126401.

35. J. D. Capelouto, "Statue of Thomas Jefferson in Downtown Decatur Removed," *Atlanta Journal Constitution*, June 22, 2020, https://www.ajc.com/news /local/statue-thomas-jefferson-downtown-decatur-removed/t2sW24ZnjXPdTr uQrwFRKN/.

36. Jeffrey C. Mays and Zachary Small, "Jefferson Statue Will Be Removed from N.Y.C. Council Chambers," *New York Times*, October 4, 2021 (updated November 15, 2021), https://www.nytimes.com/2021/10/18/nyregion/thomas-jeffer son-statue-ny-city-council.html.

37. Quoted in Mays and Small, "Jefferson Statue."

38. Latisha Jensen, "Portland Man Describes Tearing Down Thomas Jefferson Statue: 'It's Not Vandalism,'" *Willamette Week*, June 20, 2020, https://www.wwe ek.com/news/2020/06/20/portland-man-describes-tearing-down-thomas-jeffer son-statue-its-not-vandalism/.

39. Jensen, "Portland Man."

40. Brad Kutner, "The History of the Arthus Ashe Monument in Richmond," *Style Weekly*, August 22, 2017, https://www.styleweekly.com/richmond/the-histo ry-of-the-arthur-ashe-monument-in-richmond/Content?oid=4237161.

41. Other statues have met similar fates. See Teo Armus and Hadley Green, "Charlottesville's Lee Statue Meets Its End, in a 2,250 Degree Furnace," *Washington Post*, October 26, 2023, https://www.washingtonpost.com/dc-md-va/interac tive/2023/civil-war-monument-melting-robert-e-lee-confederate/.

42. Autumn Childress, "Graffiti-Riddled Jefferson Davis Statue on Display at the Valentine," June 22, 2022, https://www.wric.com/news/local-news/richmond /graffiti-riddled-jefferson-davis-statue-on-display-at-the-valentine/.

43. Alan Suderman, "Virginia Evicts Confederate Monuments from Its State Capitol," *Washington Post*, July 24, 2020, https://www.washingtonpost.com /national/virginia-evicts-confederate-monuments-from-its-state-capitol/2020 /07/24/a47204bc-cda5-11ea-99b0-8426e26d203b_story.html.

44. Norma Evenson, "Monumental Spaces," 19–34, in Richard Longstreth, ed., *The Mall in Washington, 1791–1991* (New Haven, CT: Yale University Press, 2002), 33.

45. Lisa Benton-Short, *The National Mall: No Ordinary Public Space* (Toronto: University of Toronto Press, 2016), 3.

46. Peter Gardella, *American Civil Religion: What Americans Hold Sacred* (New York: Oxford University Press, 2014), 323.

47. National Park Service, "Foundation Document: National Mall and Memorial Parks," accessed February 28, 2025, npshistory.com/nama-fd-2017.pdf, 3.

48. National Park Service, "Foundation Document: National Mall and Memorial Parks," 4.

49. National Park Service, "Foundation Document: National Mall and Memorial Parks," 4, 15; Roger C. Aden, "Introduction: The Soul of a Nation," 1–10, in Roger C. Aden, ed., *US Public Memory, Rhetoric, and the National Mall* (Lanham, MA: Lexington Books, 2018), 1.

50. Aden, "Introduction: The Soul of a Nation," 1.

51. For an insightful history of the Mall, see Savage, *Monumental Wars.*

52. Savage, *Monumental Wars,* 25, 171.

53. Aden, "Introduction: The Soul of a Nation," 3.

54. Benton-Short, *The National Mall,* 4, 201–203.

55. See, for example, John Y. Cole, *America's Greatest Library: An Illustrated History of the Library of Congress* (London: D. Giles, 2017), 16.

56. Archibald MacLeish, "Letter to the President," December 6, 1942, President's Personal File, 255–268, "PPF 259, Jefferson, Thomas, 1938–1942," Franklin D. Roosevelt Library (hereinafter FDRL).

57. Cole, *America's Greatest Library,* 130–131.

58. This is true as of this writing, but it is also important to note that this is one of the places that President Trump's executive order applies to, and the exhibits discussed here will be changed if the order survives predicted legal challenges on First Amendment grounds.

59. Smithsonian Books, *Official Guide to the Smithsonian National Museum of African American History and Culture* (Washington, DC: Smithsonian Books, n.d.), 35.

60. Smithsonian Books, *Official Guide,* 44.

61. National Park Service, "Cultural Landscapes Inventory: Jefferson Memorial," accessed January 20, 2025, nps.gov/JEME_CLrevised2009.pdf, 54.

62. Richard Longstreth, "Introduction: Change and Continuity of the Mall, 1791–1991," 11–17, in Longstreth, *The Mall in Washington, 1791–1991,* 15.

63. National Park Service, "Cultural Landscapes Inventory: Jefferson Memorial," 16.

64. For a good history of the memorial, see Andrew Burstein, *Democracy's Muse: How Thomas Jefferson Became an FDR Liberal, a Reagan Republican, and a Tea Party Fanatic, All the While Being Dead* (Charlotteville: University of Virginia Press, 2015), 13–26. For correspondence related to the creation, staffing, and mission of the commission, see OF 1491-OF 1504; OF 1505, Box 1, "Thomas Jefferson Memorial Commission, 1933–1935," and OF 1505 Box 2, Thomas Jefferson Memorial Commission Miscellaneous, "Thomas Jefferson Memorial Commission, 1936–1937," FDRL.

65. Thomas Ludlow, "Remarks in the House of Representatives," June 3, 1936, OF 1505, Box 2, Thomas Jefferson Memorial Commission Miscellaneous, "Thomas Jefferson Memorial Commission, 1936–1937," FDRL, 1.

66. Ludlow, "Remarks," 2–3.

67. See, for example, FDR's response to correspondence from Alexander Legare, February 17, 1937, and the memo from Representative John J. Bolan to Marvin McIntyre, April 4, 1937, in OF 1505, Box 2 Thomas Jefferson Memorial Commission Miscellaneous, "Thomas Jefferson Memorial Commission, 1936–1937," FDRL.

68. Franklin D. Roosevelt, "Memo to Stuart Gibboney," January 24, 1940, OF 1505, Box 2, Thomas Jefferson Memorial Commission Miscellaneous, "Thomas Jefferson Memorial Commission, 1939–1940," FDRL; Franklin D. Roosevelt,

"Memo to Fiske Kimball," March 12, 1941, OF 1505, Box 2, Thomas Jefferson Memorial Commission Miscellaneous, "Thomas Jefferson Memorial Commission, 1941–1945," FDRL.

69. Franklin D. Roosevelt, "Memo to Stuart G. Gibboney, January 31, 1940, OF 1505, Box 2, Thomas Jefferson Memorial Commission Miscellaneous, "Thomas Jefferson Memorial Commission, 1939–1940," FDRL.

70. There were ongoing issues with design. See, for example, Frederic A. Delano, "Letter to James Roosevelt," February 24, 1937, OF 1505, Box 2, Thomas Jefferson Memorial Commission Miscellaneous, "Thomas Jefferson Memorial Commission, 1936–1937," FDRL. See also the various documents in OF 1505, Box 2, Thomas Jefferson Memorial Commission Miscellaneous, "Thomas Jefferson Memorial Commission, 1938," FDRL.

71. Gardella, *American Civil Religion*, 324.

72. For discussion, see Burstein, *Democracy's Muse*, 14–17.

73. See, among many similar examples, , "Citizens Fight to Save Trees," *Washington Herald*, November 12, 1938, OF 1505, Box 2, Thomas Jefferson Memorial Commission Miscellaneous, "Thomas Jefferson Memorial Commission, 1938," FDRL.

74. Many people were moved to write to Roosevelt personally. See the correspondence filed in OF 1505, Box 2, Thomas Jefferson Memorial Commission Miscellaneous, "Thomas Jefferson Memorial Commission, 1936–1937," FDRL; OF 1505, Box 2, Thomas Jefferson Memorial Commission Miscellaneous, "Thomas Jefferson Memorial Commission, 1938," FDRL.

75. C. Marshall Finnan, "Memo to MH McIntyre," November 17, 1938, OF 1505, Box 2, Thomas Jefferson Memorial Commission Miscellaneous, "Thomas Jefferson Memorial Commission, 1938," FDRL.

76. Richard Guy Wilson, "High Noon on the Mall: Modernism versus Totalitarianism, 1910–1970," 143–163, in Longstreth, *The Mall in Washington, 1791–1991*, 144–145.

77. Wilson, "High Noon on the Mall," 152.

78. See Eugene Masselink, "Letter to Missy LeHand," April 1, 1937, OF 1505, Box 2, Thomas Jefferson Memorial Commission Miscellaneous, "Thomas Jefferson Memorial Commission, 1936–1937," FDRL.

79. James W. Loewen, *Lies Across America: What Our Historic Sites Get Wrong* (Chicago: Touchstone Press, 2000), 344–349.

80. Loewen, *Lies Across America*, 346. As William Jeremiah Moses notes of the quotation on the memorial: "'Nothing is more certainly written in the book of fate than that these people are to be free . . .' is actually followed by ' . . . nor is it less certain that the two races, equally free, cannot live in the same government.'" Wilson Jeremiah Moses, *Thomas Jefferson: A Modern Prometheus* (New York: Cambridge University Press, 2019), 44. On Jefferson's beliefs and actions regarding slavery and race, see, among many others, Annette Gordon-Reed, "Afterword," 91–96, in Jon Meacham, ed., *In the Hands of the People: Thomas Jefferson on Equality, Faith, Freedom, and the Art of Citizenship* (New York: Random House, 2020), 92.

81. Moses, *Thomas Jefferson*.

82. That descendant wrote, "I am the sixth generation great-grandson of a sla-veowner. My cousins from Sally Hemings's family are also the great-grandchildren of a slaveowner. . . . My family owned their family. That is the American history you will not learn when you visit the Jefferson Memorial. But you will learn it at Monticello.'" Lucien K. Truscott IV, "I'm a Direct Descendant of Thomas Jeffer-son. Take Down His Memorial," *New York Times*, July 6, 2020, https://www.ny times.com/2020/07/06/opinion/thomas-jefferson-memorial-truscott.html.

83. National Park Service, "Thomas Jefferson Memorial," 2, accessed February 28, 2025, https://www.nps.gov/thje/index.htm.

84. National Park Service, "Thomas Jefferson Memorial."

85. Given the March 2025 executive order concerning historical interpretations in Smithsonian institutions, as of this writing it remains to be seen if this depic-tion remains stable.

86. Sanchez and Moore, "Reappropriating Public Memory," 5.

87. Jane Henderson, "How to View a Flawed Founder Now? Missouri His-tory Museum Reinterprets Jefferson Statue for 21st Century," *St. Louis Post Dis-patch*, April 27, 2022, https://www.stltoday.com/news/local/metro/how-to-view-a -flawed-founder-now-missouri-history-museum-reinterprets-jefferson-statue -for-21st/article_36341bfe-3284-5097-ad65-a54e4451c359.html.

88. Henderson, "How to View a Flawed Founder Now?"

89. Iker Seisdedos, "Richmond Took down Its Racist Statues, but Now City Doesn't Know What To Do with Them," *El Pais*, February 5, 2023, https://engli sh.elpais.com/usa/2023-02-05/richmond-took-down-its-racist-statues-but-now -nobody-knows-what-to-do-with-them.html.

90. Chandra A. Maldonado, "Absence and Piecemeal Approaches to Com-memorative Practice," *Howard Journal of Communication* (2024), https://doi.org .10.1080/10646175.2024.2326207.

91. For a detailed discussion of previous interpretive practices, see Mary E. Stuckey, *For the Enjoyment of the People: The Creation of National Identity in Amer-ican Public Lands* (Lawrence: University Press of Kansas, 2023), 72–80.

92. See Walter Johnson, *The Broken Heart of St. Louis and the Violent History of the United States* (New York: Basic Books, 2020), 293–294; W. Arthus Meh-rhoff, *The Gateway Arch: Fact and Symbol* (Bowling Green, OH: Bowling Green State University Press, 1992), 58; Hal K. Rothman, *Devil's Bargains: Tourism in the Twentieth-Century American West* (Lawrence: University Press of Kansas, 1998), 155.

93. For detailed timelines and history, see John Bodnar, *Remaking American Public Memory: Commemoration and Patriotism in the Twentieth Century* (Prince-ton, NJ: Princeton University Press, 1992), 186–189; Sharon A. Brown, "Jefferson National Expansion, Administrative History," accessed April 15, 2025, https:// www.nps.gov/parkhistory/online_books/jeff/adhit.htm Johnson, *Broken Heart of St. Louis*, 295; Alfred Haworth Jones, "The Search for a Useable American Past in the New Deal Era," *American Quarterly* 23, no. 5 (1971): 710–724, esp. 710–711; Charles B. Hosner Jr., *Preservation Comes of Age: From Williamsburg to the*

National Trust, 1926–1949 (Charlottesville: University of Virginia Press, 1981), 626–649; Mehrhoff, *Gateway Arch.*

94. On the relationship between museums and the frontier myth, see Greg Dickinson, Brian L. Ott, and Eric Aoki, "Memory and Myth at the Buffalo Bill Museum," *Western Journal of Communication* 69, no. 2 (2005): 85–108, esp. 85.

95. Bernard J. Dickmann, "Letter to Franklin D. Roosevelt," February 9, 1934, OF 234 Thomas Jefferson Box 1, "OF 234 Thomas Jefferson, 1933–1934," FDRL.

96. American Historical Association, Untitled, December 28, 1933, OF 234 Thomas Jefferson Box 1, "OF 234 Thomas Jefferson, 1933–1934," FDRL. The memorial was also endorsed in similar terms by the Missouri Historical Society, the St. Louis Chapter of the Sons of the Revolution, the Governing Board of the St. Louis Chapter of the Daughters of the American Revolution, the League of Women Voters of St. Louis, and (with less elaboration), by the Executive Committee of the Mississippi Valley Historical Association, as well as sundry other local and national groups and organizations. OF 234 Thomas Jefferson Box 1, "OF 234 Thomas Jefferson, 1933–1934," FDRL. See also George B. Hertzog Jr. *Battling for the National Parks* (Mt. Kisco, NY: Moyer Bell, 1988), 56–57; Mehrhoff, *Gateway Arch*, 11.

97. National Park Service, "Jefferson National Expansion Memorial: Foundation Document Overview," accessed February 28, 2025, /http://npshistory.com /publications/foundation-documents/jeff-fd-overview.pdf.

98. National Park Service, "Gateway Arch," accessed February 28, 2025, https:// www.nps.gov/jeff/faqs.htm.

99. Allan Temko, *Eero Saarinen* (New York: George Braziller, 1962), 123.

100. Carole Blair, Marsha S. Jepperson, and Enrico Pucci Jr., "Public Memorializing in Postmodernity: The Vietnam Veterans' Memorial as Prototype," *Quarterly Journal of Speech* 77, no. 3 (1991): 263–288; Temko, *Eero Saarinen*, 18.

101. Blair, Jepperson, and Pucci, "Public Memorializing," 290.

102. Again, the interpretation here may change given Trump's executive order.

103. I was told by one that it is unusual to get more than twenty or so people on any of their museum tours. Another told me that they do not challenge the widespread belief that the Louisiana Purchase doubled the size of the nation because too many people take that as an article of faith, and trying to correct this information isn't worth the effort in the short time they have visitors' attention.

104. The DAR is best known for refusing to allow renowned soprano Marian Anderson to hold a concert in its hall adjacent to the library building because she was Black.

105. Consider, for example, the sites related to slavery in Montgomery, Alabama, that were once largely ignored and are now an explicit part of the commemorative landscape.

106. Simon Winchester, *The Men Who United the States* (New York: Harper Perennial, 2013), 11.

107. Katharyne Mitchell, "Monuments, Memorials, and the Politics of Memory," *Urban Geography* 24, no. 5 (2003): 442–459, esp. 446.

Chapter 3: The Collective Jefferson

1. Phyllis Young, "The Story of the Thomas Jefferson Statue," January 11, 2022, *Lawton Constitution*, https://www.swoknews.com/styles/the-story-of-the-thomas-jefferson-statue/article_def7942e-2fc4-5d5e-8c62-1b878ce3740a.html.

2. United States Capitol Historical Society, *We, the People: The Story of the United States Capitol* (Washington, DC: National Geographic Society, 2016), 71.

3. Carole Blair, "Contemporary US Memorial Sites as Exemplars of Rhetoric's Materiality," 16–27, in Jack Seltzer and Shaun Crowley, eds., *Rhetorical Bodies* (Madison: University of Wisconsin Press, 1999), 39. See also Brooke Covington, "Unpacking the Vernacular Camouflage of Virginia Tech's April 16th Memorial," *Western Journal of Communication* (2022): 1–21; Theresa Ann Donofrio, "Ground Zero and Place-Making Authority: The Conservative Metaphors in 9/11 Families' 'Take Back the Memorial' Rhetoric," *Western Journal of Communication* 74, no. 2 (2010): 150–169; Megan Irene Fitzmaurice, "Commemorative Privilege in National Statuary Hall: Spatial Constructions of Racial Citizenship," *Southern Communication Journal* 81, no. 4 (2016): 252–262.

4. For an insightful discussion of the politics of these kinds of spaces, see Fitzmaurice, "Commemorative Privilege."

5. Mary E. Stuckey, "'To Preserve Unimpaired': The Presidency, National Parks, and the Preservation of the US Settler Colonialist State," *Rhetoric & Public Affairs* 27, no. 1 (2024): 1–26.

6. For terrific discussions of these points, see Christa J. Olson, "The Democratic Hemisphere," 23–38, in Adrianna Angel, Michael L. Butterfield, and Nancy R. Gomez, eds., *Rhetorics of Democracy in the Americas* (University Park: Penn State University Press, 2021); Christa J. Olson, *American Magnitude: Hemispheric Vision and Public Feeling in the United States* (Columbus: Ohio State University Press, 2021).

7. Megan Gambino, "The True Story behind Plymouth Rock," *Smithsonian Magazine*, November 20, 2017, https://www.smithsonianmag.com/smithsonian-institution/the-true-story-behind-plymouth-rock-639690/.

8. See, for example, National Park Service, "Lincoln and Thanksgiving," accessed March 1, 2025, https://www.nps.gov/liho/learn/historyculture/lincoln-and-thanksgiving.htm#:~:text=Lincoln%20issued%20onine%20proclamations%20while,States%20has%20celebrated%20Thanksgiving%20Day.

9. Gregory Clark, *Rhetorical Landscapes in America: Variations on a Theme from Kenneth Burke* (Columbia: University of South Carolina Press, 2004), 25.

10. Athinodoros Chronis, "The Staging of Contested Servicescapes," *Journal of Service Research* 22, no. 4 (2019): 456–473, esp. 459; John Urry, *The Tourist Gaze*, 2nd ed. (Thousand Oaks, CA: Sage, 2002), 1.

11. Kirk Savage, *Standing Soldiers, Kneeling Slaves: Race, War, and Monument in Nineteenth Century America* (Princeton, NJ: Princeton University Press, 1997), 7.

12. John A. Agnew, "Introduction," 1–18, in John A. Agnew and Jonathan M. Smith, eds., *American Space/American Place: Geographies of the Contemporary United States* (Edinburgh: Edinburgh University Press, 2002), 7.

13. Agnew, "Introduction," 6.

14. Thomas F. Gieryn, *Truth Spots: How Places Make People Believe* (Chicago: University of Chicago Press, 2018), 2–3; David Jacobson, *Place and Belonging in America* (Baltimore: Johns Hopkins University Press, 2002), 3; Patricia A. Stokowski, "Languages of Place and Discourses of Power: Constructing New Senses of Place," *Journal of Leisure Research* 38, no. 4 (2002): 368–382, esp. 373.

15. For a detailed discussion of how this works, see Fitzmaurice, "Commemorative Privilege."

16. On public memory and the frontier myth, see, among many others, Zoë Hess Carney and Mary E. Stuckey, "The World as the American Frontier: Racialized Presidential War Rhetoric," *Southern Communication Journal* 80, no. 3 (2015): 163–188; Leah Ceccarelli, *On the Frontier of Science: An American Rhetoric of Exploration and Exploitation* (East Lansing: Michigan State University Press, 2013); Leroy G. Dorsey, "The Frontier Myth and Presidential Rhetoric: Theodore Roosevelt's Campaign for Conservation," *Western Journal of Communication* 59, no. 1 (1995): 1–19; Leroy G. Dorsey and Rachel M. Harlow, "'We Want Americans Pure and Simple': Theodore Roosevelt and the Myth of Americanism," *Rhetoric & Public Affairs* 6, no. 1 (2003): 55–78; Janice Hocker Rushing, "The Rhetoric of the American Western Myth," *Communications Monographs* 50, no. 1 (1983): 14–32; Richard Slotkin, "Nostalgia and Progress: Theodore Roosevelt's Myth of the Frontier," *American Quarterly* 33, no. 5 (1981): 608–637; David A. Smith, *Cowboy Presidents: The Frontier Myth and US Politics Since 1900* (Norman: University of Oklahoma Press, 2021).

17. For pictures and details of the rotunda, see Architect of the Capitol, "Capitol Rotunda," accessed March 1, 2025, https://www.aoc.gov/explore-capitol-cam pus/buildings-grounds/capitol-building/rotunda.

18. There is a statue of Jefferson inside the capitol itself. Located in the rotunda, the bronze statue portrays Jefferson holding plans for the building, which he designed. See "The Virginia State Capitol," revised summer 2022.

19. Information sheet, Richmond Capitol, n.d.

20. National Park Service, "Foundation Document Overview, Independence National Historic Park," accessed January 20, 2025, npshistory.com/inde-fd-over view.pdf, 2.

21. National Park Service, "Foundation Document Overview," 2.

22. National Park Service, "Independence Hall," accessed March 1, 2025, https://www.nps.gov/inde/learn/historyculture/places-independencehall.htm. For a discussion of why this distinction is important, see Olson, "The Democratic Hemisphere; Olson, *American Magnitude.*

23. National Park Service, "Foundation Document Overview," 5–7.

24. Again, given President Trump's March 2025 executive order on the interpretation of national history, it remains to be seen if this interpretation remains.

25. National Park Service, "Foundation Document Overview," 7.

26. National Park Foundation, "Independence National Historical Park," accessed March 1, 2025, https://www.nationalparks.org/explore/parks/independen ce-national-historical-park.

27. Robert C. Aden, *Upon the Ruins of Liberty: The President's House at Independence National Historical Park and Public Memory* (Philadelphia: Temple University Press, 2015), 35.

28. Stephen E. Lucas, "The Rhetorical Ancestry of the Declaration of Independence," *Rhetoric & Public Affairs* 1, no. 2 (1998): 143–184.

29. Peter Gardella, *American Civil Religion: What Americans Hold Sacred* (New York: Oxford University Press, 2014), 98.

30. Alphonse J. Beitzinger, *A History of American Political Thought* (New York: Harper & Row, 1972), 161–166; Joseph Ellis, *American Sphinx: The Character of Thomas Jefferson* (New York: Alfred A. Knopf, 1997), 11; Jean H. Yarborough, *American Virtues: Jefferson on the Character of a Free People* (Lawrence: University Press of Kansas, 1998), 1–26.

31. Jefferson himself acknowledged this. See, among many others, Joyce Appleby, "Introduction: Jefferson and His Complex Legacy," 1–16, in Peter S. Onuf, ed., *Jeffersonian Legacies* (Charlottesville: University of Virginia Press, 1993), 7; Winston Groom, *The Patriots: Alexander Hamilton, Thomas Jefferson, John Adams, and the Making of America* (Washington, DC: National Geographic, 2020), 137; Jon Meacham, *Thomas Jefferson. The Art of Power* (New York: Random House, 2013), 102–103; Ray Raphael, *Founding Myths: Stories That Hide Our Patriotic Past* (New York: MJF Books, 2004), 108–109.

32. Eric Foner, *The Story of American Freedom* (New York: Norton, 1999), 12.

33. Foner, *The Story of American Freedom*, 89.

34. Tim Gruenwald, *Curating America's Painful Past: Memory, Museums, and the National Imagination* (Lawrence: University Press of Kansas, 2021).

35. Gary B. Nash, "For Whom Will the Liberty Bell Toll? From Controversy to Cooperation," 75–101, in James Oliver Horton and Lois E. Horton, eds., *Slavery and Public History: The Tough Stuff of American Memory* (New York: New Press, 2006), 75; Gardella, *American Civil Religion*, 74–77.

36. Nash, "For Whom Will the Liberty Bell Toll?," 77–78.

37. Aden, *Upon the Ruins of Liberty*, xii–xiii.

38. Aden, *Upon the Ruins of Liberty*, 7; Nash, "For Whom Will the Liberty Bell Toll?," 79.

39. Marie Tyler-McGraw, "Southern Comfort Levels: Race, Heritage Tourism, and the Civil War in Richmond," 151–167, in Horton and Horton, *Slavery and Public History*, 159.

40. Gardella, *American Civil Religion*, 67.

41. Gardella, *American Civil Religion*, 67.

42. Aden, *Upon the Ruins of Liberty*, 38–39.

43. For more on the museum, see https://www.amrevmuseum.org/.

44. Aden, *Upon the Ruins of Liberty*, 4–42.

45. The guide is available for download here: https://www.visitrapidcity.com/things-to-do/all-things/attractions/city-presidents.

46. Jefferson's summary is here: https://www.blackhillsbadlands.com/public-sculptures/thomas-jefferson.

47. There are a remarkable number of vistas from which to view the monument,

which include several pullouts on nearby highways, and even a viewing point at Badlands National Park, some seventy-five miles away.

48. For more on the controversy, see Teresa Bergman, *Exhibiting Patriotism: Creating and Contesting Interpretations of American Historic Sites* (Walnut Creek, CA: Left Coast Press, 2013), 14–53.

49. Annette McGivney, "The Battle for Mount Rushmore: It Should be Turned into Something Like the Holocaust Museum," *The Guardian*, July 3, 2021, https://www.theguardian.com/environment/2021/jul/03/mount-rushmore -south-dakota-indigenous-americans.

50. The Crazy Horse Memorial has its own set of interpretive issues. See, for example, Carole Blair and Neil Michael, "The Rushmore Effect: Ethos and National Collective Identity," 156–196, in Michael Hyde, ed., *The Ethos of Rhetoric* (Columbia: University of South Carolina Press, 2004), 175–179; Brooke Jarvis, "Who Speaks for Crazy Horse?," *New Yorker*, September 16, 2019, https://www .newyorker.com/magazine/2019/09/23/who-speaks-for-crazy-horse.

51. Jarvis, "Who Speaks for Crazy Horse?"

52. On the controversies surrounding the site, see, among many others, Jarvis, "Who Speaks for Crazy Horse?"; Gardella, *American Civil Religion*, 232; Mc-Givney, "The Battle for Mount Rushmore."

53. National Park Service, "Foundation Document Overview," accessed March 1, 2025, https://www.nps.gov/moru/learn/management/foundation-docu ment-overview.htm, 5.

54. National Park Service, "Foundation Document Overview," 5.

55. National Park Service, "Foundation Document Overview," 3.

56. Michael Billig, *Banal Nationalism* (London: Sage, 1995).

57. On the relationship between the two sculptures, see Blair and Michael, "Rushmore Effect," 160–163.

58. Blair and Michael, "Rushmore Effect," 170.

59. Blair and Michael, "Rushmore Effect," 156.

60. National Park Service, "Be a Junior Ranger: Mount Rushmore National Memorial, South Dakota," accessed January 20, 2025, https://npshistory.com/pub lications/interpretation/junior-ranger/index.htm.

61. Bergman, *Exhibiting Patriotism*, 149.

62. Blair and Michael, "Rushmore Effect," 180–181.

63. For more on the US interventions in Panama and the Canal, see Ovidio Diaz-Espino, *How Wall Street Created a Nation: JP Morgan, Teddy Roosevelt, and the Panama Canal* (Primedia E-launch, 2014); Julie Greene, *The Canal Builders: Making America's Empire at the Panama Canal* (New York: Penguin, 2009).

64. Garry Wills, *"Negro President": Jefferson and the Slave Power* (Boston: Houghton Mifflin, 2003), 118.

65. Britannica, "Louisiana Purchase," accessed March 1, 2025, https://www.br itannica.com/event/Louisiana-Purchase. See also Keith Thompson, *Jefferson's Shadow: The Story of His Science* (New Haven, CT: Yale University Press, 2012), 217.

66. Wills, *"Negro President,"* 119.

67. Peter S. Onuf, *Jefferson's Empire: The Language of American Nationhood* (Charlottesville: University Press of Virginia, 2000), 1.

68. Mary E. Stuckey, *Defining Americans: The Presidency and National Identity* (Lawrence: University Press of Kansas, 2023), 33–39.

69. Walter Johnson, *The Broken Heart of St. Louis and the Violent History of the United States* (New York: Basic Books, 2020), 16.

70. Robert J. Miller, "The Doctrine of Discovery, Manifest Destiny, and American Indians," 87–100, in Susan Sleeper-Smith et al., eds., *Why You Can't Teach History without American Indians* (Chapel Hill: University of North Carolina Press, 2015), 92; Thompson, *Jefferson's Shadow*, 218.

71. Ellis, *American Sphinx*, 212; Miller, "The Doctrine of Discovery, Manifest Destiny, and American Indians," 95–96; Garry Wills, *"Negro President,"* xiii.

72. Miller, "The Doctrine of Discovery, Manifest Destiny, and American Indians," 95–96; Wilson Jeremiah Moses, *Thomas Jefferson: A Modern Prometheus* (New York: Cambridge University Press, 2019), 62.

73. See, among many others, Meacham, *Thomas Jefferson*, 392; Onuf, *Jefferson's Empire*, 49; Robert M. Owens, *Mr. Jefferson's Hammer: William Henry Harrison and the Origins of American Indian Policy* (Norman: University of Oklahoma Press, 2007); Ronald Takaki, *A Different Mirror: A History of Multicultural America* (Boston: Little, Brown, 1993), 48.

74. Onuf, *Jefferson's Empire*, 19–20. See also Francis D. Cogliano, *Thomas Jefferson: Reputation and Legacy* (Charlottesville: University of Virginia Press, 2006), 12–13; Moses, *Thomas Jefferson*, 271–272.

75. Adam Dahl, *Empire of the People: Settler Colonialism and the Foundations of Modern Democratic Thought* (Lawrence: University Press of Kansas, 2018), 2.

76. Dahl, *Empire of the People*, 4.

77. Blair and Michael, "The Rushmore Effect," 180.

78. See, among many others, Cogliano, *Thomas Jefferson*, 59–60.

79. David Sehat, *The Jefferson Rule: How the Founding Fathers Became Infallible and Our Politics Inflexible* (New York: Simon & Schuster, 2015), 1.

80. Sehat, *Jefferson Rule*, 36–37.

81. Joseph J. Ellis, "Introduction," 1–12, in Encyclopedia Britannica, *The Founding Fathers: The Essential Guide to the Men Who Made America* (Hoboken, NJ: John Wiley & Sons, 2007), 2.

82. Nikole Hannah-Jones, "Democracy," 7–36, in Nikole Hannah-Jones et al., eds. *The 1619 Project: A New American Origin Story* (London: W. H. Allen, 2021), 19.

83. Joseph J. Ellis, *The Quartet: Orchestrating the Second American Revolution* (New York: Vintage, 2015), xi–xiii.

Chapter 4: The Popular Jefferson

1. Jefferson asks "Sally" to open the letter announcing his appointment as secretary of state in the opening scene of Act II, for example. Lin-Manuel Miranda and Jeremy McCarter, *Hamilton: The Revolution* (New York: Grand Central Publishing, 2016), 152.

2. Gregory Clark, *Rhetorical Landscapes in America: Variations on a Theme from Kenneth Burke* (Columbia: University of South Carolina Press, 2004), 25.

3. Kirk Savage, *Standing Soldiers, Kneeling Slaves: Race, War, and Monument in Nineteenth Century America* (Princeton, NJ: Princeton University Press, 1997), 7.

4. Athinodoros Chronis, "The Staging of Contested Servicescapes," *Journal of Service Research* 22, no. 4 (2019): 456–473, esp. 459.

5. John A. Agnew, "Introduction," 1–18, in John A. Agnew and Jonathan M. Smith, eds., *American Space/American Place: Geographies of the Contemporary United States* (Edinburgh: Edinburgh University Press, 2002), 6–7.

6. Thomas F. Gieryn, *Truth Spots: How Places Make People Believe* (Chicago: University of Chicago Press, 2018), 2–3.

7. David Jacobson, *Place and Belonging in America* (Baltimore: Johns Hopkins University Press, 2002), 3.

8. See, for example, Barry Brummett, *Rhetoric in Popular Culture* (Thousand Oaks, CA: Sage Publications, 2022); Jennifer C. Dunn, "Critical Rhetoric in the Age of the (First) Reality TV President: A Critique of Freedom and Domination," *International Journal of Communication* 14 (2020): 813–830; John Louis Lucaites and Robert Hariman, "Visual Rhetoric, Photojournalism, and Democratic Public Culture," *Rhetoric Review* 20, no. 1/2 (2001): 37–42.

9. See, among many others, Kendall R. Phillips, *A Cinema of Hopelessness: The Rhetoric of Rage in 21st Century Popular Culture* (New York: Springer Nature, 2021).

10. Examples include Bonnie J. Dow, "Fixing Feminism: Women's Liberation and the Rhetoric of Television Documentary," *Quarterly Journal of Speech* 90, no. 1 (2004): 53–80; Deborah Harris-Moore, *Media and the Rhetoric of Body Perfection: Cosmetic Surgery, Weight Loss and Beauty in Popular Culture* (New York: Routledge, 2016); Casey Ryan Kelly, "The Wounded Man: Foxcatcher and the Incoherence of White Masculine Victimhood," *Communication and Critical/Cultural Studies* 15, no. 2 (2018): 161–178; Tammie M. Kennedy, Joyce Irene Middleton, and Krista Ratcliffe, eds., *Rhetorics of Whiteness: Postracial Hauntings in Popular Culture, Social Media, and Education* (Carbondale: Southern Illinois University Press, 2017).

11. For a sampling of such work, see Karrin Vasby Anderson, *Women, Feminism, and Pop Politics: From "Bitch" to "Badass" and Beyond* (New York: Peter Lang, 2018); Barry Brummett, *Uncovering Hidden Rhetorics: Social Issues in Disguise* (Thousand Oaks, CA: Sage, 2008); Celeste Michelle Condit, *Decoding Abortion Rhetoric: Communicating Social Change* (Champaign-Urbana: University of Illinois Press, 1990); Linda Fuller, *Sport, Rhetoric, and Gender: Historical Perspectives and Media Representations* (New York: Springer, 2006); Heather Latimer, "Popular Culture and Reproductive Politics: *Juno, Knocked Up* and the enduring legacy of *The Handmaid's Tale*," *Feminist Theory* 10, no. 2 (2009): 211–226; Kent A. Ono, *Critical Rhetorics of Race* (New York: NYU Press, 2011); Thomas Rosteck and Thomas S. Frentz, "Myth and Multiple Readings in Environmental Rhetoric: The Case of *An Inconvenient Truth*," *Quarterly Journal of Speech* 95, no. 1 (2009): 1–19; Phaedra C. Pezzullo, *Toxic Tourism: Rhetorics of Pollution, Travel, and Environmental Justice* (Tuscaloosa: University of Alabama Press, 2009); Deanna D. Sellnow, *The*

Rhetorical Power of Popular Culture: Considering Mediated Texts (Thousand Oaks, CA: Sage, 2017).

12. On *Hamilton*, see especially Jeffrey P. Mehltretter Drury and Sara A. Mehltretter Drury, eds., *Rhetoric, Politics, and Hamilton: An American Musical* (New York: Peter Lang, 2021); on *The West Wing*, see especially Trevor Parry-Giles and Shawn J. Parry-Giles, *The Prime-Time Presidency: The West Wing and US Nationalism* (Champaign-Urbana: University of Illinois Press, 2010); and Christopher J. Wernecke and Ann E. Burnette, "'That Was the First Time in History That Anyone Bothered to Write That Down': Mythologizing the Declaration of Independence in *The West Wing*," in Mary E. Stuckey, ed., *Used, Abused, and Sidelined: Debating the Declaration* (University Park: Penn State University Press, forthcoming).

13. Wernecke and Burnette, "'That Was the First Time in History That Anyone Bothered to Write That Down.'"

14. For a clear and concise summary of this historiography, see Bradford J. Vivian, "Jefferson's Other," *Quarterly Journal of Speech* 88, no. 3(2002): 284–302, esp. 285–287.

15. Barbara Oberg, "Introduction," 1–21, in Robert M. S. McDonald, ed., *Thomas Jefferson Lives: Biographers and the Battle for History* (Charlottesville: University of Virginia Press, 2019), 5–6.

16. Fawn M. Brodie, *Thomas Jefferson: An Intimate History* (New York: Norton, 1974).

17. Annette Gordon-Reed, "Introduction," xv–xxiv, in Brodie, *Thomas Jefferson*.

18. For the best discussion of the historiography of Jefferson's private life and Brodie's contribution to it, see Annette Gordon-Reed, "'That Woman': Fawn Brodie and Thomas Jefferson's Intimate History," 265–278, in McDonald, *Thomas Jefferson Lives*.

19. Annette Gordon-Reed, *Thomas Jefferson and Sally Hemings: An American Controversy* (Charlottesville: University Press of Virginia, 1997).

20. Annette Gordon-Reed and Peter S. Onuf, *"Most Blessed of the Patriarchs": Thomas Jefferson and the Empire of the Imagination* (New York: Liveright, 2016), xiv–xv.

21. Gordon-Reed and Onuf, *"Most Blessed of the Patriarchs,"* 146.

22. Mary E. Stuckey, *Defining Americans: The Presidency and National Identity* (Lawrence: University Press of Kansas, 2023), 28–32.

23. Moses considers Jefferson to favor a kind of ethnic nationalism. See William Jeremiah Moses, *Thomas Jefferson: A Modern Prometheus* (New York: Cambridge University Press, 2019), 41.

24. Keith Thompson, *Jefferson's Shadow: The Story of His Science* (New Haven, CT: Yale University Press, 2012), 134.

25. Jon Meacham, *Thomas Jefferson: The Art of Power* (New York: Random House, 2013), 477.

26. Joseph J. Ellis, *The Quartet: Orchestrating the Second American Revolution* (New York: Vintage, 2015), xix; Richard Hofstadter, *The American Political Tradition: And the Men Who Made It* (New York: Vintage, [1948] 1973), 26.

27. Roger C. Kennedy, *Mr. Jefferson's Lost Cause: Land, Farmers, Slavery, and the Louisiana Purchase* (New York: Oxford University Press, 2003), 73.

28. Garry Wills, *"Negro President": Jefferson and the Slave Power* (Boston: Houghton Mifflin, 2003), 8–9.

29. Wills, *"Negro President,"* 9.

30. See, for example, Eric Foner, *The Story of American Freedom* (New York: Norton, 1998), 3.

31. Eva Sheppard Wolfe, *Race and Liberty in the New Nation: Emancipation in Virginia from the Revolution to Nat Turner's Rebellion* (Baton Rouge: Louisiana State University Press, 2006), xiii.

32. See, for example, Michael J. Lee and R. Jarrod Atchison. *We Are Not One People: Secession and Separatism in American Politics Since 1776* (New York: Oxford, 2022); James W. Loewen and Edward W. Sebesta, eds., *The Confederate and Neo-Confederate Reader: The "Great Truth" about the "Lost Cause"* (Jackson: University Press of Mississippi, 2010).

33. See, for example, Nikole Hannah-Jones et al., eds. *The 1619 Project: A New American Origin Story* (London: W. H. Allen, 2021).

34. Wills, *"Negro President,"* xiii.

35. Wolfe, *Race and Liberty in the New Nation*, ix–xi.

36. Jon Meacham, ed., *In the Hands of the People: Thomas Jefferson on Equality, Faith, Freedom, and the Art of Citizenship* (New York: Random House, 2020), 3. See also Kevin R. C. Gutzman, *The Jeffersonians: The Visionary Presidencies of Jefferson, Madison, and Monroe* (New York: St. Martin's Press, 2022), 16.

37. Francis D. Cogliano, *Thomas Jefferson: Reputation and Legacy* (Charlottesville: University of Virginia Press, 2006), 200.

38. Ellis, *The Quartet*, xix, 145.

39. Meacham, *Thomas Jefferson*, 8.

40. Thomas Jefferson, *Notes on the State of Virginia*, ed. Thomas Shuffleton (New York: Penguin, 1998), Query XVIII.

41. That letter is available here: https://www.loc.gov/exhibits/jefferson/159.html.

42. Wolfe, *Race and Liberty in the New Nation*, 102–103.

43. Meacham, *Thomas Jefferson*, 475; Garry Wills, *"Negro President,"* 24.

44. You can see a video of the attraction at https://www.youtube.com/watch?v=nkxOdzVbrrs.

45. Robert Ebert, Review of *Jefferson in Paris*, April 7, 1995, https://www.rogerebert.com/reviews/jefferson-in-paris-1995.

46. Eve Zibart, Review of *Jefferson in Paris*, April 7, 1995, https://www.washingtonpost.com/wp-srv/style/longterm/movies/videos/jeffersoninparispg13zibart_c01065.htm.

47. CBS Productions, *Sally Hemings: An American Scandal*, 2000.

48. On the agency exercised by enslaved people, see Eugene Genovese, *Roll Jordan Roll: The South That the Sales Made* (New York: Vintage, 1976); Daive A. Dunkley, *Agency of the Enslaved: Jamaica and the Culture of Freedom in the Atlantic World* (New York: Lexington Books, 2012); Karen Cook Bell, "Fugitivity and

Enslaved Women's Agency in the Age of Revolution." *Journal of Women's History* 34, no. 4 (2022): 58–80.

49. Vivian, "Jefferson's Other," 293–294.

50. On plantations as memory sites, see Justine Wells, "Monumentality, Ruination, and the Milieux of Memory's Lessons from WEB DuBois," *Western Journal of Communication* 87, no. 3 (2023): 281–303.

51. Perry E. Carter, David Butler, and Owen Dwyer, "Defetishizing the Plantation: African Americans in the Memorialized South," *Historical Geography* 39, no. 1 (2011): 128–146, esp. 128.

52. Carter, Butler, and Dwyer, "Defetishizing the Plantation," 128–129.

53. Columbia Pictures, Jack Warner Production, *1776*, 1972.

54. He freed only a handful of slaves in his lifetime or in his will. Most of those he freed were members of the Hemings family.

55. See, for example, Merrill D. Peterson, *The Jefferson Image in the American Mind* (Charlottesville, VA: Thomas Jefferson Memorial Foundation, 1989), viii.

56. Ken Burns, *Thomas Jefferson*, PBS, 1997.

57. Nikole Hannah-Jones, "Democracy," 7–36, in Hannah-Jones et al., *The 1619 Project*, 11–12.

58. Miranda and McCarter, *Hamilton*, 52.

59. Miranda and McCarter, *Hamilton*, 161.

60. These criticism are reinforced in the text. Jefferson is willing to cut a deal with Hamilton on economic policy so that he can "work a little closer to home"; Miranda and McCarter, *Hamilton*, 188.

61. Christopher Bell, "*Hamilton* as Cosmoginic Myth," 69–85, in Mehltretter Drury and Mehltretter Drury, *Rhetoric, Politics, and Hamilton*, 81.

62. For the various complexities of Hamilton as a model and the role of race in *Hamilton*, see Mehltretter Drury and Mehltretter Drury, *Rhetoric, Politics, and Hamilton*.

63. For a detailed history of Monticello, see Stuart Gibboney, "Letter to the President, enclosing a report of the Thomas Jefferson Memorial Foundation," April 12, 1938, President's Personal File, 5285–5328, "PPF 5319, Thomas Jefferson Memorial Foundation," FDRL.

64. Carter, Butler, and Dwyer, "Defetishizing the Plantation," 130.

65. Meredith Stone et al., "Searching for the Enslaved in the 'Cradle of Democracy': Virginia's James River Plantation Websites and the Reproduction of Local Histories," *Southeastern Geographer* 56, no. 2 (2016): 203–222, esp. 203. For further discussions of how plantation tourist sites position life on plantations, see Edward E. Baptist, *The Half Has Never Been Told: Slavery and the Making of American Capitalism* (New York: Basic Books, 2014); Candace F. Bright and David L. Butler, "Webwashing the Tourism Plantation: Using Historic Websites to View Changes in the Representation of Slavery at Tourism Plantations," 31–47, in S. P. Hanna et al., eds., *Social Memory and Heritage Tourism Methodologies* (Abingdon, UK: Routledge, 2015); David L. Butler, "Whitewashing Plantations: The Commodification of a Slave-Free Antebellum South," *International Journal of Hospitality & Tourism Administration* 2, no. 3-4 (2001): 163–175; Jennifer

L. Eichstedt and Stephen Small, *Representations of Slavery: Race and Ideology in Southern Plantation Museums* (Washington, DC: Smithsonian, 2002); Antoinette T. Jackson, *Speaking for the Enslaved: Heritage Interpretation at Antebellum Plantation Sites* (New York: Routledge, 2016); Thomas C. Hubka, *Big House, Little House, Back House, Barn: The Connected Farm Buildings of New England* (Lincoln: University Press of Nebraska, 2004).

66. Shevaun E. Watson and Cathy Rex, "New Directions for Research: Bringing Together Public Memory, Early America, and Tourism Studies," 1–17, in Cathy Rex and Shevaun E. Watson, eds., *Public Memory, Race, and Heritage Tourism of Early America* (New York: Routledge, 2022), 6.

67. On tourism sites depicting "the South," see Kristin Poirot and Shevaun E. Watson, "Memories of Freedom and White Resilience: Place, Tourism, and Urban Slavery," *Rhetoric Society Quarterly* 45, no. 2 (2015): 91–116.

68. E. Arnold Modlin, Derek H. Alderman, and Glenn W. Gentry, "Tour Guides as Creators of Empathy: The Role of Affective Inequality in Marginalizing the Enslaved at Plantation House Museums," *Tourist Studies* 11, no. 1 (2011):3–19, esp. 15.

69. Ira Berlin, "Coming to Terms with Slavery in Twenty-First Century America," 1–17, in James Oliver Horton and Lois E. Horton, eds., *Slavery and Public History: The Tough Stuff of American Memory* (New York: New Press, 2006), 1–6.

70. Some sites are dedicated to primarily focusing on slavery and the enslaved. See, for example, the Whitney Plantation, https://whitneyplantation.org/.

71. On the importance of Monticello to Jefferson, see Gordon-Reed and Onuf, *"Most Blessed of the Patriarchs,"* 27, 57.

72. You can see its mission statement here: https://www.monticello.org/thomas-jefferson-foundation/mission-and-vision-statement/.

73. Thomas Jefferson Foundation, "Site of Conscience," accessed March 3, 2025, https://www.monticello.org/thomas-jefferson-foundation/site-of-conscience/.

74. James W. Loewen, *Lies Across America: What Our Historic Sites Get Wrong*, 20th anniversary ed. (New York: New Press, 2009), 355.

75. Thomas Jefferson Foundation, "Thomas Jefferson's Monticello," accessed March 3, 2025, https://www.monticello.org/.

76. Information about the tours is available here: https://www.monticello.org/visit/tickets-tours/?ref=pnav.

77. Modlin, Alderman, and Gentry, "Tour Guides as Creators of Empathy," 8.

78. Gayle Jessup White, *Reclamation: Sally Hemings, Thomas Jefferson, and a Descendant's Search for Her Family's Lasting Legacy* (New York: Harper Collins, 2021), xv–xvi.

79. Clint Smith, *How the Word Is Passed: A Reckoning with the History of Slavery Across America* (New York: Back Bay Books, 2021), 42.

80. Meacham, *In the Hands of the People*, 76.

81. On this question, I'm thinking, for example, of the criticism of Oliver Stone's *JFK*. See William D. Romanowski, "Oliver Stone's JFK: Commercial

Filmmaking, Cultural History, and Conflict," *Journal of Popular Film and Televi-sion* 21, no. 2 (1993): 63–71.

82. Moses, *Thomas Jefferson*, 97.

Chapter 5: The Children's Jefferson

1. An oath of allegiance has been required since 1790, but the words of the current oath date to 1929 and were emended in 1950. The oath can be found on the website of the U.S. Citizenship and Immigrations Services (accessed March 4, 2025), https://www.uscis.gov/citizenship/learn-about-citizenship/the-naturali zation-interview-and-test/naturalization-oath-of-allegiance-to-the-united-sta tes-of-america#:~:text=%22I%20hereby%20declare%2C%20on%20oath,the%20 United%20States%20of%20America.

2. YouTube, "Thomas Jefferson for Kids," November 10, 2016, https://www .google.com/search?q=teach+chldren+thomas+jefferson&rlz=1C1GCEB_enUS9 76US976&oq=teach+chldren+thomas+jefferson&gs_lcrp=EgZjaHJvbWUyBgg AEEUYOTIHCAEQIRifBdIBCDgzMTNqMG05qAIAsAIA&sourceid=chr ome&ie=UTF-8#fpstate=ive&vld=cid:dc25dedo,vid:uL_6b-k7aVI,st:o.

3. See, for example, "4th of July for Kids," https://www.youtube.com/watch?v= XoNIsoqT5so; PBS, "Independence Day," https://www.google.com/search?q=te ach+chldren+independece+day&rlz=1C1GCEB_enUS976US976&oq=teach+ch ldren+independece+day&gs_lcrp=EgZjaHJvbWUyBggAEEUYOTIHCAEQI RifBdIBCDU1MTNqMG03qAIAsAIA&sourceid=chrome&ie=UTF-8#fpsta te=ive&vld=cid:f6d19df4,vid:BvS58YqMzRM,st:o.

4. Sara VanderHaagen, "Political Truths: Black Feminist Agency and Public Memory in Biographies of Children," *Women's Studies in Communication* 35, no. 1 (2012): 18–41; Sara C. VanderHaagen, *Children's Biographies of African Ameri-can Women: Rhetoric, Public Memory, and Agency* (Columbia: University of South Caroline Press, 2018).

5. For more on these controversies, see Francesca Lopez and Christine E. Sleeter, *Critical Race Theory and Its Critics: Implications for Teaching and Research* (New York: Teachers College Press, 2023); Bradford Vivian, *Campus Misinfor-mation: The Real Threat to Free Speech in American Higher Education* (New York: Oxford University Press, 2023).

6. Kay E. Vandergrift, "Introduction," vii–xi, in Kay E. Vandergrift, ed., *Ways of Knowing: Literature and the Intellectual Life of Children* (Lanham, MD: Scarecrow Press, 1996), vii.

7. Margaret Mailett, *Choosing and Using Fiction and Non-Fiction 3–11: A Com-prehensive Guide for Teachers and Student Teachers* (New York: Routledge, 2010), 7.

8. For discussions of this argument from various points of view, see, for exam-ple, Timothy E. Cook, "The Newberry Award as Political Education: Children's Literature and Cultural Reproduction," *Polity* 17, no. 3 (1985): 421–425; Gale Ea-ton, *Well-Dressed Role Models: The Portrayal of Women in Biographies for Children* (Lanham, MD: Scarecrow, 2006); William H. Epstein, "Inducing Biography," *Children's Literature Association Quarterly* 12, no. 4 (1987): 177–179; Perry Nodel-man, *The Pleasures of Children's Literature* (New York: Longman, 1992); John E.

Wills, "Lives and Other Stories: Neglected Aspects of the Teacher's Art," *History Teacher*, no. 1 (1992): 33–49; Rob Wilson, "Producing American Selves: The Form of the American Biography," *boundary 2*, 18, no. 2 (1991): 104–129.

9. See Virginia Department of Education, "Standards of Learning for History and Social Science," accessed March 4, 2025, https://www.doe.virginia.gov/teach ing-learning-assessment/k-12-standards-instruction/history-and-social-science /standards-of-learning.

10. Pat Brisson, "Writing for Children: One Author's Experience," 289–302, in Vandergrift, *Ways of Knowing*, 297.

11. On the persuasiveness of illustrations, see Mailett, *Choosing and Using Fiction and Non-Fiction 3–11*, 220.

12. See, for example, Peggy Thomas, *Thomas Jefferson Grows a Nation* (Honesdale, PA: Calkins Creek Books, 2015), 2.

13. Although they are never directly juxtaposed, see, for example, the various activities Jefferson and his family and those he enslaved are depicted as participating in by Elizabeth V. Chew, *Thomas Jefferson: A Day at Monticello* (New York: Abrams Books for Young Readers, 2014).

14. Mailett, *Choosing and Using Fiction and Non-Fiction 3–11*, 255.

15. Mailett, *Choosing and Using Fiction and Non-Fiction 3–11*, 257. See also Vandergrift, "Introduction," vii.

16. I am thinking here primarily of Edward Coles; there are likely others of whom I am not aware. On Coles, see Thomas Jefferson Foundation, "Edward Coles," accessed March 5, 2025, https://www.monticello.org/research-education /thomas-jefferson-encyclopedia/edward-coles/.

17. Gail Boldt and Felicity McArdle, "Introduction: Young Children, Pedagogy, and the Arts: Ways of Seeing," 3–18, in Felicity McArdle and Gail Boldt, eds., *Young Children, Pedagogy, and the Arts: Ways of Seeing* (New York: Routledge, 2013), 11. See also Evelyn Arizpe and Morag Styles, *Children Reading Picture Books: Interpreting Visual Texts*, 2nd ed. (New York: Routledge, 2016).

18. See, for example, the biographies of Sojourner Truth studied by Sara VanderHaagen. VanderHaagen, "Practical Truths"; VanderHaagen, *Children's Biographies of African American Women*.

19. For example, the editors of American Heritage produced a book titled *Thomas Jefferson and His World*, in which they claim, "Slavery presented an even greater challenge [than religious freedom]. Jefferson thought it to be as bad for masters as for slaves. He never bought a slave himself, but he had acquired approximately 150 by inheritance and marriage. He did not free them because the practice 'as far as I can judge from the experiments . . . made to give liberty, or rather, to abandon persons whose habits have been framed in slavery, is like abandoning children.'" Editors of American Heritage, *Thomas Jefferson and His World* (New York: Golden Press, 1960), 52. For a similar treatment see Anne Colver, *Thomas Jefferson: Author of Independence* (Champaign, IL: Garrard Publishing, 1963).

20. On the rhetorical aspects of borders, see, among many others, Josue David Cisneros, "(Re)Bordering the Civic Imaginary: Rhetoric, Hybridity, and

Citizenship in *La Gran Marcha*," *Quarterly Journal of Speech* 97, no. 1 (2011): 26–49; Lisa A. Flores, "Constructing Rhetorical Borders: Peons, Illegal Aliens, and Competing Narratives of Immigration," *Critical Studies in Media Communication* 20, no. 4 (2003): 362–387.

21. See, for example, the discussions found in Vanessa Beasley, *You, the People: American National Identity in Presidential Rhetoric* (College Station: Texas A&M University Press, 2011); Mary E. Stuckey, *Defining Americans: The Presidency and National Identity* (Lawrence: University Press of Kansas, 2023).

22. It also required a series of court cases, but that is too long a story to tell here.

23. Eleni Andreouli and Caroline Howarth. "National Identity, Citizenship and Immigration: Putting Identity in Context," *Journal for the Theory of Social Behaviour* 43, no. 3 (2013): 361–382.

24. Leslie A. Hahner, *To Become an American: Immigrants and Americanization Campaigns of the Early Twentieth Century* (East Lansing: Michigan State University Press, 2017).

25. Ideally, belonging as a paradigm can help overcome those hierarchies. See John A. Powell and Stephen Menendian, *Belonging without Othering: How We Save Ourselves and the World* (Stanford, CA: Stanford University Press, 2024.

26. Gary Gerstle, *American Crucible: Race and Nation in the Twentieth Century* (Princeton, NJ: Princeton University Press, 2017); Rogers M. Smith, *Civic Ideals: Conflicting Visions of Citizenship in US History* (New Haven, CT: Yale University Press, 1997).

27. Rogers M. Smith, "'The American Creed' and American Identity: The Limits of Liberal Citizenship in the United States," *Western Political Quarterly* 41, no. 2 (1988): 225–251.

28. Joan Holub and Daniel Roode, *This Little President: A Presidential Primer* (New York: Little Simon, 2016), 3.

29. See, for example, Sonia W. Black, *Thomas Jefferson: Man of the People* (New York: Scholastic, 2021), 4; Maira Kalman, *Thomas Jefferson: Life, Liberty, and the Pursuit of Everything* (New York: Nancy Paulson Books, 2014), 7–16; Carol Greene, *Thomas Jefferson: Author, Inventor, President* (Danbury, CT: Children's Press, 1991), 5–6.

30. See, for example, Monica L. Rausch, *Great Americans: Thomas Jefferson* (Pleasantville, NY: Weekly Reader Books, 2007), 8.

31. Elizabeth Sirimarco, *Presidents of the United States: Thomas Jefferson Our Third President* (Mankato, MN: Child's World, 2009).

32. Sirimarco, *Presidents of the United States*, 7.

33. Black, *Thomas Jefferson*, 15. For similar treatments, see James Cross Giblin, *Thomas Jefferson: A Picture Book Biography* (New York: Scholastic, 1994), 20; Dennis Brindell Fradin, *Who Was Thomas Jefferson?* (New York: Random House, 2003), 3.

34. Greene, *Thomas Jefferson*, 21–22.

35. For a discussion of the moose story, see Keith Thompson, *Jefferson's Shadow: The Story of His Science* (New Haven, CT: Yale University Press, 2012), 9. For the

children's version, see Mara Rockliff, *Jefferson Measures a Moose* (Somerville, MA: Candlewick Press, 2020). See also Carrie Clickard, *Thomas Jefferson and the Great Mammoth Hunt: The True Story of the Quest for America's Biggest Bones* (New York: Simon & Schuster, 2019).

36. Rockliff, *Jefferson Measures a Moose*, 6.

37. Rockliff, *Jefferson Measures a Moose*, 11.

38. Rockliff, *Jefferson Measures a Moose*, 26.

39. Rockliff, *Jefferson Measures a Moose*, 30.

40. Rockliff, *Jefferson Measures a Moose*, 32.

41. Barb Rosenstock, *Thomas Jefferson Builds a Library* (Honesdale, PA: Calkins Creek, 2013), 8.

42. Rosenstock, *Thomas Jefferson Builds a Library*, 21.

43. Rosenstock, *Thomas Jefferson Builds a Library*, 25.

44. Rosenstock, *Thomas Jefferson Builds a Library*, 28.

45. Thomas, *Thomas Jefferson Grows a Nation*, esp. 7–11.

46. Thomas, *Thomas Jefferson Grows a Nation*, 1.

47. Thomas, *Thomas Jefferson Grows a Nation*, 1.

48. Thomas, *Thomas Jefferson Grows a Nation*, 2.

49. Thomas, *Thomas Jefferson Grows a Nation*, 22–24.

50. Thomas, *Thomas Jefferson Grows a Nation*, 26.

51. Thomas, *Thomas Jefferson Grows a Nation*, 35.

52. Sirimarco, *Presidents of the United States*, 11.

53. Thomas, *Thomas Jefferson Grows a Nation*, 36.

54. Thomas, *Thomas Jefferson Grows a Nation*, 37.

55. Miller, *Thomas Jefferson for Kids*, 123.

56. Miller, *Thomas Jefferson for Kids*, 124.

57. See, for example, John B. Severance, *Thomas Jefferson: Architect of Democracy* (New York: Clarion Books, 1998).

58. Black, *Thomas Jefferson*, 11.

59. Miller, *Thomas Jefferson for Kids*, 8.

60. Miller, *Thomas Jefferson for Kids*, 23.

61. Miller, *Thomas Jefferson for Kids*, 27.

62. Miller, *Thomas Jefferson for Kids*, 104.

63. Miller, *Thomas Jefferson for Kids*, 104.

64. Chew, *Thomas Jefferson*, iv.

65. Chew, *Thomas Jefferson*, 23.

66. Chew, *Thomas Jefferson*, 24–25.

67. See, for example, Jelani Memory, *A Kids Book About Racism* (akidsbookabout.com, 2019).

68. White House Historical Association and Untold History, "Untold History: The Enslaved Household of Thomas Jefferson," accessed March 4, 2025, https://www.whitehousehistory.org/videos/the-enslaved-household-of-thomas-jefferson.

69. Hasan Davis, *The Journey of York: The Unsung Hero of the Lewis and Clark Expedition* (North Mankato, ND: Capstone, 2019).

70. Davis, *The Journey of York*, 2.

71. Davis, *The Journey of York*, 19.

72. Davis, *The Journey of York*, 22, 31.

73. Davis, *The Journey of York*, 36.

74. Davis, *The Journey of York*, 38.

75. During the New Deal, for example, the Federal Writers Project, part of the Works Progress Administration, conducted a number of interviews with those who had been enslaved. See Library of Congress, "The WPA and the Slave Narrative Collection," accessed March 4, 2025, https://www.loc.gov/collections /slave-narratives-from-the-federal-writers-project-1936-to-1938/articles-and -essays/introduction-to-the-wpa-slave-narratives/wpa-and-the-slave-narrative -collection/.

76. Jonah Winter and Terry Widener, *My Name Is James Madison Hemings* (New York: Schwartz Wade Books, 2016). The interview was preserved by the Thomas Jefferson Heritage Society, "Madison Hemings Interview," accessed March 4, 2025, https://www.tjheritage.org/madison-hemings-interview.

77. Winter and Widener, *My Name Is James Madison Hemings*, flyleaf.

78. Winter and Widener, *My Name Is James Madison Hemings*, 1.

79. Winter and Widener, *My Name Is James Madison Hemings*, 6.

80. Winter and Widener, *My Name Is James Madison Hemings*, 22.

81. Winter and Widener, *My Name Is James Madison Hemings*, 23.

82. Judith St. George, *What Was the Lewis and Clark Expedition?* (New York: Penguin Workshop, 2014).

83. St. George, *What Was the Lewis and Clark Expedition*, 24.

84. VanderHaagen, "Plain Truths"; VanderHaagen, *Children's Biographies of African American Women*.

Conclusion

1. According to the American Presidency Project, he mentioned "Roosevelt" some three hundred times as president.

2. See, for example, Erika Doss, *Memorial Mania: Public Feeling in America* (Chicago: University of Chicago Press, 2012).

3. Valeska Hilbig, "Horatio Greenough's George Washington," August 1, 2017, Smithsonian Institution, https://www.si.edu/newsdesk/factsheets/horatio-gre enough-s-george-washington.

4. Franklin D. Roosevelt Presidential Library and Museum, "A Mighty Endeavor: D-Day," accessed March 4, 2025, https://www.fdrlibrary.org/d-day.

5. Michael E. Ruane, "FDR's Moving Fireside D Day Prayer to be Added to World War II Memorial," *Washington Post*, October 15, 2020, https://www.wash ingtonpost.com/history/2020/10/15/fdr-dday-fireside-chat-prayer/.

6. It is telling, for example, that a Confederate memorial was recently replaced by a statue of congressman and civil rights icon John Lewis. See Amanda Holpuch, "Statue of John Lewis Replaces a Confederate Memorial in Georgia," *New York Times*, August 18, 2024, https://www.nytimes.com/2024/08/18/us/john-lewis -statue-decatur-georgia.html.

7. Jon Meacham, *Thomas Jefferson: The Art of Power* (New York: Random House, 2013), 499.

8. Quoted in Andrew Burstein, *Democracy's Muse: How Thomas Jefferson Became an FDR Liberal, a Reagan Republican, and a Tea Party Fanatic, All the While Being Dead* (Charlottesville: University of Virginia Press, 2015), 196.

9. Burstein, *Democracy's Muse*, 128.

10. Burstein, *Democracy's Muse*, 194.

11. Jack N. Rakove, "What Remains of Thomas Jefferson?," *Wall Street Journal*, July 1, 2022, C1.

Selected Bibliography

Archival Sources
Authenticated transcripts of presidential speeches can be found at the American Presidency Project, a fully searchable online database. All speeches are identified by node number and can be found at https://www.presidency.ucsb.edu. It is abbreviated as APP.
Considerable material is also available from the Franklin D. Roosevelt Presidential Library in Hyde Park, New York. That material is cited by collection, box, and file name, and is abbreviated as FDRL.
National Park Service material can be found online, and includes web page information. All those links were operative as of August 2024.

Secondary Sources
Aden, Robert C., ed. *Rhetorics Haunting the National Mall: Displaced and Ephemeral Public Memories.* Lanham, MD: Lexington Books, 2018.
Aden, Robert C. *Upon the Ruins of Liberty: The President's House at Independence National Historical Park and Public Memory.* Philadelphia: Temple University Press, 2015.
Aden, Robert C., ed. *US Public Memory, Rhetoric, and the National Mall.* Lanham, MD: Lexington Books, 2018.
Aden, Roger C., Min Wa Han, Stephanie Norander, Michael E. Pfahl, Timothy P. Pollock Jr., and Stephanie L. Young. "Re-Collection: A Proposal for Refining the Study of Collective Memory and Its Places." *Communication Theory* 19, no. 3 (2009): 219–350.
Agnew, John A., and Jonathan M. Smith, eds. *American Space American Place: Geographies of the Contemporary United States.* Edinburgh: Edinburgh University Press, 2002.
Anderson, Benedict. *Imagined Communities.* London: Verso Books, 2016.
Anderson, Karrin Vasby. *Women, Feminism, and Pop Politics: From "Bitch" to "Badass" and Beyond.* New York: Peter Lang, 2018.
Andreouli, Eleni, and Caroline Howarth. "National Identity, Citizenship and Immigration: Putting Identity in Context." *Journal for the Theory of Social Behaviour* 43, no. 3 (2013): 361–382.

Angel, Adrianna, Michael L. Butterfield, and Nancy R. Gomez, eds. *Rhetorics of Democracy in the Americas*. University Park: Penn State University Press, 2021.

Arizpe, Evelyn, and Morag Styles. *Children Reading Picture Books: Interpreting Visual Texts*, 2nd ed. New York: Routledge, 2016.

Armitage, David. *The Declaration of Independence: A Global History*. Cambridge, MA: Harvard University Press, 2007.

Asen, Robert. "A Discourse Theory of Citizenship." *Quarterly Journal of Speech* 90, no. 2 (2004): 189–211.

Balthrop, V. William, Carole Blair, and Neil Michael. "The Presence of the Present: Hijacking 'the Good War'"? *Western Journal of Communication* 74, no. 2 (2010): 170–207.

Baptist, Edward E. *The Half Has Never Been Told: Slavery and the Making of American Capitalism*. New York: Basic Books, 2014.

Beasley, Vanessa. "The Rhetoric of Ideological Consensus in the United States: American Principles and American Pose in Presidential Inaugurals." *Communication Monographs* 68, no. 2 (2001): 169–183.

Beasley, Vanessa. *You, the People: American National Identity in Presidential Rhetoric*. College Station: Texas A&M University Press, 2011.

Bederman, Gail. *Manliness and Civilization: A Cultural History of Gender and Race in the United States, 1880–1917*. Chicago: University of Chicago Press, 1995.

Beitzinger, Alphonse J. *A History of American Political Thought*. New York: Harper & Row, 1972.

Bell, Karen Cook. "Fugitivity and Enslaved Women's Agency in the Age of Revolution." *Journal of Women's History* 34, no. 4 (2022): 58–80.

Benton-Short, Lisa. *The National Mall: No Ordinary Public Space*. Toronto: University of Toronto Press, 2016.

Bergman, Teresa. *Exhibiting Patriotism: Creating and Contesting Interpretations of American Historic Sites*. Walnut Creek, CA: Left Coast Press, 2013.

Biesecker, Barbara A. "Remembering World War II: The Rhetoric and Politics of National Commemoration of the 21st Century." *Quarterly Journal of Speech* 88, no. 4 (2002): 393–409.

Billig, Michael. *Banal Nationalism*. London: Sage, 1995.

Black, Sonia W. *Thomas Jefferson: Man of the People*. New York: Scholastic, 2021.

Blair, Carole, Marsha S. Jepperson, and Enrico Pucci Jr. "Public Memorializing in Postmodernity: The Vietnam Veterans' Memorial as Prototype." *Quarterly Journal of Speech* 77, no. 3 (1991): 263–288.

Bodnar, John. *Remaking American Public Memory: Commemoration and Patriotism in the Twentieth Century*. Princeton, NJ: Princeton University Press, 1992.

Boles, John. *Jefferson: Architect of American Liberty*. New York: Basic Books, 2017.

Brodie, Fawn M. *Thomas Jefferson: An Intimate History*. New York: Norton, 1974.

Browne, Stephen H. "'The Circle of Our Felicities': Thomas Jefferson's First Inaugural Address and the Rhetoric of Nationhood." *Rhetoric & Public Affairs* 5, no. 3 (2002): 409–438.

Browne, Stephen H. *Jefferson's Call for Nationhood*. College Station: Texas A&M University Press, 2003.

Browne, Stephen H. "Reading Public Memory in Daniel Webster's *Plymouth Rock Oration.*" *Western Journal of Communication* 57, no. 4 (1993): 464–477.

Brummett, Barry. *Rhetoric in Popular Culture.* Thousand Oaks, CA: Sage , 2022.

Brummett, Barry. *Uncovering Hidden Rhetorics: Social Issues in Disguise.* Thousand Oaks, CA: Sage, 2008.

Burke, Kenneth. *Language as Symbolic Action.* Berkeley: University of California Press, 1966.

Burstein, Andrew. *Democracy's Muse: How Thomas Jefferson Became an FDR Liberal, a Reagan Republican, and a Tea Party Fanatic, All the While Being Dead.* Charlottesville: University of Virginia Press, 2015.

Bush, Howard K., Jr. *American Declarations: Rebellion and Resistance in American Cultural History.* Champaign-Urbana: University of Illinois Press, 1999.

Butler, David L. "Whitewashing Plantations: The Commodification of a Slave-Free Antebellum South." *International Journal of Hospitality & Tourism Administration* 2, no. 3-4 (2001): 163–175.

Campbell, Karlyn Kohrs, and Kathleen Hall Jamieson. *Presidents Creating the Presidency: Deeds Done in Words.* Chicago: University of Chicago Press, 2008.

Carney, Zoë Hess, and Mary E. Stuckey. "The World as the American Frontier: Racialized Presidential War Rhetoric." *Southern Communication Journal* 80, no. 3 (2015): 163–188.

Carter, Perry E., David Butler, and Owen Dwyer. "Defetishizing the Plantation: African Americans in the Memorialized South." *Historical Geography* 39 no. 1 (2011): 128–146.

Casey, Edward S. *Remembering: A Phenomenological Study.* Bloomington: Indiana University Press, 2000.

Ceccarelli, Leah. *On the Frontier of Science: An American Rhetoric of Exploration and Exploitation.* East Lansing: Michigan State University Press, 2013.

Charland, Maurice. "Constitutive Rhetoric: The Case of the *Peuple Quebecois.*" *Quarterly Journal of Speech* 73, no. 2 (1987): 133–150.

Charland, Maurice. "The Rhetoricians' Identity." *Rhetor: The Journal of the Canadian Society for the Study of Rhetoric* 8, no. 1 (2021): 26–32.

Chew, Elizabeth V. *Thomas Jefferson: A Day at Monticello.* New York: Abrams Books for Young Readers, 2014.

Chronis, Athinodoros. "The Staging of Contested Servicescapes." *Journal of Service Research* 22, no. 4 (2019): 456–473.

Cisneros, Josue David. "(Re)Bordering the Civic Imaginary: Rhetoric, Hybridity, and Citizenship in *La Gran Marcha.*" *Quarterly Journal of Speech* 97, no. 1 (2011): 26–49.

Clark, Gregory. *Rhetorical Landscapes in America: Variations on a Theme from Kenneth Burke.* Columbia: University of South Carolina Press, 2004.

Clickard, Carrie. *Thomas Jefferson and the Great Mammoth Hunt: The True Story of the Quest for America's Biggest Bones.* New York: Simon & Schuster, 2019.

Cogliano, Francis D. *Thomas Jefferson: Reputation and Legacy.* Charlottesville: University of Virginia Press, 2006.

Cole, John Y. *America's Greatest Library: An Illustrated History of the Library of Congress.* London: D. Giles, 2017.

Colver, Anne. *Thomas Jefferson: Author of Independence.* Champaign, IL: Garrard Publishing, 1963.

Condit, Celeste Michelle. *Decoding Abortion Rhetoric: Communicating Social Change.* Champaign-Urbana: University of Illinois Press, 1990.

Condit, Celeste Michelle, and John Louis Lucaites. *Crafting Equality: America's Anglo-African word.* Chicago: University of Chicago Press, 1993.

Confino, Alon. "Collective Memory and Cultural History: Problems of Method." *American Historical Review* 102, no. 5 (1997): 1386–1403.

Cook, Timothy E. "The Newberry Award as Political Education: Children's Literature and Cultural Reproduction." *Polity* 17, no. 3 (1985): 421–425.

Covington, Brooke. "Unpacking the Vernacular Camouflage of Virginia Tech's April 16th Memorial." *Western Journal of Communication* (2022): 1–21.

Cox, Karen L. *No Common Ground: Confederate Monuments and the Ongoing Fight for Racial Justice.* Chapel Hill: University of North Carolina, 2021.

Craughwell, Thomas J. *Thomas Jefferson's Crème Brûlée: How a Founding Father and His Slave James Hemings Brought French Cuisine to America.* Philadelphia: Quirk Books, 2012.

Crowe, Julie Homchick. "Correction to: Contagion, Quarantine and Constitutive Rhetoric: Embodiment, Identity and the 'Potential Victim' of Infectious Disease." *Journal of Medical Humanities* 43, no. 3 (2022): 529–530.

Dahl, Adam. *Empire of the People: Settler Colonialism and the Foundations of Modern Democratic Thought.* Lawrence: University Press of Kansas, 2018.

Davis, Hasan. *The Journey of York: The Unsung Hero of the Lewis and Clark Expedition.* North Mankato, ND: Capstone, 2019.

Diaz-Espino, Ovidio. *How Wall Street Created a Nation: JP Morgan, Teddy Roosevelt, and the Panama Canal.* Primedia E-launch, 2014.

Dickinson, Greg, Brian L. Ott, and Eric Aoki. "Memory and Myth at the Buffalo Bill Museum." *Western Journal of Communication* 69, no. 2 (2005): 85–108.

Dickinson, Greg, Carole Blair, and Brian L. Ott, eds. *Places of Public Memory: The Rhetoric of Museums and Memorials.* Tuscaloosa: University of Alabama Press, 2010.

Donofrio, Theresa Ann. "Ground Zero and Place-Making Authority: The Conservative Metaphors in 9/11 Families' 'Take Back the Memorial' Rhetoric." *Western Journal of Communication* 74, no. 2 (2010): 150–169.

Dorsey, Leroy G. "The Frontier Myth and Presidential Rhetoric: Theodore Roosevelt's Campaign for Conservation." *Western Journal of Communication* 59, no. 1 (1995): 1–19.

Dorsey, Leroy G., and Rachel M. Harlow. "'We Want Americans Pure and Simple': Theodore Roosevelt and the Myth of Americanism." *Rhetoric & Public Affairs* 6, no. 1 (2003): 55–78.

Doss, Erika. *Memorial Mania: Public Feeling in America.* Chicago: University of Chicago Press, 2012.

Dow, Bonnie J. "Fixing Feminism: Women's Liberation and the Rhetoric of Television Documentary." *Quarterly Journal of Speech* 90, no. 1 (2004): 53–80.

Dunkley, Daive A. *Agency of the Enslaved: Jamaica and the Culture of Freedom in the Atlantic World.* New York: Lexington Books, 2012.

Dunn, Jennifer C. "Critical Rhetoric in the Age of the (First) Reality TV President: A Critique of Freedom and Domination." *International Journal of Communication* 14 (2020): 813–830.

Eaton, Gale. *Well-Dressed Role Models: The Portrayal of Women in Biographies for Children.* Lanham, MD: Scarecrow, 2006.

Editors of American Heritage. *Thomas Jefferson and His World.* New York: Golden Press, 1960.

Eichstedt, Jennifer L., and Stephen Small. *Representations of Slavery: Race and Ideology in Southern Plantation Museums.* Washington, DC: Smithsonian, 2002.

Ellis, Joseph. *American Sphinx: The Character of Thomas Jefferson.* New York: Alfred A. Knopf, 1997.

Ellis, Joseph. *The Quartet: Orchestrating the Second American Revolution.* New York: Vintage, 2015.

Encyclopedia Britannica. *The Founding Fathers: The Essential Guide to the Men Who Made America.* Hoboken, NJ: John Wiley &Sons, 2007.

Engels, Jeremy. "Disciplining Jefferson: The Man within the Breast and the Rhetorical Norms of Producing Order." *Rhetoric & Public Affairs* 9, no. 3 (2006): 411–435.

Epstein, William H. "Inducing Biography." *Children's Literature Association Quarterly* 12, no. 4 (1987): 177–179.

Fabre, Genevieve, and Robert O'Meally, eds. *History and Memory in American Culture.* New York: Oxford University Press, 1994.

Farrell, Thomas B. "The Weight of Rhetoric: Studies in Cultural Delirium." *Philosophy & Rhetoric* 41, no. 4 (2008): 467–487.

Fitzmaurice, Megan Irene. "Commemorative Privilege in National Statuary Hall: Spatial Constructions of Racial Citizenship." *Southern Communication Journal* 81, no. 4 (2016): 252–262.

Flores, Lisa A. "Constructing Rhetorical Borders: Peons, Illegal Aliens, and Competing Narratives of Immigration." *Critical Studies in Media Communication* 20, no. 4 (2003): 362–387.

Foner, Eric. *The Story of American Freedom.* New York: Norton, 1999.

Fradin, Dennis Brindell. *Who Was Thomas Jefferson?* New York: Random House, 2003.

Freeman, Joanne B., and Johann N. Neem. *Jeffersonians in Power: The Rhetoric of Opposition Meets the Realities of Governing.* Charlottesville: University of Virginia Press, 2019.

Fuller, Linda. *Sport, Rhetoric, and Gender: Historical Perspectives and Media Representations.* New York: Springer, 2006.

Gallagher, Victoria. "Memory and Reconciliation in the Birmingham Civil Rights Institute." *Rhetoric & Public Affairs* 2, no. 2 (1999): 303–320.

Gardella, Peter. *American Civil Religion: What Americans Hold Sacred.* New York: Oxford University Press, 2014.

Garrison, Justin D. *An Empire of Ideals: The Chimeric Imagination of Ronald Reagan.* New York: Routledge, 2013.

Genovese, Eugene. *Roll Jordan Roll: The South That the Sales Made.* New York: Vintage, 1976.

Gerstle, Gary. *American Crucible: Race and Nation in the Twentieth Century.* Princeton, NJ: Princeton University Press, 2017.

Giblin, James Cross. *Thomas Jefferson: A Picture Book Biography.* New York: Scholastic, 1994.

Gieryn, Thomas F. *Truth Spots: How Places Make People Believe.* Chicago: University of Chicago Press, 2018.

Gillis, John R., ed., *Commemoration: The Politics of National Identity.* Princeton, NJ: Princeton University Press, 1994.

Goehring, Charles, and George N. Dionisopoulos. "Identification by Antithesis: *The Turner Diaries* as Constitutive Rhetoric." *Southern Communication Journal* 78, no. 5 (2013): 369–386.

Goggins, Sydney. "Reshaping Public Memory in the *1619 Project*: Rhetorical Interventions Against Selective Forgetting." *Museums and Social Issues* 14, no. 102 (2019): 60–73.

Golden, James L., and Alan L. Golden. *Thomas Jefferson and the Rhetoric of Virtue.* Lanham, MD: Rowman & Littlefield, 2002.

Gordon-Reed, Annette. *Thomas Jefferson and Sally Hemings: An American Controversy.* Charlottesville: University of Virginia Press, 1998.

Gordon-Reed, Annette, and Peter S. Onuf. *"Most Blessed of the Patriarchs": Thomas Jefferson and the Empire of the Imagination.* New York: Liveright, 2016.

Grahame-Smith, Seth. *Abraham Lincoln, Vampire Hunter.* London: Hackett, 2010.

Greene, Carol. *Thomas Jefferson: Author, Inventor, President.* Danbury, CT: Children's Press, 1991.

Greene, Julie. *The Canal Builders: Making America's Empire at the Panama Canal.* New York: Penguin, 2009.

Groom, Winston. *The Patriots: Alexander Hamilton, Thomas Jefferson, John Adams, and the Making of America.* Washington, DC: National Geographic, 2020.

Gross, Alan G. "Lincoln's Use of Constitutive Metaphors." *Rhetoric & Public Affairs* 7, no. 2 (2004): 173–189.

Gruenwald, Tim. *Curating America's Painful Past: Memory, Museums, and the National Imagination.* Lawrence: University Press of Kansas, 2021.

Gutzman, Kevin R. C. *The Jeffersonians: The Visionary Presidencies of Jefferson, Madison, and Monroe.* New York: St. Martin's Press, 2022.

Hahner, Leslie A. *To Become an American: Immigrants and Americanization Campaigns of the Early Twentieth Century.* East Lansing: Michigan State University Press, 2017.

Halbwachs, Maurice. *On Collective* Memory, edited, translated, and with an introduction by Lewis A. Coser. Chicago: University of Chicago Press, 1992.

Hanna, S. P., E. A. Modlin Jr., A. P. Carter, and D. L. Butler, eds. *Social Memory and Heritage Tourism Methodologies*. Abingdon, UK: Routledge, 2015.

Hannah-Jones, Nikole, Caitlin Roper, Ilena Sherman, and Jake Silverstein, eds. *The 1619 Project: A New American Origin Story*. London: W. H. Allen, 2021.

Harris-Moore, Deborah. *Media and the Rhetoric of Body Perfection: Cosmetic Surgery, Weight Loss and Beauty in Popular Culture*. New York: Routledge, 2016.

Hartnett, Stephen J., Patrick Shaou-Whea Dodge, and Lisa B. Keranen. "Postcolonial Remembering in Taiwan: 228 and Transitional Justice as 'The End of Fear.'" *Journal of International and Intercultural Communication* 13, no. 3 (2020): 238–256.

Haskins, Ekatarina. *Popular Memories: Participatory Culture and Democratic Citizenship*. Columbia: University of South Carolina Press, 2015.

Hoerl, Kristen. "Selective Amnesia and Racial Transcendence in News Coverage of President Obama's Inauguration." *Quarterly Journal of Speech* 98, no. 2 (2012): 178–202.

Hofstadter, Richard. *The American Political Tradition: And the Men Who Made It*. New York: Vintage, [1948] 1973.

Holub, Joan, and Daniel Roode. *This Little President: A Presidential Primer*. New York: Little Simon, 2016.

Horton, James Oliver, and Lois E. Horton, eds. *Slavery and Public History: The Tough Stuff of American Memory*. New York: New Press, 2006.

Hubka, Thomas C. *Big House, Little House, Back House, Barn: The Connected Farm Buildings of New England*. Lincoln: University Press of Nebraska, 2004.

Hyde, Michael, ed. *The Ethos of Rhetoric*. Columbia: University of South Carolina Press, 2004.

Irwin-Zarecka, Iwona. *Frames of Remembrance: The Dynamics of Collective Memory*. New Brunswick, ME: Transaction, 1994.

Jackson, Antoinette T. *Speaking for the Enslaved: Heritage Interpretation at Antebellum Plantation Sites*. New York: Routledge, 2016.

Jacobson, David. *Place and Belonging in America*. Baltimore: Johns Hopkins University Press, 2002.

Jasinski, James. "Constitutive Rhetoric," in *Sourcebook on Rhetoric: Key Concepts in Rhetorical Studies*. Thousand Oaks, CA: Sage, 2001.

Jayne, Allen. *Jefferson's Declaration of Independence: Origins, Philosophy, and Theology*. Lexington: University Press of Kentucky, 1998.

Jefferson, Thomas. *Notes on the State of Virginia*, ed. Thomas Shuffleton. New York: Penguin, 1998.

Johnson, Nuala C., Richard H. Schein, and Jamie Winders, eds. *The Wiley-Blackwell Companion to Cultural Geography*. New York: John Wiley & Sons, 2013.

Johnson, Walter. *The Broken Heart of St. Louis and the Violent History of the United States*. New York: Basic Books, 2020.

Jones, Alfred Haworth. "The Search for a Useable American Past in the New Deal Era." *American Quarterly* 23, no. 5 (1971): 710–724.

Hertzog, George B., Jr. *Battling for the National Parks.* Mt. Kisco, NY: Moyer Bell, 1988.

Hosner, Charles B., Jr. *Preservation Comes of Age: From Williamsburg to the National Trust, 1926–1949.* Charlottesville: University of Virginia Press, 1981.

Jorgensen-Earp, Cheryl, and Lori Lanziotti. "Public Memory and Private Grief: The Construction of Shrines at the Sites of Public Tragedy." *Quarterly Journal of Speech* 84, no. 2 (1998): 150–170.

Kalman, Maira. *Thomas Jefferson: Life, Liberty, and the Pursuit of Everything.* New York: Nancy Paulson Books, 2014.

Kammen, Michael. *Mystic Chords of Memory: The Transformation of Tradition in American Culture.* New York: Vintage, 1993.

Kaplan, Lawrence S. *Thomas Jefferson: Westward the Course of Empire.* Wilmington, DE: Scholarly Resources, 1998.

Kelly, Casey Ryan. "The Wounded Man: Foxcatcher and the Incoherence of White Masculine Victimhood." *Communication and Critical/Cultural Studies* 15, no. 2 (2018): 161–178.

Kennedy, Roger C. *Mr. Jefferson's Lost Cause: Land, Farmers, Slavery, and the Louisiana Purchase.* New York: Oxford University Press, 2003.

Kennedy, Tammie M., Joyce Irene Middleton, and Krista Ratcliffe, eds. *Rhetorics of Whiteness: Postracial Hauntings in Popular Culture, Social Media, and Education.* Carbondale: Southern Illinois University Press, 2017.

Kirshenblatt-Gimblett, Barbara. *Destination Culture: Tourism, Museums, and Heritage.* Berkeley: University of California Press, 1998.

Krebs, Ronald R. "Tell Me a Story: FDR, Narrative, and the Making of the Second World War." *Security Studies* 24, no. 1 (2015): 131–170.

Laracey, Mel. *Informing a Nation: The Newspaper Presidency of Thomas Jefferson.* Ann Arbor: University of Michigan Press, 2021.

Latimer, Heather. "Popular Culture and Reproductive Politics: *Juno, Knocked Up* and the Enduring Legacy of *The Handmaid's Tale*," *Feminist Theory* 10, no. 2 (2009): 211–226.

Lee, Michael J., and R. Jarrod Atchison. *We Are Not One People: Secession and Separatism in American Politics Since 1776.* New York: Oxford, 2022.

Loewen, James W. *Lies Across America: What Our Historic Sites Get Wrong*, 20th anniversary ed. New York: New Press, 2009.

Loewen, James W., and Edward W. Sebesta, eds. *The Confederate and Neo-Confederate Reader: The "Great Truth" About the "Lost Cause."* Jackson: University Press of Mississippi, 2010.

Longstreth, Richard, ed. *The Mall in Washington, 1791–1991.* New Haven, CT: Yale University Press, 2002.

Lopez, Francesca, and Christine E. Sleeter. *Critical Race Theory and Its Critics: Implications for Teaching and Research.* New York: Teachers College Press, 2023.

Lowenthal, David. *Possessed by the Past: The Heritage Crusade and the Spirit of History.* New York: Free Press, 1996.

Lucaites, John Louis, and Robert Hariman. "Visual Rhetoric, Photojournalism, and Democratic Public Culture." *Rhetoric Review* 20, no. 1/2 (2001): 37–42.

Lucas, Stephen E. "The Rhetorical Ancestry of the Declaration of Independence." *Rhetoric & Public Affairs* 1, no. 2 (1998): 143–184.

Mailett, Margaret. *Choosing and Using Fiction and Non-Fiction 3–11: A Comprehensive Guide for Teachers and Student Teachers.* New York: Routledge, 2010.

Malone, Dumas. *Jefferson and His Time.* 6 vols. Boston: Little, Brown, 1948.

Maxson, J. David. "'Second Line to Bury White Supremacy': Take 'Em Down NOLA,' Monument Removal, and Residual Memory," *Quarterly Journal of Speech* 106, no. 1 (2020): 48–71.

McAlister, Faber. "An Uncanny Architope: Impossible Ghosts of Empire at the Bronte Parsonage Museum." *Quarterly Journal of Speech* 109, no. 3 (2023): 230–253.

McArdle, Felicity, and Gail Boldt, eds. *Young Children, Pedagogy, and the Arts: Ways of Seeing.* New York: Routledge, 2013.

McDonald, Robert M. S., ed. *Thomas Jefferson Lives: Biographers and the Battle for History.* Charlottesville: University of Virginia Press, 2019.

McGeough, Ryan Erik, Catherine Helen Palczewski, and Randall A. Lake. "Oppositional Memory Practices: US Memorial Spaces as Arguments over Public Memory." *Argumentation and Advocacy* 51, no. 4 (2015): 231–254.

Meacham, Jon. *Thomas Jefferson: The Art of Power.* New York: Random House, 2013.

Meacham, Jon. *Thomas Jefferson: President and Philosopher.* New York: Crown, 2014.

Meacham, Jon, ed. *In the Hands of the People: Thomas Jefferson on Equality, Faith, Freedom, and the Art of Citizenship.* New York: Random House, 2020.

Medhurst, Martin J., Robert L. Ivie, Philip Wander, and Robert L. Scott. *Cold War Rhetoric: Strategy, Metaphor, and Ideology.* East Lansing: Michigan State University Press, 1997.

Mehltretter Drury, Jeffrey P., and Sara A. Mehltretter Drury, eds. *Rhetoric, Politics, and Hamilton: An American Musical.* New York: Peter Lang, 2021.

Mehrhoff, Arthus. *The Gateway Arch: Fact and Symbol.* Bowling Green, OH: Bowling Green State University Press, 1992.

Miranda, Lin-Manuel, and Jeremy McCarter. *Hamilton: The Revolution.* New York: Grand Central Publishing, 2016.

Mitchell, Katharyne. "Monuments, Memorials, and the Politics of Memory." *Urban Geography* 24, no. 5 (2003): 442–459.

Modlin, E. Arnold, Derek H. Alderman, and Glenn W. Gentry. "Tour Guides as Creators of Empathy: The Role of Affective Inequality in Marginalizing the Enslaved at Plantation House Museums." *Tourist Studies* 11, no. 1 (2011): 3–19.

Moses, Wilson Jeremiah. *Thomas Jefferson: A Modern Prometheus.* New York: Cambridge University Press, 2019.

Newmyer, R. Kent. *The Treason Trial of Aaron Burr: Law, Politics, and the Character Wars of the New Nation.* New York: Cambridge University Press, 2012.

Nodelman, Perry. *The Pleasures of Children's Literature.* New York: Longman, 1992.

Nora, Pierre. "Between History and Memory: Les Lieux de Mémoire." *Representations* 26, no. 9 (1989): 7–25.

O'Keefe, Kieran. "Monuments to the American Revolution." *Journal of the American Revolution*, September 17, 2019, https://allthingsliberty.com/2019/09/monuments-to-the-american-revolution/.

Olson, Christa J. *American Magnitude: Hemispheric Vision and Public Feeling in the United States*. Columbus: Ohio State University Press, 2021.

Olson, Christa J. *Jefferson's Empire: The Language of American Nationhood*. Charlottesville, VA: University of Virginia Press, 2000.

Ono, Kent A. *Critical Rhetorics of Race*. New York: NYU Press, 2011.

Onuf, Peter S. *Jefferson's Empire: The Language of American Nationhood*. Charlottesville, VA: University of Virginia Press, 2000.

Onuf, Peter S, ed. *Jeffersonian Legacies*. Charlottesville: University of Virginia Press, 1993.

Owens, Robert M. *Mr. Jefferson's Hammer: William Henry Harrison and the Origins of American Indian Policy*. Norman: University of Oklahoma Press, 2007.

Paliewicz, Nicholas, and Marouf Hasian Jr. "Mourning Absences: Melancholic Commemoration and the Contested Public Memories of the National September 11 Memorial and Museum." *Western Journal of Communication* 80, no. 2 (2016): 140–162.

Parry-Giles, Shawn J., and J. Michael Hogan, eds. *Rhetoric and Public Address in the Twenty-First Century: A Handbook*. Malden, MA: Wiley-Blackwell, 2010.

Parry-Giles, Trevor, and Shawn J. Parry-Giles. *The Prime-Time Presidency: The West Wing and US Nationalism*. Champaign-Urbana: University of Illinois Press, 2010.

Pavković, Aleksandar A., and Peter Radan, eds. *The Ashgate Research Companion to Secession*. Burlington, VT: Ashgate, 2011.

Peterson, Merrill J. *The Jefferson Image in the American Mind*. Charlottesville: University Press of Virginia, 1998.

Peterson, Merrill J. *Thomas Jefferson and the New Nation: A Biography*. New York: Oxford, 1975.

Pezzullo, Phaedra C. *Toxic Tourism: Rhetorics of Pollution, Travel, and Environmental Justice*. Tuscaloosa: University of Alabama Press, 2009.

Phillips, Kendall R. *A Cinema of Hopelessness: The Rhetoric of Rage in 21st Century Popular Culture*. New York: Springer Nature, 2021.

Phillips, Kendall R., ed. *Framing Public Memory*. Tuscaloosa: University of Alabama Press, 2004.

Pineda, Richard D., and Stacey K. Sowards. "Flag Waving as Visual Argument 2006: Immigration Demonstrations and Cultural Citizenship." *Argumentation and Advocacy* 43, no. 3–4 (2007): 164–174.

Poirot, Kristin, and Shevaun E. Watson. "Memories of Freedom and White Resilience: Place, Tourism, and Urban Slavery." *Rhetoric Society Quarterly* 45, no. 2: (2015) 91–116.

Powell, John A., and Stephen Menendian. *Belonging without Othering: How We Save Ourselves and the World*. Stanford, CA: Stanford University Press, 2024.

Pretes, Michael. "Tourism and Nationalism." *Annals of Tourism Research* 30, no. 1 (2003): 125–142.

Raphael, Ray. *Founding Myths: Stories That Hide Our Patriotic Past.* New York: MJF Books, 2004.

Rausch, Monica L. *Great Americans: Thomas Jefferson.* Pleasantville, NY: Weekly Reader Books, 2007.

Rex, Cathy, and Shevaun E. Watson, eds. *Public Memory, Race, and Heritage Tourism of Early America.* New York: Routledge, 2022.

Reyes, G. Mitchell, ed. *Public Memory, Race, and Ethnicity.* New York: Cambridge Scholars Publishing, 2010.

Rockliff, Mara. *Jefferson Measures a Moose.* Somerville, MA: Candlewick Press, 2020.

Romanowski, William D. "Oliver Stone's JFK: Commercial Filmmaking, Cultural History, and Conflict." *Journal of Popular Film and Television* 21, no. 2 (1993): 63–71.

Rosenstock, Barb. *Thomas Jefferson Builds a Library.* Honesdale, PA: Calkins Creek, 2013.

Rosteck, Thomas, and Thomas S. Frentz. "Myth and Multiple Readings in Environmental Rhetoric: The Case of *An Inconvenient Truth.*" *Quarterly Journal of Speech* 95, no. 1 (2009): 1–19.

Rothburg, Michael. *Multidirectional Memory: Remembering the Holocaust in the Age of Decolonization.* Stanford, CA: Stanford University Press, 2009.

Rothman, Hal K. *Devil's Bargains: Tourism in the Twentieth-Century American West.* Lawrence: University Press of Kansas, 1998.

Ruane, Michael E. "FDR's Moving Fireside D Day Prayer to be Added to World War II Memorial." *Washington Post,* October 15, 2020. https://www.washingtonpost.com/history/2020/10/15/fdr-dday-fireside-chat-prayer/.

Rushing, Janice Hocker. "The Rhetoric of the American Western Myth." *Communications Monographs* 50, no. 1 (1983): 14–32.

Sanchez, James Chase, and Kristen R. Moore. "Reappropriating Public Memory: Racism, Resistance, and Erasure of the Confederate Defenders of Charleston Monument." *Present Tense* 5, no. 2 (2015): 1–9.

Savage, Kirk. *Monumental Wars: Washington DC, the National Mall, and the Transformation of the Memorial Landscape.* Berkeley: University of California Press, 2005.

Savage, Kirk. *Standing Soldiers, Kneeling Slaves: Race, War, and Monument in Nineteenth Century America.* Princeton, NJ: Princeton University Press, 1997.

Sehat, David. *The Jefferson Rule: How the Founding Fathers Became Infallible and Our Politics Inflexible.* New York: Simon & Schuster, 2015.

Sellnow, Deanna D. *The Rhetorical Power of Popular Culture: Considering Mediated Texts.* Thousand Oaks, CA: Sage, 2017.

Seltzer, Jack, and Shaun Crowley, eds. *Rhetorical Bodies.* Madison: University of Wisconsin Press, 1999.

Severance, John B. *Thomas Jefferson: Architect of Democracy.* New York: Clarion Books, 1998.

Shaffer, Marguerite S. *See America First: Tourism and National Identity, 1880–1940.* Washington, DC: Smithsonian Books, 2001.

Sheckel, Paul A. *Memory in Black and White: Race, Commemoration, and the Post-Bellum Landscape.* Walnut Creek, CA: Alta Mira, 2003.

Shepherd, Gregory J., Jeffrey St. John, and Ted Striphas, eds. *Communication as . . . : Perspectives on Theory.* Thousand Oaks, CA: Sage, 2006.

Sirimarco, Elizabeth. *Presidents of the United States: Thomas Jefferson Our Third President.* Mankato, MN: Child's World, 2009.

Sleeper-Smith, Susan, Juliana Barr, Jean M. O'Brien, Nancy Shoemaker, and Scott Manning Stevens, eds. *Why You Can't Teach History without American Indians.* Chapel Hill: University of North Carolina Press, 2015.

Sloane, Thomas O., ed. *Encyclopedia of Rhetoric.* New York: Oxford University Press, 2001.

Slotkin, Richard. "Nostalgia and Progress: Theodore Roosevelt's Myth of the Frontier." *American Quarterly* 33, no. 5 (1981): 608–637.

Smith, Clint. *How the Word Is Passed: A Reckoning with the History of Slavery Across America.* New York: Back Bay Books, 2021.

Smith, David A. *Cowboy Presidents: The Frontier Myth and US Politics Since 1900.* Norman: University of Oklahoma Press, 2021.

Smith, Rogers M. "The American Creed" and American Identity: The Limits of Liberal Citizenship in the United States." *Western Political Quarterly* 41, no. 2 (1988): 225–251.

Smith, Rogers M. *Civic Ideals: Conflicting Visions of Citizenship in US History.* New Haven, CT: Yale University Press, 1997.

Smithsonian Books. *Official Guide to the Smithsonian National Museum of African American History and Culture.* Washington, DC: Smithsonian Books, n.d.

St. George, Judith. *What Was the Lewis and Clark Expedition?* New York: Penguin Workshop, 2014.

St. John de Crèvecoeur, J. Hector. *Letters from an American Farmer and Sketches of Eighteenth-Century America.* New York: Penguin, 1981.

Stokowski, Patricia A. "Languages of Place and Discourses of Power: Constructing New Senses of Place." *Journal of Leisure Research* 38, no. 4 (2002): 368–382.

Stone, Meredith, Ian Spangler, Xavier Griffin, and Stephen P. Harina. "Searching for the Enslaved in the 'Cradle of Democracy': Virginia's James River Plantation Websites and the Reproduction of Local Histories." *Southeastern Geographer* 56, no. 2 (2016): 203–222.

Stuckey, Mary E. *Defining Americans: The Presidency and National Identity.* Lawrence: University Press of Kansas, 2023.

Stuckey, Mary E. *Deplorable: The Worst Presidential Campaigns from Jefferson to Trump.* Lawrence: University Press of Kansas, 2021.

Stuckey, Mary E. "The Donner Party and the Rhetoric of Westward Expansion." *Rhetoric & Public Affairs* 14, no. 2 (2011): 229–260.

Stuckey, Mary E. *For the Enjoyment of the People: The Creation of National Identity in American Public Lands.* Lawrence: University Press of Kansas, 2023.

Stuckey, Mary E. *The Good Neighbor: Franklin D. Roosevelt and the Rhetoric of American Power.* East Lansing: Michigan State University Press, 2013.

Stuckey, Mary E. "One Nation (Pretty Darn) Divisible: National Identity in the 2004 Conventions," *Rhetoric & Public Affairs* 8, no. 4 (2005): 639–656.

Stuckey, Mary E. "'To Preserve Unimpaired': The Presidency, National Parks, and the Preservation of the US Settler Colonialist State." *Rhetoric & Public Affairs* 27, no. 1 (2024): 1–26.

Stuckey, Mary E., ed. *Used, Abused, and Sidelined: Debating the Declaration.* University Park: Penn State University Press, forthcoming.

Sturges, Mark. "Founding Farmers: Jefferson, Washington, and the Rhetoric of Agricultural Reform." *Early American Literature* 50, no. 3 (2015): 681–709.

Sturken, Marita. *Tangled Memories: The Vietnam War, the AIDS Epidemic, and the Politics of Remembering.* Berkeley: University of California Press, 1997.

Sturken, Marita. *Tourists of History: Memory, Kitsch, and Consumerism from Oklahoma City to Ground Zero.* Durham, NC: Duke University Press, 2007.

Sullivan, Shannon, and Nancy Tuana. *Race and the Epistemologies of Ignorance.* New York: SUNY Press, 2007.

Sweet, Derek, and Margret McCue-Enser. "Constituting 'the People' as Rhetorical Interruption: Barack Obama and the Unfinished Hopes of an Imperfect People." *Communication Studies* 61, no. 5 (2010): 602–622.

Takaki, Ronald. *A Different Mirror: A History of Multicultural America.* Boston: Little, Brown, 1993.

Taylor, Andrew. "Barry Goldwater: Insurgent Conservatism as Constitutive Rhetoric." *Journal of Political Ideologies* 21, no. 3 (2016): 242–260.

Temko, Allen. *Eero Saarinen.* New York: George Braziller, 1962.

Thomas, Peggy. *Thomas Jefferson Grows a Nation.* Honesdale, PA: Calkins Creek Books, 2015.

Thompson, Keith. *Jefferson's Shadow: The Story of His Science.* New Haven, CT: Yale University Press, 2012.

United States Capitol Historical Society. *We, the People: The Story of the United States Capitol.* Washington, DC: National Geographic Society, 2016.

Urry, John. *The Tourist Gaze,* 2nd ed. Thousand Oaks, CA: Sage, 2002.

Vandergrift, Kay E., ed. *Ways of Knowing: Literature and the Intellectual Life of Children.* Lanham, MD: Scarecrow Press, 1996.

VanderHaagen, Sara. *Children's Biographies of African American Women: Rhetoric, Public Memory, and Agency.* Columbia: University of South Caroline Press, 2018.

VanderHaagen, Sara. "Political Truths: Black Feminist Agency and Public Memory in Biographies of Children." *Women's Studies in Communication* 35, no. 1 (2012): 18–41.

Vivian, Bradford J. *Campus Misinformation: The Real Threat to Free Speech in American Higher Education.* New York: Oxford University Press, 2023.

Vivian, Bradford J. "Jefferson's Other." *Quarterly Journal of Speech* 88, no. 3 (2002): 284–302.

Vivian, Bradford J. *Public Forgetting: The Rhetoric and Politics of Beginning Again.* University Park: Penn State Press, 2011.

Warner, Benjamin R., Diane G Bystrom, Mitchell S. McKinney, and Mary C. Banwart, eds. *Democracy Disrupted: Communication in the Volatile 2020 Presidential Election*. New York: Praeger, 2022.

Wells, Justine. "Monumentality, Ruination, and the Milieux of Memory's Lessons from WEB DuBois." *Western Journal of Communication* 87, no. 3 (2023): 281–303.

White, Gayle Jessup. *Reclamation: Sally Hemings, Thomas Jefferson, and a Descendant's Search for her Family's Lasting Legacy*. New York: Harper Collins, 2021.

White, James Boyd. *Heracles' Bow: Essays on the Rhetoric and Poetics of the Law*. Madison: University of Wisconsin Press, 1985.

White, Leanne, ed. *Commercial Nationalism and Tourism: Selling the National Story*. Bristol, UK: Channel View Publications, 2017.

Whittenburg, Cari. "The Oklahoma City National Memorial and Museum: Materiality, Trauma, and the Comfort of Catharsis." *Western Journal of Communication* 88, no. 4 (2024): 782–801.

Wills, Garry. *"Negro President": Jefferson and the Slave Power*. Boston: Houghton Mifflin, 2003.

Wills, John E. "Lives and Other Stories: Neglected Aspects of the Teacher's Art." *History Teacher* 26, no. 1 (1992): 33–49.

Wilson, G. S. *Jefferson on Display: Attire, Etiquette, and the Art of Presentation*. Charlottesville: University of Virginia Press, 2018.

Wilson, Rob. "Producing American Selves: The Form of the American Biography." *boundary 2*, 18, no. 2 (1991): 104–129.

Winchester, Simon. *The Men Who United the States*. New York: Harper Perennial, 2013.

Winter, Jonah, and Terry Widener. *My Name Is James Madison Hemings*. New York: Schwartz Wade Books, 2016.

Wolfe, Eva Sheppard. *Race and Liberty in the New Nation: Emancipation in Virginia from the Revolution to Nat Turner's Rebellion*. Baton Rouge: Louisiana State University Press, 2006.

Yarborough, Jean H. *American Virtues: Thomas Jefferson on the Character of a Free Republic*. Lawrence: University Press of Kansas, 1998.

Zarefsky, David. "Presidential Rhetoric and the Power of Definition." *Presidential Studies Quarterly* 34, no. 3 (2004): 607–619.

Zelizer, Barbie. "Competing Memories: Reading the Past against the Grain: The Shape of Memory Studies." *Critical Studies in Media Communication* 12, no. 2 (1995): 213–239.

Zelizer, Barbie. *Remembering to Forget: Holocaust Memory Through the Camera's Eye*. Chicago: University of Chicago Press, 1998.

Index

Adams, John: Alien and Sedition Acts, 17; books about, 176n11; bust of, 81; death of, 21, 46; fictional representation of, 120; Jefferson and, 18, 122; in political rhetoric, 21; on slavery, 121. *See also* founding generation

African Americans: American Revolution and, 137; claims to equality, 141; exclusion of, 103; Jefferson's legacy and, 16, 34; views of national ideals, 26

Alamo, 84

Alien and Sedition Acts, 17

American Exceptionalism, 36

American Heritage, 208n19

American President, The (film), 130–131

American Revolution: Black Americans and, 137; in Capitol Rotunda, paintings of, 87; commemorations of, 56; heroes and villains of, 12, 13–14, 85; idea of human equality and, 83; peoplehood and, 106; places associated with, 85

Anderson, Marian, 196n104

André, John, 12

Apsáalooke (Crow) people, 157

Arnold, Benedict, 12, 13, 16

Articles of Confederation, 17

Ashe, Arthur, 136

Atchison, R. Jarrod, 28

Badlands National Park, 98

Banneker, Benjamin, 62, 113

Bear Flag Rebellion, 24

Bederman, Gail, 11

Biden, Joe, 43

Billig, Michael, 100

Bill of Rights, 30–31, 89

Black Elk Peak (Harney Peak), 98

Blair, Carole, 100, 101, 104

Borglum, Gutzon, 100, 101, 102

Boston's Freedom Trail, 85

Boston Tea Party, 11

Brodie, Fawn: *Jefferson: An Intimate History*, 111, 112

Brokaw, Tom: *The Greatest Generation*, 100

Buffon, Georges-Louis Leclerc, Comte de, 145, 146

Bunker Hill, 84, 85

Burns, Ken, 7, 121, 122, 123, 124, 172

Burr, Aaron, 19, 107

Burstein, Andrew, 176n11

Bush, George W.: Middle East policy, 38–39; at naturalization ceremony at Monticello, 5; promotion of democracy, 38; use of Jefferson's legacy, 38, 40, 43

Bush, George W. H., 40, 42, 47

Butler, David, 120

Byrd, Harry, 59

Cabot, John, 87, 88

Capitol Hill, 86

Capitol Rotunda: commemoration of women's suffrage, 88; foundational narrative in, 86–89; Jefferson statue in, 80, 81, 85, 88, 104–105; location of, 86; wall paintings and sculptures in, 86, 87–88

Carter, Jimmy, 34, 45

Carter, Perry E., 120
Charbonneau, Toussaint, 156
Chief Joseph (wal-lam-wat-kain leader), 99
children's books: circulation of, 139–140; depiction of slavery in, 138, 149–154; didactic nature of, 136, 137–138, 159; idea of citizenship in, 136–137, 154–155; illustrations, 138–139; national ideals in, 136–137, 144–145, 148, 155; Sally Hemings in, 151; targeted audience, 138, 139; teaching hard things in, 154–159; treatment of Jefferson in, 138–139, 148–159; US founding in, 136
Chinese Exclusion Act (1882), 140
citizenship: as belonging, 140, 141; in children's books, discussion of, 136–137, 154–155; dilemmas of, 19; immigrants' access to, 141; legal and social aspects of, 140–141; meaning of, 12; national identity and, 125, 140–142; as product of history, 137; rhetoric and, 6
civic identity, 141–142
civil rights, 40
Civil War, 21, 27, 29, 46, 58, 153
Clark, William, 19, 103
Clérisseau, Charles-Louis, 58
Cleveland, Grover, 96
Clinton, Bill: statue in Rapid City, 97; treatment of Jefferson by, 35, 40, 41, 42, 43, 188n79
Coglinano, Joseph, 27
cognate stories, 158, 170
Colbert, Burwell, 128
Cold War: end of, 38; Jefferson's legacy in context of, 32, 36, 166; proxy wars, 37
collective memory, 9–10, 11, 12–13, 89
Columbus, Christopher, 86, 87, 88
commemorations and commemorative sites, 3, 10, 12–13, 50, 52, 54–55. See also monuments and memorials
communal identity, 84, 163, 165
communities: claims to belonging, 25; collective choices, 82; creation through rhetoric, 9, 22–24; exclusions from, 23, 24, 25–26; formation of, 140; hierarchies within, 24; origin stories and, 24, 25–26
Concord, Massachusetts, 85

Confederate monuments and commemorative sites, 11, 56, 58, 59, 74, 100, 211n6
Congress Hall in Philadelphia, Pennsylvania, 90
Congress of the Confederation, 16
constitutive rhetoric, 9, 23, 27, 31
Continental Congress, 87, 90, 91, 92, 93, 104, 137. See also American Revolution
Corby, William, 67
Cornwallis, Charles, 87
Corps of Discovery, 103, 156
Cosway, Maria, 117
Crazy Horse (Lakota war leader), 98
Custer, George Armstrong, 99
Custer State Park, 98

Daniels, Josephus, 30–31
Daughters of the American Revolution (DAR) Library, 75, 196n104
Davis, Jefferson, 58, 59, 68
Declaration of Independence: 250th anniversary of the signing of, 128; artefacts related to, 62; Committee of Five, 16, 93; draft of, 115, 121; first reading to the public, 134; ideals of equality and human rights, 29, 150; importance of, 92–93, 134–135; at Independence National Historical Park, quote from, 95; Jefferson and, 4, 7, 28, 41–42, 60, 92, 93, 122, 142, 143, 144, 150, 166, 172–173; in museum exhibits, 75; national identity in, 106; painting in Capitol Rotunda, 87; in political rhetoric, 92–93, 166; principles of, 41, 42; school curriculum on, 136–137; secession and, 28, 166; signing of, 6, 21, 137; slavery and, 114, 115
democracy, 2, 188n79
Democrats: attitude to Jefferson, 35, 36; views of the nation, 26
Dickmann, Bernard, 70
Diggs, Daveed, 108
Douglass, Frederick, 26, 62
Dyer, Owen, 120

East Liverpool, Ohio, 76
Ebert, Roger, 117
Eisenhower, Dwight D., 33, 36, 39, 88
Ellis, Joseph, 106, 122

enslaved people, 23, 26, 119, 126, 211n75
Eppes, Maria (Polly) Jefferson, 17
Executive Committee of the Mississippi
    Valley Historical Association, 196n96

Federal Writers Project, 211n75
First and Second National Banks in
    Philadelphia, Pennsylvania, 90
Floyd, George, 19, 45, 50
Ford, Gerald: health policy, 40;
    introduction of "Thomas Jefferson
    Day," 33; on principles of Declaration
    of Independence, 42; statues of, 88, 97;
    use of Jefferson's legacy, 33–34, 40, 41
Forest, Edith Hern, 155
Fort Clatsop in Astoria, Oregon: Black
    history at, 157; children's books at, 139,
    156, 158
founding generation: books dedicated
    to, 176n11; in children stories, 135–136,
    144; founding fathers replaced with,
    82–83, 110, 167–168; memorialization
    of, 4, 19, 20, 82–83, 88, 94, 108, 140;
    memorials and statues dedicated to,
    2, 80, 99; misconceptions about, 91;
    representations of, 57, 81; slavery and,
    92, 94, 130, 138, 150, 151, 169; view of
    liberty, 114; view of the nation, 103
Fourth of July celebration, 10, 25, 135
Franklin, Benjamin, 75, 91, 121. See also
    founding generation
Franklin, John Hope, 123–124
Freeman, Elizabeth, 62
Friends of the National World War II
    Memorial, 164

Garfield, James A., 88
Gateway Arch National Park. See
    Jefferson National Expansion
    Memorial (JNEM)
George III, King of Great Britain, 115, 121
Geronimo (Bedonkohe military leader), 99
Gettysburg memorial site, 84
Gibboney, Stuart, 64
Gordon-Reed, Annette, 57; Thomas
    Jefferson and Sally Hemings: An
    American Controversy, 112
Grant, Ulysses S., 88
Great Depression, 29
Groom, Walter, 8

Haitian Revolution, 18, 62
Hamilton (musical): controversies of,
    6; depiction of founders, 107–108;
    productions of, 110; treatment of
    Jefferson in, 107–108
Hamilton, Alexander, 30, 88, 124. See also
    founding generation
Hamilton: The Revolution (McCarter and
    Miranda), 201n1, 205n60
Hancock, John, 87
Hannah-Jones, Nikole, 13, 122
Hemings, Betty, 151
Hemings, James Madison, 157–158
Hemings, Robert, 122
Hemings, Sally: background of, 16;
    children of, 151, 153, 157–158, 181n68;
    fictional representations of, 118–119,
    124, 131; Jefferson's relations with, 5,
    17, 66, 111–112, 117–118, 120, 127, 166,
    168–169, 181n68, 195n182
Henry, Patrick, 8, 89
Hill, A. P., 58
historical tourism, 54–55, 109
History Museum in St. Louis, 53
Holmes, John, 116
Hoover, Herbert, 39
Horn, Frances Gillette, 155
House of Burgesses, 15
Hughes, Ursula Granger, 155
human rights, 29, 166
Hungarian Revolution of 1956, 36

immigration, 140
Independence Day: celebrations, 26; in
    children stories, 134–135
Independence Hall in Philadelphia,
    Pennsylvania, 90, 91, 93, 95, 99,
    134
Independence National Historical Park
    (INHP): affiliated sites of, 90, 168;
    approach to slavery at, 92, 93–94,
    96, 168; archeological site at, 93, 94;
    foundational narrative of, 85–86, 89,
    90–91, 94, 95, 168; gift shop in, 139;
    historical misconceptions at, 91–92,
    134–135; interpretive themes of, 91;
    location of, 90, 91; mission of, 90,
    91; renovation of, 93; treatment of
    Jefferson in, 81, 86, 92, 105; visitors to,
    95–96, 139–140

Indigenous peoples: assimilation of, 18, 103; children's books about, 139; depiction of Penn's treaty with, 87; dispossession of, 17, 82, 97, 98, 100, 165; exclusion from community, 23; Jefferson on, 16; warfare, 87–88, 98
Irving, Washington, 12

Jackson, Andrew, 31, 82, 88, 162
Jackson, Stonewall, 58, 59
Jarvis, Brooke, 98
Jefferson, Martha Skelton (née Wayles), 16, 151
Jefferson, Peter, 152
Jefferson, Thomas: Act for Religious Freedom, 65; Adams and, 17, 18; advocacy of emancipation, 115–116; on American Exceptionalism, 36; approach to politics, 34, 176n11; as archetype of US democracy, 36, 136, 162–163, 171; association with the Confederacy, 29; biographies of, 14, 111–112, 123, 143, 176n11; birth of, 16; children of, 16, 17, 20, 151, 153, 157–158, 181n68; in collective memory, 1, 3, 13–15, 161, 162; commemorative sites, 53–54, 109–110; as complicated figure, 112, 113, 116, 120–125; correspondence of, 65, 116; death of, 21, 46; Declaration of Independence and, 28, 142, 143, 144, 150, 166, 172–173; dedication to education, 40; on economic opportunities, 112–113, 124–125, 166; on equality of all men, 43, 114, 132; fictional representations of, 5; films and documentaries about, 7, 100–101, 110, 117–118, 121–124, 130–131; foreign policy of, 18; as founding father, 2, 19, 54, 66, 142, 161; in France, 17, 146; grave of, 49; Hamilton's disputes with, 124; headstone of, 49, 51; Hemings and, 5, 17, 111–112, 151, 153, 166, 168–169, 181n68; heroization of, 163; on Indian Removal, 76; Indigenous policy of, 18, 103, 104; on individual liberty, 8; interests of, 142, 145, 147; interpretations of, 40, 111, 159, 170–173; legacies of, 18–19, 35–36, 41, 133, 148–154, 160, 173; legal career of, 15–16; Lewis and Clark Expedition and, 18, 19, 142; Library of Congress and, 146–147, 148; local meaning of, 58–59; Louisiana Purchase and, 34, 101, 102–103, 163, 164; love of books, 146–147; Madison and, 163; marriage of, 16, 17; on money, depiction of, 33, 164; Monticello home, 8, 16, 18, 130; musicals about, 6, 107–108, 201n11; national meaning of, 59–67; *Notes on the State of Virginia*, 16, 115–116, 145; personality of, 7–8, 122–123, 145–146, 149–150; personal library of, 61; political career of, 16, 17, 92; in political rhetoric, 7, 18–19, 42, 162–163; in popular culture, 2, 19–20, 107–109, 110–111, 116, 130–132, 171, 172, 182n84; popularity of, 27; on popular sovereignty, 46; posthumous praise of, 33; presidency of, 18–19; on private land ownership, 77; relationship to slavery, 8, 15–16, 18, 42, 61–62, 65, 92, 108, 112–116, 126–130, 132–133, 149–153, 169, 208n19; as romantic figure, 116, 117–120, 132; schools named after, 53; statues of, 49–50, 53, 55, 57, 62, 72, 73, 75, 80–81, 86, 89, 96–97; as symbol of human rights, 36–37; on territorial expansion, 77, 103–104; US national identity and, 3–4, 6–7, 8, 14, 22, 32–33, 36, 66, 78–79, 163–164, 165; videos on, 135, 155, 156; vision of the nation, 31, 34, 45, 103. *See also* founding generation; Jefferson in children's books; Jefferson's monuments and memorials
Jefferson: An Intimate History (Brodie), 111, 112
Jefferson hotels, 53
Jeffersonians of America, 31
Jefferson in children's books: as active hero, 143–145; flaws of, 149–150; illustrations of, 138–139, 159–160; as model citizen, 142, 145, 148, 149, 154–155; as person who thinks about the nation, 145–148; as slave-owner, 138, 144, 148–153
Jefferson in Paris (film, 1995), 7, 110, 117–118, 124
Jefferson Measures a Moose (Rockliff), 146
Jefferson Memorial in Washington, D.C.: construction of, 63, 64; design

of, 32, 65; FDR's interest in, 18, 31, 32, 64–65; idea of national identity and, 52; interior walls of, 63; Obama with his daughter at, *44*; presentation of Jefferson in, 4, 67; protection of, 78; size of, 62–63

Jefferson National Expansion Memorial (JNEM) in St. Louis, Missouri: construction of, 69; design of, 71; endorsements of, 70, 196n96; galleries, 72; Indigenous peoples and, 71; interpretive history of, 52; museums, 71; park of, 71; promotion of, 69–70; renaming of, 6; statue of Jefferson at, 72, *73*; tours, 196n103; visitors to, 72, 74, 167

Jefferson Pier Stone, 75–76, 167

Jefferson's monuments and memorials: commemoration of Jefferson in, 19; creation of, 1–2, 4, 68; list of, 6; reflection of American history in, 105–106, 195n82; removal of, 165, 171; visitors' interaction with, 167. *See also individual monuments*

Jenkinson, Clay, 123

Johnson, Lyndon, 37, 40–41

Johnston, Joseph E., 59

Jones, Absalom, 62

Journey of York, The (Davis), 156–157

Juneteenth celebration, 10–11

Kennedy, John F., 6, 36–37

Kentucky Resolution, 17, 28, 166

King, Martin Luther, Jr., 43, 88

La Fayette, Gilbert Du Motier, Marquis de, 88

Lafayette, James Armistead, 137

Land Ordinance of 1784, 16

La Salle, Robert Cavelier, sieur de, 87, 88

League of Women Voters of St. Louis, 196n96

Leapheart, Roman, 50

Lee, Michael J., 28

Lee, Robert E., 58, 59, 81

Levy, Jonas, 80

Levy, Uriah, 80

Lewis, Andrew, 89

Lewis, John, 211n6

Lewis, Meriwether, 19, 103

Lewis and Clark Expedition, 18, 19, 39, 70, 72, 103, 142, 158

Lexington, KY: historical significance of, 85

LGBTQ+ people: claims to equality, 141

Liberty Bell: controversy over, 93–94, 168; crack at, 93, 96; display of, 90, 92, 93, 168; symbolism of, 91, 93, 96; visitors to, 95–96

Library of Congress: collections of, 147; Jefferson and, 33, 53, 60–61, 67, 146–147, 148; location of, 86

Lilly Endowment, 164

Lincoln, Abraham: on Declaration of Independence, 172; legacy of, 31, 182n82; on Mount Rushmore National Monument, 101, 102, 168; national identity and, 6; popularity of, 6, 162; in presidential speeches, 42; reflection on Jefferson and Adams, 46–47, 114; statue in Capitol Rotunda, 88; Thanksgiving celebration, 84; use of founding documents, 46; view of the nation, 47

Lincoln Memorial, 86

Loewen, James W., 65

Louisiana Purchase: 150th anniversary of, 33; commemoration of, 68, 69; Jefferson's role in, 14, 17, 34, 49, 70, 71, 101, 102–103, 163, 164; misconceptions about, 196n103

Louverture, Toussaint, 19, 62

Ludlow, Thomas, 63

MacLeish, Archibald, 18, 61

Madison, James, 14, 17, 28, 31, 65, 97, 163. *See also* founding generation

Malone, Dumas, 7

Marshall, John, 89

MASH (television show), 130

Mason, George, 13, 89

Maury, Matthew Fontaine, 50

Mayflower (ship), 84, 87

Meacham, Jon, 114, 172

memorial emplacement, 85, 164

memorializing collectives, 82–83

Michael, Neil, 100, 101, 104

minoritized and excluded people: stories of, 158–159

Miranda, Lin-Manuel, 107, 124, 125

Missouri Compromise, 21, 116

Missouri Historical Society, 196n96

Missouri History Museum, 68–69, 78

Monroe, James, 31, 47

Montgomery, Alabama: slavery sites in, 196n105

Montgomery, Richard, 13

Montgomery Monument, St. Paul's Chapel in New York, 13

Monticello plantation: as "always a work in progress," 129; burial place at, 165; cemetery, 129; children's books at, 152; cinematic depiction of life in, 119; docents and guides, 128; enslaved people at, 125, 126–127, 129; forced-labor camp, 122; fruits and vegetables grown at, 147; gift shop in, 139; Jefferson's life in, 8, 16, 18, 130; Levy's purchase of, 80; location of, 125; as metaphor for Jeffersonian democracy, 132; Mulberry Row, 127; naturalization ceremonies at, 5; removal of statues from, 165; as tourist attraction, 126–128, 129, 172; visitor experiences, 6, 127–129, 130; website, 127

monumental adaptation, 52, 67–74

monumental detritus, 52, 74–77

monumental stability, 52, 56–58, 78

monuments and memorials: aesthetics of, 3; civic tourism and, 54; commemorations and commemorative sites, 3, 10, 12–13, 50, 52, 54–55; emplacement of, 85; historical frame of, 55, 85–86; ideological meaning of, 74; interpretations of, 19, 77–78, 104; national identity and, 77; as part of the public landscape, 56–57, 74, 172; patriotism and, 84, 85; pedagogical role of, 12; physical context of, 104; political use of, 3, 55–56, 77, 182n83; purpose of, 54, 55; removal of, 59; risk becoming detritus, 78; as sites of collective memory, 56; as sites of national citizenship, 4–5, 11–12; as social practice, 4; stability of, 66, 165; studies of, 182n83; Trump's executive order on, 176n5, 193n58, 195n85, 196n102; values of, 78. *See also* statues

Moses, William Jeremiah, 132, 194n80

Mount Rushmore National Monument: 50th anniversary of, 47; advocacy of, 104; carvers' studio behind, 102; creation of, 100–101; film about, 100–101; Indigenous presence at, 98, 99; Junior Ranger Handbook on, 100; location of, 86; NPS interpretation of, 99, 104; patriotism of, 99–100, 168; politics of, 100, 101; Presidential Trail to, 102; presidents depicted on, 6, 47, 53, 81, 86, 97–98, 101, 102–103, 168; public perception of, 161, 172; purpose of, 99; treatment of Jefferson, 47, 81, 86, 101, 102, 105–106; visitors to, 97–98, 99

Museum of African American History and Culture (MAAHC), 4

Museum of the American Revolution in Philadelphia, Pennsylvania, 90, 96

My Name Is James Madison Hemings (Winter and Widener), 157–158

narratives of belonging, 109

National Archives, 41, 139

national hypocrisy, 142

National Liberty Museum in Philadelphia, Pennsylvania, 90

National Mall in Washington, D.C., 59–60, 86, 139, 164, 167

National Museum of African American History and Culture (NMAAHC), 60, 62, 67

National Museum of the American Indian, 62, 76

National Park Service (NPS): approach to Native history, 98–99; "Foundation Document," 70; interpretation of Mount Rushmore National Memorial, 99, 104; Jefferson Memorial and, 63, 64, 66; list of Jefferson sites, 6; preservation of National Mall, 60

National Presidential Wax Museum in Keystone, South Dakota, 99

national stories, 170

nation-building, 109, 110

naturalization ceremonies, 4, 5, 135, 140

Nelson, Thomas, Jr., 89

New Deal, 30, 31, 34, 166, 211n75

Nixon, Richard, 37–38, 40, 164

Nora, Pierre, 54
Northwest Ordinance (1787), 16, 77

oath of allegiance, 207n1
Obama, Barack, 39, 40, *44*, 164
Oceti Sakowin Nation (Great Sioux Nation), 86
Old City Hall in Philadelphia, Pennsylvania, 90
origin stories, 24, 25–26. *See also* US national identity

Padover, Saul, 65
Paha Sapa (Black Hills), 98. *See also* Mount Rushmore National Monument
patriotism, 27, 84
Penn, William, 87, 88
Pennsylvania: slavery in, 94
Peterson, Merrill, 27
Philadelphia, Pennsylvania: Jefferson's statue in, 81; museums and historical sites, 90
Pilgrims, 86–87
places: associated with historical events, 84–85; construction of, 83–84
Plymouth Rock, 84
Pocahontas, 86, 87, 136
popular culture, 5, 110, 130, 131, 182n84
Portland, Oregon, 57
Powhatan people, 136
presidents: appeal to national ideals, 24–25; authority to speak for entire nation, 26; children's books about, 142–143; commemoration of, 4, 6, 162–164; cynicism of, 171–172; on patriotism, 27; policy preferences, 46; references to historical figures in speeches, 162, 171, 182n82; as slave-owners, 92, 94, 97; treatment of Jefferson, 3, 22, 46, 47–48, 171; visions of national identity, 27, 166
Presidents of the United States: Thomas Jefferson Our Third President (Sirimarco), 143
public memory, 136. *See also* collective memory

race, 14, 23, 120, 136
Raleigh, Walter, 87, 88

Randolph, Martha Jefferson, 17, 117, 118, 120
Rapid City, South Dakota: as "City of Presidents," 97; patriotism of, 97; Self-Guided Walking Tour, 97; statues of presidents in, 81, 96–97
Reagan, Ronald: domestic policy, 166; Fourth of July speech, 47; memorialization of, 162; popularity of, 162, 182n82; references to FDR, 162; statue in Capitol Rotunda, 88; use of Jefferson, 22, 34–35, 40, 41, 42, 47, 48, 166
Red Cloud (Oglala Lakota leader), 99
religious iconography, 67
Republicans, 26, 31, 35, 36, 105
rhetoric: commemorations and, 3; community creation through, 9, 22–24; educational capacities of, 5–6, 159, notion of, 2–3, politics and, 22
Richmond, Virginia, 58–59, 165
Roadside Presidents app, 53
Roosevelt, Franklin D.: attitude toward partisan politics, 185n28; correspondence of, 61; "D-Day Prayer," 164; influence of, 182n82; Jefferson National Memorial in Washington and, 18, 31, 63, 64, 65; message to Thomas Jefferson Memorial Foundation, 30, 185n23; presidency of, 29; Reagan on, 162; use of Jefferson, 22, 29–32, 33, 48, 166, 167, 185n23, 185n28; view of the nation, 29, 30
Roosevelt, Theodore: depicted on Mount Rushmore, 168; economic policy of, 101, 102; popularity of, 6, 182n82; use of Jefferson, 29, 47

Saarinen, Eero, 71. *See also* Jefferson National Expansion Memorial (JNEM)
Sacagawea, 156, 158
Sally Hemings (film), 7, 124
Sally Hemings: An American Scandal (television miniseries): depiction of Jefferson in, 118–119; ideological commitments, 119–120
Schlag, Felix, 164
Second Continental Congress, 16

Seven Council Fires of the Great Sioux Nation, 86
1776 (Broadway play), 120–121
"Sites of Conscience," 126–127
Sitting Bull (Hunkpapa Lakota leader), 99
slave power, 115
slavery: abolition of, 149, 169–170; in children's books, treatment of, 138, 149–154, 157–158; consequences of, 120; economic realities and, 121; expansion of, 113; Jefferson relation with, 8, 15–16, 18, 42, 208n19; legacies of, 14; memorial sites of, 168, 194n80, 196n105; public statements on, 115; romantic view of, 119, 168–169. *See also* enslaved people
Sleepy Hollow, New York, 12
Smith, John, 87, 88
Smithsonian institutions: executive order on historical interpretations of, 195n85
Sorkin, Aaron, 130–131
South Dakota: Indian reservations in, 98
Southern plantations, 126
Speedwell (ship), 86
statues: ideological meaning of, 74; removals of, 57; vandalism of, 50
Stephens, Alexander, 59
St. John de Crèvecoeur, J. Hector: *Letters from an American Farmer*, 23
St. Louis, Missouri, 68, 69, 70; statue of Jefferson, 72, *73*
St. Louis Chapter of the Sons and Daughters of the Revolution, 196n96
Stuart, J. E. B., 58, 59
Superman: in popular culture, depictions of, 182n84

Thanksgiving celebration, 84
theaters of ideology, 109
This Little President (Holub and Roode), 143
Thomas Jefferson (documentary), 7
Thomas Jefferson (film), 121, 122, 123, 124
Thomas Jefferson: A Day at Monticello (Chew), 152
Thomas Jefferson and His World, 208n19
Thomas Jefferson and Sally Hemings: An American Controversy (Gordon-Reed), 112
Thomas Jefferson Builds a Library (Rosenstock), 146

Thomas Jefferson for Kids (Miller), 149
"Thomas Jefferson for Kids" (YouTube video), 135
Thomas Jefferson Foundation, 30, 64, 125, 126–127, 185n23
Thomas Jefferson Grows a Nation (Thomas), 147
Thomas Jefferson's World (virtual tour), 127, 129
Trail of Tears, 82
Tremain, Johnny, 110
Truman, Harry, 88
Trump, Donald: executive order "Restoring Truth and Sanity to American History," 176n5, 193n58, 195n85, 196n102; quotes of Jefferson, 39–40; reelection of, 96; on vandalism of Jefferson's statue, 57; vision of the nation, 45; visit to Vietnam, 39
Tubman, Harriet, 62

United States: exclusions and inequality, 141–142; foundation of, 13; global ambitions of, 167; globalization of democracy and, 36; immigration policies, 140; international mission of, 39; nation character of, 8; territorial expansion of, 39, 70–71, 77, 81–83, 103 (*see also* US national identity; American Revolution); threat to federal union, 29.
University of Missouri, 49, 50
University of Notre Dame, 67
University of Virginia: creation of, 113; Jefferson statues in, 53, 75
US Constitution, 17, 106
US history: in children's education, 136; interpretations of, 176n5
US national identity: celebration of, 45; children's literature and, 135–137; claim of uniqueness of, 23; Constitution and, 106; context of, 81; contradictions of, 122; definitions of, 19; fluid aspect of, 52; formation of, 135–137, 161; historically important places and, 85–86; Jefferson and, 4, 14, 22, 32–33, 36, 42, 130, 163–164, 165; national hypocrisy, 142; popular culture and, 5; presidents and, 166; principles of, 43; race and, 14, 121; visions of, 8–9

VanderHaagen, Sara, 158
Vietnam War, 34, 36, 37
Virginia: Act for Religious Freedom, 65; books about, 145; Commonwealth of, 136; history of, 16–17, 136–137; House of Delegates, 16; people and nature of, 16, 145; role in American Revolution, 89; Virginia State Capitol, 89
Virginia Resolution, 17, 28, 166

Walker, Maggie, 136
Walt Disney World's Hall of Presidents, 116
War on Terror, 38
Washington, George: as archetype of US democracy, 136; books dedicated to, 176n11; commemoration of, 58, 163; Farewell Address, 102; as heroic figure, 13; Jefferson and, 17, 92; Memorial of, 52; on Mount Rushmore, depiction of, 47, 101, 102, 168; popularity of, 6; as slave-owner, 92, 94, 102; statues of, 57, 59, 88, 89. *See also* founding generation
Washington Monument, 75, 76, 86
Watergate scandal, 34
Wayles, John, 151

Webster, Daniel, 8, 21–22
Weems, Parson, 163
Weizman National Museum of Jewish History in Philadelphia, 90
West Wing, The (television drama series), 131
What Was the Lewis and Clark Expedition? (St. George), 158
Wheatley, Phillis, 62, 113
White, Gayle Jessup, 129
White House: Jefferson's statue on the grounds of, 80, 81
white supremacy, 25, 85, 100, 101, 114, 166, 167, 168
William & Mary College, 15
Wills, Garry, 103, 114
Wilson, Woodrow, 97
Winchester, Simon, 77
Wind Cave National Park, 98
women, claims to equality, 141; commemoration of suffrage, 88
Works Progress Administration, 211n75
World's Fair of 1904, 68

Yorktown, 85

Zibart, Eve, 117, 118

www.ingramcontent.com/pod-product-compliance
Lightning Source LLC
Chambersburg PA
CBHW020333100426

42812CB00029B/3105/J